Naming God

Avinu Malkeinu—Our Father, Our King

Edited By Rabbi Lawrence A. Hoffman, PhD

16pt

Copyright Page from the Original Book

Naming God: *Avinu Malkeinu*—Our Father, Our King
2015 Hardcover Edition, First Printing
© 2015 by Lawrence A. Hoffman

All rights reserved. No part of this book may be reproduced or transmitted in any form or by any means, electronic or mechanical, including photocopying, recording, or by any information storage and retrieval system, without permission in writing from the publisher.

For information regarding permission to reprint material from this book, please mail or fax your request in writing to Jewish Lights Publishing, Permission Department, at the address / fax number listed below, or email your request to permissions@jewishlights.com.

Library of Congress Cataloging-in-Publication Data
Naming God : avinu malkeinu—our father, our king / edited by Rabbi Lawrence A. Hoffman, PhD.
 pages cm. — (Prayers of awe)
 Includes bibliographical references.
 ISBN 978-1-58023-817-5 (hardcover) — ISBN 978-1-58023-842-7 (ebook)
 1. God (Judaism) —Name. I. Hoffman, Lawrence A., 1942– editor.
 BM610.N36 2015
 296.3'112—dc23
                              2015009936

10 9 8 7 6 5 4 3 2 1

Manufactured in the United States of America
Jacket Design: Tim Holtz
Jacket Art: © Igor Rogozhnikov/Shutterstock.com

Published by Jewish Lights Publishing
A Division of LongHill Partners, Inc.
Sunset Farm Offices, Route 4, P.O. Box 237
Woodstock, VT 05091
Tel: (802) 457-4000   Fax: (802) 457-4004
www.jewishlights.com

TABLE OF CONTENTS

Introduction : Why This Book: And Why It Is the Way It Is ... iii

PART I: Two Overviews
- The History, Meaning, and Varieties of Avinu Malkeinu ... 3
- "Our Father and King" ... 25

PART II : The Liturgy
- Editor's Introduction to Avinu Malkeinu ... 65
- Translator's Introduction to Avinu Malkeinu ... 69
- Avinu Malkeinu ... 72
- Translator's Introduction to Ki Hinei Kachomer ... 88
- Ki Hinei Kachomer ... 92

PART III : Avinu Malkeinu
- The Music of Avinu Malkeinu ... 100
- Who's Your Daddy? ... 107

PART IV : Precursors, Foundations, and Parallels
- Biblical Precursors ... 117
- Father or King ... 130
- Why "Our Father"? ... 138
- Prayer and Character ... 150
- Divine Epithets and Human Ambivalence ... 163
- Our Father, Our King ... 172
- Empowerment, Not Police ... 182
- Why We Say Things We Don't Believe ... 215

PART V : How Prayer Book Editors Deal with Naming God
- A British Father and a British King? ... 227
- Avinu Malkeinu and the New Reform Machzor (Mishkan HaNefesh) ... 238
- What Is God's Name? ... 254
- Changing God's Names ... 266

PART VI : Masculine Imagery; Feminist Critique
- So Near and Oh So Far ... 277
- Our Rock, Our Hard Place ... 284
- What's in a Word? ... 294
- Rescuing the Father-God from Delray Beach ... 299

I Do Not Know Your Name	306

PART VII : What's in a Name?

Abracadabra	315
My Name Is Vulnerability	323
We Are But Dust	330
Two Pockets	337
Re-imaging God	345
"Would You Still Love Me If...?"	352
Celebrating a Conflicted Relationship with God	360
God the Cashier	367
Piety and Protest	372
The Most Difficult Name for God, "You"—Or, How Is Prayer Possible?	382
Machzor and Malkhut	389
"We Guess; We Clothe Thee, Unseen King"	400
From Direct Experience to a World of Words	407
Appendix A : Avinu Malkeinu through Time	415
Appendix B: Alternatives to Avinu Malkeinu*	447
Notes	459
Glossary	493
Front Cover Flap	503
Back Cover Flap	505
Back Cover Material	507

Also in the Prayers of Awe Series

Who by Fire, Who by Water—Un'taneh Tokef

All These Vows—Kol Nidre

We Have Sinned: Sin and Confession in Judaism—Ashamnu and Al Chet

May God Remember: Memory and Memorializing in Judaism—Yizkor

All the World: Universalism, Particularism and the High Holy Days

Other Jewish Lights Books by Rabbi Lawrence A. Hoffman, PhD

My People's Prayer Book: Traditional Prayers, Modern Commentaries, Vols. 1–10

My People's Passover Haggadah: Traditional Texts, Modern Commentaries, Vols. 1 & 2
(coedited with David Arnow, PhD)

The Art of Public Prayer, 2nd Ed.: *Not for Clergy Only*

(A book from SkyLight Paths, Jewish Lights' sister imprint)

*Rethinking Synagogues:
A New Vocabulary for Congregational Life*

*Israel—A Spiritual Travel Guide:
A Compoanion for the Modern Jewish Pilgrim*

The Way Into Jewish Prayer

What You Will See Inside a Synagogue
(coauthored with Dr. Ron Wolfson)

Introduction

Why This Book: And Why It Is the Way It Is

Rabbi Lawrence A. Hoffman, PhD

Rabbi Lawrence A. Hoffman, PhD, has served for more than three decades as professor of liturgy at Hebrew Union College – Jewish Institute of Religion in New York. He is a world-renowned liturgist and holder of the Stephen and Barbara Friedman Chair in Liturgy, Worship and Ritual. He has written and edited many books, including the *My People's Prayer Book: Traditional Prayers, Modern Commentaries* series, winner of the National Jewish Book Award; and the *Prayers of Awe* series; and he is coeditor of *My People's Passover Haggadah: Traditional Texts, Modern Commentaries*, a finalist for the National Jewish Book Award. He cofounded and developed Synagogue 2/3000, a transdenominational project designed to envision and implement the ideal synagogue of the spirit for the twenty-first century.

Of all the books in the *Prayers of Awe* series so far, this one has proved most surprising. When books are planned, one never knows what the research will turn up, and the topic of *Avinu Malkeinu* has turned out to be quite amazing.

I wondered at the outset if *Avinu Malkeinu* should even make it into this series. The original plan was to focus on prayers that present modern worshipers with significant difficulties—a criterion under which *Avinu Malkeinu* certainly qualified, on account of its redundant masculine imaging of God as a father and king. I worried, however, that the prayer might not have enough about it to fill up an entire volume. Secondary literature on it is exceptionally sparse. Halakhic discussion about its use is sparse to nonexistent.

But further consideration suggested that *Avinu Malkeinu* was part of a larger issue of naming God. So I added to the book's content the medieval poem *(piyyut)* known as *Ki Hinei Kachomer* ("Like clay in the hand of the potter")—a composition that supplements "Our Father" and "Our King" with a great many other ways to conceptualize the divine.

To my surprise, *Avinu Malkeinu* alone presented far more depth than I had anticipated. This book therefore presents both *Avinu Malkeinu* and *Ki Hinei Kachomer*, but overwhelmingly contributors have focused on *Avinu Malkeinu* as their primary topic. And for good reason. I can think of few prayers that demonstrate so clearly the process by which Jewish liturgy grew through the ages. The images of God as father and king go back to the Bible; a prayer addressed to *Avinu Malkeinu* is presented in the Talmud as going back to the second century; a full prayer based on that early Rabbinic paradigm turns up only in the ninth century; not until later in the Middle Ages does that prayer make its way into Jewish liturgy worldwide, and it now can be found in many different versions. This process of growth and diversification is itself a valuable corrective to the common assumption that the wording of our prayers goes back unfailingly to antiquity.

In addition, there is the issue that recommended *Avinu Malkeinu* in the first place: the feminist critique expanded to include the larger question of how we have the audacity to name God altogether. One after another, contributors have shed important light on how we ought to think this matter through.

Each book in the *Prayers of Awe* series is organized according to the content of the various contributions, a matter that cannot be determined in advance of their being written. I collect what people have to say and then arrange it all in an order that best sheds light on the nature of the topic. The very organization of this volume demonstrates the surprising depth of its subject.

We begin with my own two editorial overviews of the topic. The first ("The History, Meaning, and Varieties of *Avinu Malkeinu*") provides the story behind *Avinu Malkeinu*—how it developed through time to become what it is today, and how that history illustrates Jewish liturgical creativity in general. Important liturgical landmarks turned out to be *Seder Rav Amram,* our first comprehensive prayer book from the ninth century; *Machzor Vitry*, our first large-scale glimpse of Franco-German liturgy that became the Ashkenazi tradition; and assorted evidence for the the Sephardi tradition, emanating from Jews who were exiled from Spain in 1492 and who then carried their tradition northward through Holland, England, and the New World or eastward through the Mediterranean, where it was transformed by medieval Kabbalah from the Land of Israel.

My second overview ("'Our Father and King': The Many Ways That Liturgy Means") supplements the historical record by adding liturgical theory from the disciplines of philosophy, literature, and linguistics. People mistakenly think that the liturgy describes reality in the same way that science does. In reality, prayers do a whole lot more than that. Naming God, then, is far more complex than meets the eye. This second introduction provides the theoretical backdrop necessary to discuss the matter of naming, intelligently.

With these overviews behind us, we turn to the liturgy itself: "*Avinu Malkeinu:* A New and Annotated Translation" and "*Ki Hinei Kachomer:* A New and Annotated Translation" by Dr. Joel M. Hoffman, who combines his expertise in linguistics and in Hebrew to give a fresh understanding of what these prayers have to say. Every one of our volumes features such a translation, but in this case, the variety of *Avinu*

Malkeinu's many versions posed a unique challenge. Rather than provide one version alone, we provide several—all the way from the very first one (in the ninth century) to alternative contemporary versions in the Ashkenazi, Sephardi, and even Yemenite communities. The Hebrew version that results is a combination of them all, with each line numbered so as to let the reader know the source from which it is drawn. This book thus provides not just one *Avinu Malkeinu* but many different versions of it.

Part 3 turns immediately to the music of *Avinu Malkeinu*, probably the feature that most recommends the prayer to worshipers. Gordon Dale, MA, gives us the history behind the melodies we are most accustomed to hearing, and a contemporary composer, Chazzan Danny Maseng, provides rare insight into the way new music comes into being by describing the process behind his own remarkable composition.

With the discussion of music behind us, we return in part 4 ("Precursors, Foundations, and Parallels") to the history of *Avinu Malkeinu*. How and why did we begin referring to God as father and king in the first place? A series of exceptional essays provides answers to that question. Dr. Marc Zvi Brettler, Rabbi Jonathan Magonet, PhD, and Dr. Annette M. Boeckler look closely at biblical beginnings; Rabbi Elie Kaunfer, DHL, examines the Talmudic tale of *Avinu Malkeinu's* origin. Rabbi Reuven Kimelman, PhD, supplies the historical context of the regal Roman world in late antiquity. Dr. Wendy Zierler continues the analysis of biblical and Rabbinic parallels but then enriches the conversation by looking carefully at the way the themes of *Avinu Malkeinu* find their way even into contemporary literature, particularly the work of Nobel Prize winner S.Y. Agnon. Rabbi Dalia Marx, PhD, explores the way Jews have handled problematic texts in the past and then offers her own solution—as a Reform rabbi, a woman, a scholar, and an Israeli for whom language (Hebrew) is always gendered. And Rabbi Karyn D. Kedar introduces the larger question of metaphoric naming in general.

With this historical and foundational background behind us, we move on to the contemporary moment, in a remarkable dialogue by actual editors of contemporary prayer books, who discuss the way they and their communities have dealt with translating *Avinu Malkeinu*. Rabbi David A. Teutsch, PhD (Reconstructionist), and Rabbi Edwin Goldberg, DHL (North American Reform), are joined by Rabbi Paul Freedman (British Reform) and Rabbi Andrew Goldstein, PhD, with Rabbi Charles H. Middleburgh, PhD (British Liberal), in this conversation across two continents. We get something of the flavor of the discussion from some of the titles: "A British Father and a British King?" (Freedman), for instance. Does it make a difference to have an actual monarch, as British Jews do? "What is God's name" anyway? asks Teutsch. How do we go about "changing God's name"? Goldstein and Middleburgh wonder.

At last we get to part 6, "Masculine Imagery; Feminist Critique," the heart of the question that haunts worshipers as they recite *Avinu Malkeinu*. The issue was summarized historically by Dalia Marx from Israel (in part 4), but here several congregational rabbis in America add their own experience. Two of the earliest women to be ordained, Rabbi Laura Geller (Reform) and Rabbi Sandy Eisenberg Sasso, DMin (Reconstructionist), provide reflections titled "So Near and Oh So Far" and "I Do Not Know Your Name," respectively; and Rabbi Jeffrey K. Salkin, DMin, meditates on "Rescuing the Father-God from Delray Beach." Two lay worshipers round out the analysis beautifully. Catherine Madsen, who has authored liturgies herself, hints at the enigma involved by naming her piece "Our Rock, Our Hard Place." Ruth Messinger, the president of American Jewish World Service, reminds us of the seriousness of the issue in her autobiographical recollection of growing up as a woman saying this prayer. "What's in a word?" she wonders. How, indeed, do we read and hear our prayers?

Part 7 expands on the feminist critique by enlarging the question to read, "What's in a Name?" The bulk of our contributions are located here. One by one, men and women—primarily rabbis, from Reform, Conservative, Liberal, Reconstructionist, and

Orthodox movements, and from England, Canada, and the United States—expand our horizons by thoughtful perspectives on the way we approach God and how we conceptualize the divine.

A series of appendices round out the book, not simply as afterthoughts but as the means to go deeper into the story of *Avinu Malkeinu* and all it represents. Appendix A provides the actual texts in translation, all the way from the original prayer book of 860CE to contemporary versions in Ashkenazi, Sephardi, Yemenite, and Hasidic traditions, with stop-offs in medieval France and Italy. Appendix B provides alternative compositions of today, for Israel, the UK, and North America.

As a supplement to the book, available as a free download on the *Naming God* book page at www.jewishlights.com, readers can view the last hundred years and more of *Avinu Malkeinu* translations in chart form. Arranged by Rabbi April Peters, this online addendum allows readers to see the entire panoply of modern prayer-book translations at a single glance.

As always, I am indebted beyond measure to the many contributors of this volume. No single one of us knows much more than a tiny piece of the puzzle that this volume seeks to explore. Together, however, the overall picture of the way Jews name God begins to take shape. I continue to be blessed with support from my extraordinary publisher, Stuart M. Matlins, founder of Jewish Lights, and from Emily Wichland, vice president of Editorial and Production there. It was Stuart who first approached me with the idea for the Prayers of Awe series, as suggested to him by Dan Adler in response to a High Holy Day program developed by Rob Eshman, editor in chief of the *Jewish Journal of Greater Los Angeles*, and David Suissa. Their program sprang from an idea first conceived by Rabbi Elazar Muskin of Young Israel of Century City, California. Emily continues to amaze me in all she does: her abundant wisdom, skill, patience, and perseverance are precisely what an author most desires. For her copyediting, my thanks go again to Debra Corman. I happily include as well all the others at Jewish Lights, especially Tim Holtz, director of Production, who designed the cover for this book and typeset the English text.

Finally, on a more personal note, I offer thanks to Dr. Joel M. Hoffman, translator, linguist, and scholar, but also (as it happens) my son, with whom I regularly consult on matters Hebrew and linguistic. Last, but altogether first in my thoughts, I acknowledge my wife, Gayle Hoover, to whom I dedicate this effort.

PART I
Two Overviews

The History, Meaning, and Varieties of Avinu Malkeinu

Rabbi Lawrence A. Hoffman, PhD

Rabbi Lawrence A. Hoffman, PhD, has served for more than three decades as professor of liturgy at Hebrew Union College – Jewish Institute of Religion in New York. He is a world-renowned liturgist and holder of the Stephen and Barbara Friedman Chair in Liturgy, Worship and Ritual. He has written and edited many books, including the *My People's Prayer Book: Traditional Prayers, Modern Commentaries* series, winner of the National Jewish Book Award; and the *Prayers of Awe* series; and he is coeditor of *My People's Passover Haggadah: Traditional Texts, Modern Commentaries*, a finalist for the National Jewish Book Award. He cofounded and developed Synagogue 2/3000, a transdenominational project designed to envision and implement the ideal synagogue of the spirit for the twenty-first century.

Avinu Malkeinu is a single prayer with many different versions, the result of centuries of liturgical development throughout the many lands where Jews have lived. Why is *Avinu Malkeinu* still subject to so much creativity? How did it begin in the first place? And what meaning has it had for Jews across the centuries?

Avinu Malkeinu, an Anomaly?

Jewish liturgy emerged out of a millennium or so of development, first in the Land of Israel (beginning in the second century BCE) and then (from the second century CE onward) in Babylonia (present-day Iraq) as well. Rabbis in both geographic centers composed vast compilations of law and lore called Talmuds, after which later rabbinic generations added commentaries, as well as other freestanding compositions, that became the basis for an ongoing rabbinic literature that continues to this day. Among the relatively early literary classics is *Seder Rav Amram* ("The Order of Prayer by Rav Amram," c. 860), a compilation representing Babylonian prayer practice at the time. *Avinu Malkeinu* makes its first appearance there.[1]

Despite its relatively early appearance in *Seder Rav Amram*, it took many centuries more for *Avinu Malkeinu* to became so intimately identified with the experience of the High Holy Days. It was just one prayer of many to Amram, and even today, it is still rather peripheral to halakhic consciousness: Rabbi Asher Lopatin, one of our commentators here, notes that it is not even halakhically demanded! However (he continues), "Even though there is no Jewish legal obligation to say *Avinu Malkeinu*—not the first line, not the last line; not any of the lines—it feels as obligatory as the *Amidah* or the *Sh'ma*. The service would not be complete without it." Indeed, it wouldn't nowadays. Although hardly at the heart of Jewish law, it has nonetheless entered the heart of the Jews who pray it.

Yet over the centuries, we have not all prayed it the same way. Unlike the *Sh'ma* and the *Amidah*, but also unlike *Un'taneh Tokef* and *Kol Nidre* (see *Prayers of Awe, Who by Fire, Who by Water*—Un'taneh Tokef *and* All These Vows—Kol Nidre), *Avinu Malkeinu* attracted remarkable variety as it traveled from place to place. That sort of variety is not altogether unique: we find it to some extent also in the "Long Confession" *(Al Chet)* that characterizes Yom Kippur and in the Memorial Service, *Yizkor* (see *Prayers of Awe, We Have Sinned: Sin and Confession in Judaism*—Ashamnu *and* Al Chet *and* May God Remember: Memory and Memorializing in Judaism—Yizkor). But there, the differences are largely between Jews from Ashkenaz (northern and central Europe) on one hand and Sepharad (Spain and Portugal, originally) on the other. With *Avinu Malkeinu*, however, the variation is especially pronounced and more widespread.

In part, that extensive variation may be precisely because *Avinu Malkeinu* did not become so halakhically fixed as to demand one particular set of words rather than another. The *Sh'ma* came directly out of the Torah—once the decision to say it had been made (first century CE), its words were no longer open to debate. A mandated *Amidah* too was fixed by the end of the first century, at least as far as the order of topics was concerned. Wording varied for quite some time, but overall the version encoded in the prayer book by Rav Amram became statutory everywhere. Even after that, the absence of printing allowed for considerable leeway in this word or that—but the differences were minor, relative to the wholesale innovation that marked *Avinu Malkeinu*.

If we look at the High Holy Day prayers mentioned thus far, we see that *Kol Nidre* and the confessions were decided upon much later than the *Sh'ma* and the *Amidah*: they are post-Talmudic (i.e., post–sixth to seventh century), but known to Amram in the ninth century, and encoded by Jewish law thereafter. *Un'taneh Tokef* is different still: it is a poem from about the fifth century that became commonplace in northern and central Europe (Ashkenaz) as a result of being associated with Jewish martyrdom at the time of the Crusades. The Memorial Service *(Yizkor)* too grew up there as a consequence of the devastation caused by the Crusaders and was expanded after the Chmielnicki massacres that devastated Ukrainian Jewry in the seventeenth century. These prayers too, however, once decided upon, tended to remain largely as they were at the time of their founding.

Avinu Malkeinu is different. Not only did it escape the attention of the codifiers, but unlike *Un'taneh Tokef*, it was not the finished work of any single author; and unlike the confessions, it was not an alphabetic acrostic either and so did not have to fit into the arbitrary confines of the Hebrew alphabet. Instead, it was, from the very outset, a simple litany of one-line "stanzas" (for "Litany," see section entitled "Avinu Malkeinu and Liturgical Poetry"), easily alterable and adaptable.

I have already used the terms "Ashkenaz" and "Sepharad," the two major geographic currents of medieval Jewish practice. I have mentioned also the work of Rav Amram, the ninth-century rabbi who first codified Jewish prayer with lasting success. Before continuing our story, I should first trace the other books, people, and places that constitute *Avinu Malkeinu's* historical evolution.

Jewish Liturgical Tradition: Its Books and Cast of Characters

Rav Amram was, in effect, the chief rabbi of Babylonia (present-day Iraq), the geographic home of the Babylonian Talmud, which had been largely completed somewhere around the sixth to seventh centuries. By 642, the area had been conquered by Islam, and in 747, the Abbasid caliphate had established its headquarters in Baghdad.

The newly centralized authority of the caliph became the model for Babylonian rabbis as well. While the earlier Talmudic rabbis had allowed considerable discrepancy in prayer practice, these newer ones—known as *geonim* (singular: *gaon*, a biblical term meaning, roughly, "your honor")—claimed authority to fix the liturgy worldwide. Rav Amram was such a *gaon*, and his prayer book (c. 860) was circulated throughout the known Jewish world as the way Jews ought to pray.

Some decades later (c. 920) another *gaon*, Saadiah, wrote his own prayer book (called *Siddur Saadiah, siddur* being a variant of *seder*, also meaning "order"). Although similar to Amram's in that it followed the broad Rabbinic precedents of days gone by, it yet differed considerably, so that Jews now had two models from which to work. Both volumes contained not just the texts of prayers but also extensive halakhic commentary on how to say them. Saadiah composed his commentary in Judeo-Arabic, however (Arabic written in Hebrew characters), while Amram had employed Talmudic Aramaic, so Saadiah's prayer book could be consulted only in other Muslim countries, while Amram became the widespread paradigm for rabbis worldwide, all of whom used the Aramaic of the Babylonian Talmud as their *lingua franca* for advanced halakhic debate.

The two very broad divisions known as Ashkenaz and Sepharad have their own histories. Sephardi Jews had come to the Iberian Peninsula alongside Roman conquerors and were enjoying a golden age of cultural efflorescence under Muslim rule by the tenth century. That century saw just the beginning of Ashkenazi Jewry, as Jews in Italy crossed the Alps and settled in the Rhineland, establishing a tradition of rabbinic scholarship that lasted until the First Crusade (1096), when Crusader armies sweeping across Europe stopped to massacre Rhineland Jewry. Jews in France escaped the carnage, and the school of Rashi, just outside of Paris, became dominant in place of the German academies where Rashi himself had studied prior to the Crusade that ended them. To be sure, German Jewry was reborn after the Crusades, but only with the memory of the Crusader armies as a dampening influence.

Christians, meanwhile, had conquered Spain and Portugal, allowing Jews another golden age before eventually expelling them in 1492. By then, Ashkenazi Jews had spread eastward into areas now associated with modern-day Germany, Austria, the Czech Republic, Hungary, and so forth.

Ashkenazi Jews are largely identified as German because of the ubiquity of German as the language of central Europe, but the first Ashkenazi prayer book (patterned on Amram's Babylonian prototype) was written in the school of Rashi (eleventh- to twelfth-century France) and called *Machzor Vitry* ("The *machzor* [written by a man named Simchah of the town of] Vitry"). In general, we call the daily and Shabbat prayer books a *siddur* (as in *Siddur Saadiah*, reserving *seder* for the name of the evening meal that introduces Passover). By contrast, Ashkenazi Jews in the Middle Ages began calling the prayer book for holidays a *machzor*, from the Hebrew root *ch.z.r*, "to go round, to return," because it contains the prayers for the annual cycle of holidays that "come round" annually—hence the regular reference in this book to *machzor*, the prayer book for the High Holy Days (there are others for the three Pilgrimage Festivals, Passover, Shavuot, and Sukkot). In the very early days of *Machzor Vitry*, however (eleventh to twelfth centuries), that distinction had not yet been made. *Machzor Vitry* did indeed contain the prayers for all the holidays, but it also contained a siddur for daily and Shabbat worship as well as a Haggadah for the Passover seder—not unlike *Seder Rav Amram* and *Siddur Saadiah*, which were also all-encompassing.

That liturgy had grown considerably since the days of Amram and Saadiah, however, as poets recorded Jewish experience in *piyyutim* (poems of prayer that got added to the inherited liturgical corpus, especially for holidays). That extensive enlargement of the holiday liturgy is the reason services normally take so long in traditional synagogues today. It also is why the liturgy eventually got divided into a siddur and several *machzorim* (plural for *machzor*) for the various holidays, especially because prior to the invention of printing, these volumes were usually calligraphed in heavy folio editions, sometimes with illustrations in gold leaf—it had become impossible to carry the whole thing around!

Ashkenazi liturgy evolved further in the sixteenth century, as Jews increasingly settled Greater Poland: modern-day Poland but also parts of Russia, the Baltic states (especially Lithuania), and many of the former Soviet republics (like Ukraine). The Polish experience was especially rich in Jewish culture and learning, so that the Ashkenazi liturgy carried there was altered sufficiently to be named the Polish Rite *(Minhag Polin)*, as opposed to the older German version that continued on in Germany and is called the Rhineland Rite *(Minhag Rinus)*.

Sephardi Jews, meanwhile, who had been expelled in 1492, moved north to the Netherlands or east across the Mediterranean to the Turkish (Ottoman) Empire, including the Land of Israel. By the early seventeenth century, Jews in the former were joining Dutch colonial forces in colonizing Brazil and later (1655) were granted the right to resettle in England, from which Jews had been expelled in 1290. The Brazilian experiment itself was relatively short-lived, however, because Portugal ousted the Dutch in 1664, bringing the Inquisition with them, and forcing Jews to move on elsewhere—to New

Amsterdam, for example (now New York), and the various colonies that became the United States.

The Turkish branch, meanwhile, was influenced by Kabbalah, which was enjoying efflorescence in the Land of Israel, so its version of the Sephardi liturgy (unlike the Dutch and British alternative) was heavily influenced by Jewish mysticism. That mystical version became widespread in the sixteenth and seventeenth centuries because of the invention of printing, which permitted mass publication and distribution, and which occurred precisely as the Mediterranean masters of Kabbalah were writing down their doctrines. It was adopted by a new group of Jews just being founded in Ukraine: the Hasidim, who combined their Ashkenazi Polish Rite with Sephardi kabbalism to constitute their own brand of prayer.

Nowadays, then, in North America, Europe, and Israel, we find five major liturgies. Each one is called a *minhag*, a "way of prayer," or, more technically, in English, a "rite."

Sephardi liturgy may be (1) the Dutch and British version of the Sephardi Rite; alternatively, it may be (2) some version of the Kabbalah-influenced Mediterranean version, known also as *Minhag Ari*, "Ari" being a short form, or nickname, for Isaac Luria, the great kabbalistic innovator in sixteenth-century Land of Israel. Specific versions of this tradition are sometimes intertwined with the name of geographic regions in the area—the Syrian Rite, for instance, for Jews who hail from Syria. Finally, however, *Minhag Ari* may be known today (3) in its mixed Ashkenazi-Sephardi form that resulted when it was adopted by Hasidic Jews in Poland.

The course of Ashkenazi liturgy is easier to follow. Polish Hasidim (as we just saw, in variant 3, above) still use it in their mixed Ashkenazi-Sephardi version of *Minhag Ari*. But in all but the Hasidic communities, it is likely to be encountered as (4) the Polish Rite, brought westward during the Great Migration from Eastern Europe that began in 1881. The Rhineland Rite from Germany proper (5) largely died with German Jews under Hitler, but it can still be found among descendants of German Jews who left Germany in time. Jews who survived the Shoah are likely either to still follow their native Polish (4) or Rhineland (5) Rite or to be Hasidic survivors, who practice one version or another of their Hasidic *Minhag Ari* (3). But Hasidism splintered, early on, into a variety of rival sects, each with its own version of *Minhag Ari*, dictated by the "rebbes" who have led it. These sometimes go by their own names—*Minhag Chabad*, for example—the prayer practice followed by Lubavitch Hasidim, known popularly today as Chabad.

So far, I have dealt only with traditional Orthodoxy, not the various groups that go by such names as Reform, Liberal, Progressive, Conservative, Masorti, Reconstructionist, and the like—the modern Jewish denominations that emerged with the dawn of Jewish modernity in the nineteenth and twentieth centuries. By and large, they all follow Ashkenazi precedents, since they tend to have begun in Germany or by German émigrés to other Western countries. But their founders were scholars who had studied Jewish liturgy historically and who had entire libraries of prayer books at their disposal. Despite their Ashkenazi origins, they valued the poetry and philosophy of the Sephardi tradition, so did not hesitate to draw freely on Sephardi practice as well, thus making the original nomenclature (which was based on geography) a moot point. What came to matter more was the particular denomination for which any given book was prepared. By now, each of these has its own liturgical tradition, sometimes going back to the nineteenth century, when denominationalism began.

How has *Avinu Malkeinu* fared during the various stages of this lengthy Jewish odyssey through time?

Avinu Malkeinu, Once Again: How a Theology of Sin Gained the Upper Hand

The prototype for *Avinu Malkeinu* goes back to a Talmudic tale (Ta'anit 25b), which is much discussed throughout this volume:[2]

Rabbi Eliezer led the *Amidah*[3] and said twenty-four blessings,[4] but was not answered. Rabbi Akiva led after him, and said,

> "Our father, our king, we have sinned before You.
> Our father, our king, we have no king other than You.
> Our father, our king, for your sake, have mercy upon us."
> And the rain fell.

It can be readily seen that the prayer contains three parallel lines, each beginning *Avinu Malkeinu* ("Our father, our king"), and that the emphasis of the prayer is on human sinfulness. The very first line says explicitly that we are sinners, and the last line pleads with God to have mercy upon us *for God's own sake*, since, presumably, we are too sinful to expect God's bounty on account of any merit of our own. The assumption behind the whole account is that natural disasters like droughts are punishment for sin. Having no good deeds of our own, we depend on God's grace for deliverance—"grace" being a theological term for the love God shows us even though we do not deserve it.

But our printed copy of the Talmud includes changes that crept into the original version over time. Sometimes these alterations reflect points of view that the authors of the Talmud did not hold. If we check the manuscripts of this story, we can see that the emphasis on sin is a medieval insertion into the original account, which read, simply:

> Our father, our king, we have no king but You.
> Our father, our king, have mercy upon us.

This shorter (and original) version is less about us and our sins than it is about God and God's obligation. Akiva argues that God is both father and king to us, and as such, God should deal mercifully with us, the way good fathers and kings normally do.

We do, of course, have another father (our birth father), but when it comes to the monarchy, Akiva maintains, God *alone* is our king. By extension, he may be saying that the Roman emperor is not. That this prayer is attributed to Akiva is in keeping with Akiva's participation in the Bar Kokhba revolt of 132–135CE, an uprising fought specifically because it denied the emperor's right to be considered king of the Jews. The shorter (and original) version of the Akiva account regarding *Avinu Malkeinu* is just an affirmation of our Jewish loyalty to God as our ruler, and God's ensuing responsibility to take care of us.

In the course of time, that lesson was muted. The Bar Kokhba revolt failed, Akiva and the other revolutionary leaders were tortured to death, and Jerusalem was declared a pagan city, off-limits to Jews. Jews had to declare fealty to earthly monarchs, not just God in heaven. Equally significantly, after the revolt they faced the need to explain the revolt's failure, especially on the heels of the war of 70, in which Roman troops had emerged victorious as well. Rather than blame God, they adopted the theological rationale that emphasized their own sin—a position that remained dominant throughout the Middle Ages. Our printed version of the Talmud reflects changes introduced into the original narrative so as to deemphasize the original claim of God as the only ruler for Jews and to highlight instead the inevitability of Jewish sin and the need for God's grace.

The theology of sin remained standard Jewish fare for centuries, all the way until the heady atmosphere of the Enlightenment, which reached Jews when they were released from ghettos under Napoleon. These nineteenth-century Jews found it hard to believe that God sends or withholds rain on account of human merit or sin. Impressed by their newly acquired freedom, the Enlightenment philosophy of human potential, and the rising tide of scientific accomplishment, they were more inclined to see human beings as positively endowed with virtue, than as inveterate sinners needing to plead constantly for favors from the divine.

But the nineteenth century was very far off when the theology of sin led medieval Jews to see *Avinu Malkeinu* as the prayer par excellence with which to address God in moments of crisis. The doctored Talmudic passage had the effect of expanding a two-line couplet into a three-line litany, a literary format that lent itself easily to expansions. For several centuries, prayer was an oral pastime, after all: worshipers had no prayer book but neither did prayer leaders, who readily improvised lines that only eventually were written down to become part of official prayer *books*—like Amram's. As new lines were added, the prayer grew, and by Amram's time, a simple Talmudic story on kingship had become the basis for a lengthy High Holy Day prayer on sin and divine mercy.

By Amram's time also, a single line of *Avinu Malkeinu* had emerged independently elsewhere—not as this lengthy High Holy Day litany, but as a statement integrated into the part of our daily weekday morning service that is known as *Tachanun*, meaning "Supplications." *Tachanun* is also called *n'filat apayim* ("falling on one's face"), a description of the idealized body posture of someone overwhelmed by sin and pleading with God for mercy. The same Enlightenment mentality that did away with the theology of sin generally also deemphasized *Tachanun*. In traditional circles it survives, but usually as something said hastily (if at all), and most Reform, Reconstructionist, and Liberal Jews got rid of it altogether. But Amram, who epitomized medieval sentiment in the making, has an extensive *Tachanun,* to the point of containing a full confession just as if each day were Yom Kippur, followed by a poem featuring God as *Avinu Malkeinu:*

> Our father, our king, your name stands forever....
>
> Our father, our king, answer us and save us [*aneinu v'hoshi'einu*].

This last line should sound familiar. In an expanded form, it is also the signal petition of our High Holy Day *Avinu Malkeinu,* the final verse that we all sing together (a conclusion found already in Amram's version). We still say this version of it in our own *Tachanun* as well:

> Our father, our king, be gracious to us and answer us, for we have no merit; act justly and lovingly with us and save us. [*Avinu malkeinu, choneinu va'aneinu ki ein banu ma'asim; aseih imanu tz'dakah vachesed v'hoshi'einu*].[5]

That single verse in *Tachanun* shows up in our second comprehensive liturgy from the Middle Ages, *Siddur Saadiah* (c. 920), in slightly modified form.[6] For some reason, however, Saadiah omits the entire *Avinu Malkeinu* poem for the High Holy Days. So does Maimonides! *Avinu Malkeinu* had not yet become "everyone's favorite prayer," apparently, even by the death of Maimonides in 1204.

It does, however, appear in *Machzor Vitry*, the first comprehensive liturgy of northern Europe (France, eleventh to twelfth centuries), and in *Sefer Abudarham*, the equivalent volume for Sephardi Jews, but composed only in the fourteenth century. The author of the latter (David Abudarham) seems to include the poem only as a part of his *Tachanun*, saying:

> "Our father, our king, You are our father; we have no king other than You" and so forth: The reason that we customarily say this after the *Amidah* is that [the Talmud] reports ... Rabbi Akiva ... said, "Our father, our king, You are our father; our father, our king, we have no king but You. Our father, our king, have compassion on us and answer us." After that, [we conclude the *Tachanun*].[7]

Abudarham's version of the Talmudic paradigm has two lines, but given Abudarham's comment "and so forth," we should conclude that it had already been expanded beyond that.

In sum, under the influence of Amram (ninth century), *Avinu Malkeinu* had become the way to name and address God in moments of trial. A single-line version shows up in the *Tachanun* ("Supplications") of the daily weekday service, the unit of everyday prayer that emphasizes human sin and dependence on God. As a High Holy Day poem, however, it did not make it into the prayer book of Saadiah (tenth century) and was not said by Maimonides (twelfth to thirteenth centuries). It was, however, adopted by the Ashkenazi *Machzor Vitry* (eleventh to twelfth centuries) and the Sephardi *Sefer Abudarham* (fourteenth century) but said in the latter only in the daily liturgy, not specifically on the High Holy Days.

To be sure, an exhaustive survey of all the medieval sources would turn up a great many alterations and possibilities, but from what we have seen already we can say that the Talmudic tale of Rabbi Akiva led to God being addressed as *Avinu Malkeinu* in moments of need. As part of that development, the poem we know so well had become standard fare for Ashkenazi and Sephardi Jews by the late Middle Ages.

Beyond Sin

Had *Avinu Malkeinu* attracted no music, it is doubtful that it would have become so central in our consciousness; but despite its curious omission by some of the greatest liturgical luminaries, it became standard fare for most Jews, who would miss it greatly were it to be omitted from the High Holy Day experience today. As a matter of fact, it actually is omitted from traditional worship when the High Holy Days fall on Shabbat but is so missed that most Liberal and Reform Jews say it then anyway. Those same Jews do not always say it in its entirety, however, even when the High Holy Days do not fall on Shabbat, and elsewhere in these pages, we provide examples of the many ways current liturgies abridge or otherwise alter it (see appendix A and Rabbi April Peters' online addendum).

By now, the music that accompanies *Avinu Malkeinu* so overwhelms the lyrics that most people remain relatively unconcerned with what it means. Were they to attend carefully to its accent on sin, they would probably be surprised at what they were saying. Even Jews who do attend High Holy Day services with a sense of their own sin foremost in their mind are likely not to agree with the literal sense that *ein banu ma'asim* ("we have no merit") and that God must heed our cries *l'ma'ankha* ("for your [God's] sake"), for we have no right to claim God's mercy on our own.

This notion of finding some merit other than our own to justify asking God for mercy is one of the aspects of *Avinu Malkeinu* that has grown most through time. Amram provides just three lines to it: God is to heed our requests, "for your sake and not for our sake" (line 40a); "for the sake of your great compassion" (line 42a); and "for the sake of your great name" (line 43a). To the line stipulating that salvation comes only *l'ma'ankha* ("for your sake," line 41) *Machzor Vitry* adds clarification, *al yakev chet v'avon et t'filateinu* ("do not let sin and transgression interrupt our prayer," line 41a).

By the age of printing, however, the accent on justification beyond our own merit grows considerably. At least in Ashkenaz, consciousness of the many years of martyrdom led Jews to insist that Jewish victims through the centuries had not died in vain—God would keep faith with those who had perished by favoring us, their descendants, who may not be worthy ourselves, but who have a claim on God because of them. These additions to *Avinu Malkeinu* never found their way into the Sephardi version and were frequently the first casualties of modern editors who were seeking to shorten the liturgy anyway and who disagreed with the idea that (first) we are essentially sinful and that (second) God listens to us anyway because of martyrs who preceded us.

Some modern liturgies go even farther. It is rare that anyone excludes the last and most plaintive line, the one that most clearly echoes the theme of human moral depravity—*choneinu va'aneinu ki ein banu ma'asim* ("be gracious to us and answer us, for we have no merit," line 44)—if for no other reason than the fact that the melody demands it. But Rabbi David Einhorn, a major Reform thinker and writer in nineteenth-century America, did. Upon arriving on these shores from Europe, Einhorn settled in Baltimore and demonstrated his unswerving obedience to principle by (among other things) preaching sermons against slavery and having to flee for his life as a result. His prayer book *Olat*

Tamid ("A Perpetual Offering") did indeed omit that all-important line on doctrinal grounds.

Contemporary prayer books have been slow in introducing a great number of new lines, probably because so much of *Avinu Malkeinu* is perfectly acceptable as it is; we say it for the music as much as for the words; and it has been felt necessary to shorten this extended litany rather than to expand it. But some editors today feel free to add petitions to the list and to translate what we have inherited in creative ways. Appendices A and B, as well as Rabbi April Peters' online addendum, "Modern Translations of *Avinu Malkeinu*" (available as a free download at www.jewishlights.com) assemble examples of this creativity across denominationallines.

Avinu Malkeinu is obviously a central prayer to us today, although it was not always so. On the face of it, it is just an overly extended litany of lines that seem redundant at best. Below the surface, however, its history is rich with intimations of Judaism's dialogue with its history and its God.

"Our Father and King"

THE MANY WAYS THAT LITURGY MEANS

Rabbi Lawrence A. Hoffman, PhD

"Here," I say to students, "is how to write a sermon: Imagine working with the two sides of your brain separately. Every time you get an idea, decide which half of the brain it is from. If the idea seems more like a *fact*, like 'The cat is on the mat,' then it comes from the left side of your brain, part of the logical and linear way of patterning reality. If it is more holistic—a cartoon, a story, some kind of *illustration*—then treat it as deriving from the right. Powerfully left-brained people risk writing sermons that sound academic, philosophical, and informational, but boring. Dominantly right-brained people sometimes compose sermons that entertain but go nowhere. Worshipers leave left-brain sermons commenting, 'Our rabbi is brilliant, but I had trouble staying with her.' They leave right-brain sermons with a joke or two in pocket but no idea what the point was.

"Good sermons," I conclude, "need a balance: left-brain logical development of an idea, and right-brain illustrations that move us."

To be sure, I am oversimplifying: left- and right-brain categorization is more complicated than I describe. But the distinction works in practice. Conversations are indeed combinations of telling people something "true or false" (what I call left-brain) and illustrating the trueor-false something-or-others in "right-brain" imagery that makes them matter. Traditionally, the study of left-brain truth or falsity is called logic; the study of right-brain motivational speaking is called rhetoric.

So what kind of statement is the characterization of God as "father" and "king"? Is it a statement of fact, like "The cat is on the mat"? Or is it an illustration that moves us to see a truth but is not exactly the truth itself. If the latter, what is the truth to which it is supposed to point? If we know what it is, however, then why not just say it directly? And if we don't know what it is, does the metaphor stand for anything at all? Or is it like a cartoon without a point, a picture of a unicorn (when there are no real unicorns to picture) or a signpost announcing "go left" when there is no left turn to take?

Unfortunately, the simple dichotomy between fact and illustration won't do either. I usually explain to students the "left-brain, right-brain" distinction and send them home to put their ideas on sticky notes and arrange them on the left or right side of their pages to chart the way the sermon is shaping up. Are there too many left-brain sticky notes? (Then find some illustrations to balance them on the right.) Are there too many right-brain images? (Then add sticky notes with the ideas they are supposed to represent on the left.) The exercise works, by and large—we do need to balance imagery on the one hand and the things being imaged on the other. But it doesn't take very long to find things that resist being pigeonholed either way.

What, for instance, do you do with Shakespeare's description of the seven ages of man *(As You Like It,* act 2, scene 7)?

> All the world's a stage,
> and all the men and women merely players.
> They have their exits and their entrances,
> And one man in his time plays many parts,
> His acts being seven ages. At first, the infant,
> Mewling and puking in the nurse's arms.
> Then the whining school-boy, with his satchel
> And shining morning face, creeping like a snail
> Unwillingly to school. And then the lover,
> Sighing like a furnace....
> Then a soldier....
> [And so forth, ending in]
> Second childishness and mere oblivion,
> Sans teeth, sans eyes, sans taste, sans everything.

At first glance this famous monologue seems to belong on the right side of the ledger: it is a vivid picture of human beings as puppets on the stage of life, acting out roles that were there before we arrived to play them and that will be there for other players long after we are gone.

Yet some of it seems left-brain enough. Old age really is a final scene in the drama we call life, and it often is the sorry condition of being "Sans teeth, sans eyes, sans taste, sans everything."

What seems to decide the issue in favor of right-brain is the beauty of the metaphor, the pictorial quality of Shakespeare's language, the way he combines "facts" with emotive judgment on those facts. Old age as "second childishness" is as much dismay as it is description. "Mere oblivion" is not just "oblivion" (bad enough) but "mere" (even worse). How important can we be, we human beings, if we but strut about a stage for seven acts, making predetermined entrances and exits? What Shakespeare gives us is a pretty contemptible summary of human vanity—the sort of thing Ecclesiastes had in mind when he called life "vanity of vanities" (another right-brain image?) some seventeen centuries before Shakespeare was born.

But here's the problem. If we decide that Shakespeare's "Seven Ages" is overwhelmingly right-brain, how would we even be able to say anything like it that was purely left-brain? Is it true that there even is a left-brain idea of which

Shakespeare's poetic masterpiece is just an illustration? Maybe the basic left-brain idea is something like, "Life is a series of developmental stages through which all human beings pass." That certainly sounds straightforward enough, and indeed it helps my student preachers if they write something like this on the left side of their page as the bare idea that they want to talk about. Then on the right, they might put Shakespeare's colorful view.

But eventually you realize that even the stripped-down statements on the left are not "just facts." The minute we put them into words, we color them. If nature has its own bias-free language of discourse, it is mathematics, not any language that is actually spoken. Real language requires choosing some words over others, and the ones we choose color what we say. We know better by now than to believe that we simply observe the world and take verbal notes on it; rather, our senses take in a world that we then craft with language, but the language with which we craft it shapes the world that we thought we merely sensed in advance.

This participational outlook on the way we experience reality holds true even in our most simple observations. Is the cat on a mat? Or is she on a carpet? Is "the cat" some ordinary nameless feline, or is it Maxie, the family's beloved pet for over a decade? Is she just "on" the mat, or is she curled up or even arching her back ready to spring into action? Then, too, how do I emphasize my words? Am I saying, "The CAT is on the mat [so we can't just lie the baby down there]"? Or do I mean, "The cat is on the MAT [*that's* where she is; go and get her]"?

All the more are we dependent on linguistic patterning when we come to less tangible observations—like the stages of life, which can be described in any number of ways, not just Shakespeare's but others, too: the rival systems of psychologists like Freud and Erikson, for example; and religious views like the medieval Christian notion of a life cycle ending in death and rebirth to heaven or to hell, or the Jewish idea of a human life-line devoted to Torah.[1] These less concrete matters—not just our life cycle but also things like loyalty, conscientiousness, beauty, and bravery—may be less substantial than cats and mats, but they are real enough, and they generate adjectives (like conscientious, beautiful, and brave) that we then attribute even to the cats upon the mats, to save them from being boring. Maybe my otherwise conscientious cat has summoned up the bravery to take up residence again on my beautiful mat.

But wait, can cats really be conscientious? Does that mean they have a conscience? Or am I just "personifying" my cat to make a point? Personification is one of those literary devices we studied in high school, like metaphor, simile, and irony. Language is not just a *map* of what we see; it is a *strategy* that helps us see more deeply and then craft a world that we never really *just saw* in any case.

At our most profound moments, the world that we craft and see is not just about whether cats sit on mats, but whether there is a God who provides us with purpose, whether we are worthy of divine care, and whether we are born into a world that matters. These are among the affirmations that characterize the High Holy Days in particular. As insubstantial statements that go deeper than the elementary observations of our senses, they depend on highly sophisticated linguistic strategies to make their point. They are, in fact, more like overall pictures with which we operate than they are simple statements of truths.[2] And that is where we encounter the poetic.

Poetry and Prose

It is notoriously hard to define exactly what a poem is. The one thing we know for sure is that it represents a highly stylized use of language—not at all the way we normally talk and write—to the point where it has even been described as "organized violence committed on ordinary speech."[3] It is said to "thicken language, 'foregrounding' its formal qualities, and consequently 'backgrounding' its capacity for sequential, discursive, and referential meaning"[4]—a technical way of saying that poetry draws attention to itself, rather than to the ostensive message of what it is supposed to be saying. Not that poetry doesn't say *any* thing, of course. But in appreciating prose we are likely to say, "How true," whereas with poetry we remark, "How beautiful." We can summarize the point of an argument made in prose, but not an observation presented in poetry. Prose argues, while poetry presents. Prose is about "the meaning of experience"; poetry gives us "the experience of meaning."[5] Archibald MacLeish puts it memorably:

> A poem should be equal to,
> Not true.[6]

But prose and poetry are not mutually exclusive, and we would do well not to force the two into arbitrary and warring linguistic camps. A piece of powerfully discursive prose may not be a poem but may still be poetic—Lincoln's Gettysburg Address, for instance, or the wartime speeches of Winston Churchill.

But how do we know these memorable addresses were not poems? Only because we already have in mind certain qualities that poems "have to" have—rhythm, perhaps, or rhyme. Children first meet poetry with these two formal qualities, often in the form of simple doggerel: "Roses are red, violets are blue...." They graduate to great poetry that, traditionally, remains true to the canons of classical rhythm and rhyme but may adopt specialized poetic formats as well—like medieval sonnets. Eventually they get to modern poetry, where neither rhythm nor rhyme is likely to figure prominently and where, at times, it is hard to say just why a piece is poetic altogether, even though (by common consent) it probably is.

But once again, it may not be quite clear *why*, as the following experiment may show.

Some years back, I came across the following sentence somewhere:

> If a Chinese calligrapher "copies" the work of an old master it is not a forged facsimile but an interpretation as personal within stylistic limits as a Samuel or Landowska performance or a Bach partita.

I copied it out and rearranged it to look like poetry:

> If a Chinese calligrapher "copies"
> The work of an old master it is not
> A forged facsimile but an interpretation
> As personal within stylistic limits
> As a Samuel or Landowska performance
> Or a Bach partita.

I then handed it out to my class, asking the students to keep what they were getting facedown until I instructed them what to do with it. They were also not to let anyone else see what they had because (I explained) they were not all necessarily getting the same thing.

Indeed, they weren't. Half the class was getting the "prose" version; the other half, the "poetic" parallel. But without seeing each other's handouts, they had no way of knowing this. At a given point, I asked them to turn over their sheets (still guarding them from others), look at them long enough to decide what I had given them, and then turn their sheets facedown again to indicate they had read enough to be able to discuss the passages before them.

What they did not know was that I was timing how long it took them until they decided they had read enough and turned their pages over. The students with the prose versions took relatively little time to digest what seemed like a rather pedestrian fact about Chinese calligraphers, a subject about which they had little interest. In the discussion that followed, they were apt to sum up the meaning of the sentence in a brief and informative, but uninteresting, way—perhaps wondering aloud why in the world I had asked them to read it.

The students with the "poetic" version of the same thing took longer to absorb the meaning of the piece before them. When asked about it, they were more animated, more drawn to the possibility that even though they saw no obvious relevance in the reading, they were certain there must be some. It was a poem, after all, and they were used to encountering poetry that seemed quite strange at first but was later shown to have deep significance. Rather than turn the page over after a cursory reading (the way the prose readers did), they had worked to unearth the poetic profundity that they assumed their reading had to contain.

The only reason students in the second group thought they had poetry was the way the sentence appeared on the page. It had neither rhythm nor rhyme nor an abundance of other qualities that would normally count as poetic. But it *looked* poetic enough to elicit the kind of respect that poems normally deserve. Was it *really* a poem on that account? And if so, did it "foreground its formal qualities" and "background its capacity for sequential, discursive, and referential meaning"? Or, more likely, isn't it the case that the readers simply *treated* it like poetry, thereby giving it the benefit of the doubt that it had some deep lesson to teach, that the lesson had been shrouded in poetic format, and that the lesson would be forthcoming if they only studied it sufficiently.

Maybe calligraphy was a metaphor for writing our fate in the book of life, someone suggested. Perhaps the old calligrapher was God, others opined. Maybe "Chinese" stood for antiquity and, therefore, tradition.

The readers of the prose passage could hardly believe what they were hearing. As far as they were concerned, all they had in front of them was a prosaic statement about an irrelevant subject handed to them by a quirky, if not downright eccentric professor.

What matters, apparently, is not just the poetic value of the things we read, but our own readiness to see them as poetic—an important distinction when it comes to liturgy, where so many of our prayers are poetic but not readily recognized as such because they did not emerge from the Western canon of literature, so do not comport with Western standards of poetic composition.

Avinu Malkeinu and Liturgical Poetry

The poetic quality of *Avinu Malkeinu* is not entirely foreign to readers of Western literature. In form, it is a litany, a liturgical term derived from the Greek *litaneuein*, "to pray, entreat, or supplicate." Its nominal form *litaneia* occurs in 2 Maccabees (a book that made it into the early church Bible but not the Jewish one) in a context that resembles *Avinu Malkeinu*. The term is used twice to describe a "supplication" that arises in connection with the Hasmonean War, the "Maccabean" revolt, as we often call it, the uprising that gave us Hanukkah.

The Jerusalem Temple of late antiquity served not just as the site of the sacrificial cult. It was also something like a national bank with funds allocated for various ends, including (says 2 Maccabees) "deposits for widows and orphans." Heliodorus, the chancellor representing the

Hellenistic occupying power, arrives there one day to loot its holdings, at which time, "There was no little distress all over the city.... The women, with sackcloth girt under their breasts, thronged the streets ... and all raised their hands to heaven and uttered their *supplication* ... prostrating themselves in a body." Later, the revolt now fully under way, "Maccabeus and his men made a *supplication* and besought God to be their ally."[7]

A "litany," then, was a public supplication arising out of a penitential mood—just like *Avinu Malkeinu*. *Avinu Malkeinu* is also said to have arisen during a communal crisis, a drought that occasioned public supplication, including Rabbi Akiva's entreaty, "Our father, our king, we have no king other than You. Our father, our king, have mercy upon us."[8]

In time, the word "litany" was taken over by the church and used technically for a set of intercessional petitions (petitions requesting divine intervention on our behalf) voiced by the prayer leader and followed by a set congregational response.[9] By now, the term is used more generally to denote any rhetorical form of prayer arranged as "a continuous repetition, or long enumeration" of variable content but with "a repeated formula" as part of it—exactly like "*Avinu malkeinu*...."

Litanies are commonplace in liturgies—all liturgies, not just Jewish ones. In an oral age, the litany-like format allowed ready participation from a congregation that could anticipate, and even recite together, the repetitive formulary words with which each line began or ended. If the variable wording of the lines was already fixed (the prayer leader might read them off a handwritten page), individuals without print before them could at least say the opening words and then wait for the reader to complete the line. But sometimes they could do more, because until the age of books, even the number of lines (let alone their exact content) was still open-ended—people could, and did, make up lines as they went along. The poem would grow with each and every person who participated.

Jewish liturgy still has remnants of such "live litanies," if we can call them that. The *Birkat Hamazon* (Blessing after Meals), for example, contains a section with petitionary lines that begin, *Harachaman,* "May the Merciful One...." By now our printed text has a fixed set of these petitions, but originally diners would compose the lines at each sitting, inventing their content to suit the occasion. Some became commonplace and found their way into print, giving us the prayer-book version that we know. But even today, in circles where people enjoy comfort and competence in prayer, it is not unusual to pause a bit and give those around the table an opportunity to improvise requests before moving on to the formal end of the prayer.

So *Avinu Malkeinu* is a litany—not enough, perhaps, to make it a poem by modern literary standards, but certainly enough if we compare it to my arbitrary "poeticization" of the Chinese Calligrapher. Is that sufficient, however, to qualify it as poetic, or should we ask for more?

Litany-like prayers are often poetic in another obvious way: they are also alphabetic acrostics. The best example from the liturgy of the High Holy Days is the long confession *Al Chet*. The lines begin with a fixed introduction, *Al chet shechatanu l'fanekha* ("For the sin we have committed against You"), making it a litany. What follows, however, is not just a random set of "sins" but sins arranged in a double acrostic form—two lines for each letter of the Hebrew alphabet. The point is purely poetic. It is not that the various lines of the prayer do not have any meaning—they do; but summing up the cognitive content of the lines does not do the prayer justice. The acrostic suggests that whatever our sins may be, they are not necessarily the specifics of the verbal content—which is governed by the alphabet, after all, not by what we think we have actually done. Rabbi Chaim Stern, editor of the North American Reform *machzor Gates of Repentance,* properly understood the message when he provided an alternative English confession, saying, "Our sins are an alphabet of woe."

Poetry does not vitiate the content of its several lines; it provides a deeper and broader meaning to them, expanding the ordinariness of the prosaic content to the point where what would otherwise seem downright wrong points us toward a reality that simple declarative sentences alone cannot convey.

Rhyme, rhythm, acrostics, and litany—these are all poetic devices, the first two common to the Western poetic tradition, the last two standard for traditional Jewish poets. *Avinu Malkeinu* represents just one of the four, however. Is that enough to let us call it poetry?

Poetry and the Poetic

Perhaps, then, it is not actually poetry. But it still may be poetic. "Poetry" and "poetic" sound the same, as if the latter describes the former, but adjectives and nouns don't always work that way. Sometimes adjectives *suggest* the related noun without referring specifically to it. A drawing can be artistic without actually being art; ethereal describes the vapid emptiness of ether, but something ethereal can still be real. Artistic, ethereal, and poetic are the names we give to qualities that make something art, ether, and poetry but may not be altogether those very things. We can say, then, that *Avinu Malkeinu* is poetic, even though it may not have enough of the poetic about it to rank as an actual poem. If we focus on the nonpoetic part, we expect it to be prose—like the prosaic version of the Chinese Calligrapher; if we focus on what is poetic about it—its redundancy as a litany—we will look for it to contain a poetic truth beyond the words themselves—as we did with the poetic version of the Chinese Calligrapher. It all depends on our expectations.

We saw before how the students who read the prose version of the Chinese Calligrapher tended to discount it as irrelevant. Reading *Avinu Malkeinu* as prose is even worse, because it is perceived not just as irrelevant but also as false. "God is not a father," people object; "Our fate is not sealed in a book of life," others complain. To be sure, these objections are relatively uncommon, because the prayer is so beloved overall. But they should not be discounted. We should wonder why worshipers who read prayers as prose think them not just irrelevant but also wrong.

This misconception arises because we have been taught to divide prose into fiction and nonfiction. Prayer cannot be fiction, we imagine—what would be the point of praying fiction? So it must be nonfiction. But we have also learned to judge nonfiction as true or false. Fiction may be untrue, we think, but deliberately so (by definition), whereas prose is deliberately intended to be true. If it turns out to be false, we dismiss it with the sense that we have been had. Good fiction, like good poetry, never gets old; we read classic novels over and over again. We do not, however, read yesterday's science textbooks the same way. When a piece of nonfiction grows old, we replace it, treating the older version as factually misleading and even morally inappropriate because it seems to be passing on a lie.

By approaching prayer as prose, then—prose that cannot be merely fiction—we automatically open it to the probability that it will sometimes seem like a lie. Ancient or medieval liturgy, after all, reflects the cosmology of people who lived before Copernicus, knew nothing of modern physics, had never heard of psychology, and imagined an extraterrestrial realm that science refuted long ago. If *Avinu Malkeinu* is prayer, it can hardly be fiction; but if it is nonfiction, it must be true or false. On the face of it, it looks false, and if it is false, then it is also a lie being passed along as if it were true.

Not so poetry, of which Sir Philip Sydney famously proclaimed (as early as 1595), "The poet nothing affirmeth, and therefore never lieth."[10] By approaching *Avinu Malkeinu* as poetry, we can judge it by altogether different standards of what counts for failure or success, because as poetry, it may be literally false but still meaningful, relevant, and valid. We readily look for metaphors, suggestive plays on words, imagery that moves us, and a host of other qualities that pure prose is not required to have.

As it happens, moreover, the choices are not just between poetry and prose. We now know that language functions in many different ways. We can appreciate *Avinu Malkeinu* even more if we look at some of these deeper ways that language takes on meaning.

What Language Does

An enormous breakthrough over the last century or so has been the decision to study language in terms of what it does, not just what it means. The by-now classic linguist Roman Jakobson (1896–1982), for example, provided a fascinating model of six different ways that language works.

Born in Moscow, Jakobson then taught in Czechoslovakia and fled the Nazis for America, ending up at a number of universities, including Harvard and MIT. His simple graph of verbal communication demonstrates the relatively tiny extent to which we use words to give actual messages that are either "true or false."

We just automatically assume that the primary purpose of communication is to convey information like "The cat is on the mat"—a statement of fact that tells you where the cat is. It was this unstated assumption that led students to think the prose version of the Chinese Calligrapher intended to say something about calligraphers—an assumption that even the poetry readers shared to some extent (even though they used their knowledge of poetry to work out deeper levels at which information was being conveyed). And likewise, the point of *Avinu Malkeinu*, we assume, must be to let us know that God is a parent and ruler who, properly petitioned, will forgive us and manage our destiny positively. All of that may indeed be the case, but it also may not be, as Jakobson demonstrated with his study of the way words work.

Imagine a horizontal line running left to right across the page:

Sender ——————— (message) ———————→ Receiver

In any communication, a sender (on the left) is addressing a message to the receiver on the right. For the message to get through, both sender and receiver have to understand a common context—as we saw above, when we noted the various things that "The cat is on the mat" might actually mean. When the sender says something about that common context with the intent that the receiver should apply what he is saying to that context, then the message is indeed what we normally think it is: the passing of information that is either true or false. We judge the communication successful if the content is true.

Fiction works differently, because it dispenses with the normal context. If, for example, I say (with the right tone of voice), "A man goes into a bar...," you recognize it as a joke and do not expect anyone really to have gone into a bar. To play it safe, I may even say, "I heard a good joke the other day. A man goes into a bar..." But normally we expect what people tell us to be nonfiction, in which case untruths are either mistakes or outright lies.

But sometimes we say things *not* to pass on information about the context, but about ourselves. If the sender shouts, "The cat is *on the mat!*" he may mostly be indicating how he feels—something like "Oh my God, the stupid cat is on my best carpet again! What am I going to do?" The proper response is not "Yes, I see, the cat is indeed on the mat," but "Calm down; it'll be OK."

The kind of communication that says something about the sender's state of mind more than about the common context can be called "emotive." We judge it successful not because it is true or false—indeed, the cat may not be on the mat at all, and the message may still be successful (the speaker may be neurotically afraid of cats and hallucinating about an invisible one who is causing his mental anguish). The listener acknowledges that she gets the point when she says, "Calm down; it'll be OK." Emotive statements are successful when they are properly *expressive* of the sender's state of being.

The opposite is also true. A speaker may send a message not to express his own state of mind but to influence the state of mind of the receiver. A husband and wife may notice simultaneously that the cat has returned to the mat. By announcing it to his wife, the husband-sender is not so much explaining the way things are but attempting to influence the receiver-wife to do something—in this case, to get the cat off the carpet. Jakobson called this kind of message "conative," from the Latin *conatio,* "to wish, to act purposefully." A "conative" communication is successful not by expressing the feeling of the sender but by influencing the mental state of the receiver. The proper response would be, "I know, I know; I'll take care of it."

Sometimes, it is the very *form* of the message that takes most of our attention, and then we have *poetry.* If ordinary *content*-driven communication is judged by its truth, then *form*-driven communication attracts attention for its beauty.

Alternatively, there are times when all we want to do is make sure someone is on the receiving end before we do the sending. When I think your cell phone has conked out, I say, "Hello? Hello?"—not to introduce myself, but to elicit your assurance, "I'm here! I'm here!" The response, as well, is not a "fact" about where you happen to be, but the guarantee that you are hearing me, so that I can go on with whatever I was saying. This linguistic function of confirming contact Jakobson called *phatic* (like the English word "emphatic," from the Greek verb meaning "to speak").

Finally, we may know we have contact but wonder if our message is getting through. Language is a code, after all, a way of putting thoughts into a verbal package, then sending them, and having the receiver unpack and decode what we have sent so as to know what we have in mind. When we wonder if the receiver is "getting the message," we say something like "Right?" or "Get it?"—meaning "Do you understand me?" These are instances of reaffirming the reliability of the code, so Jakobson called them *metalingual*, *meta* being a Greek preposition meaning "beyond" and implying "higher" (like "metaphysical," meaning "beyond the physical").

If we update the chart to include all these ways language can "mean" something, we get the following:

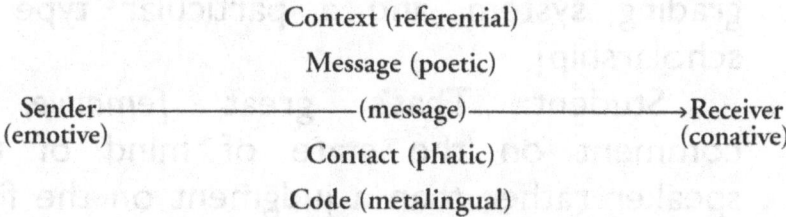

The following conversation between teacher ("me," I am imagining) and student illustrates the options:

> Me: Hello? *[phatic,* just making contact]. It's me, Rabbi Hoffman *[phatic* still, but also *contextual,* since the new information delivers vital information that presupposes the entire context of school, studenthood, and classes; my tone of voice might also have made it *conative*—if I had emphasized my authority with a view toward influencing the student to feel fearful about what I was about to say].

Student: Oh, hi. Thanks for calling [*phatic*; the student doesn't really mean to offer thanks, so much as to affirm proper contact].

Me: Listen [still *phatic*, just continuing the contact], I have graded your paper and you did exceptionally well; you stood first in the class, in fact, with a grade that allows you to apply for A1 Scholarship Assistance [*contextual*, a "true or false" statement, that presupposes the context of classroom exams, student-teacher relationships, the grading system, and a particular type of scholarship].

Student: That's great [*emotive*; a comment on the state of mind of the speaker rather than a judgment on the final test score]! I so appreciate your calling me [maybe *emotive* still, a further statement on the speaker's state of mind; but also, perhaps, *conative*, an attempt to influence me to continue acting kindly; and maybe *contextual* too, if, say, the student were on an official "Committee for Teacher Fair Play" and making a statement about how well I am obeying the new standards of teacher-student communication].

Me: I called the minute I finished grading [*contextual*, since I seem now to be referring to the new communication guidelines, but also *conative*, maybe, an attempt to curry favor with the student and influence her to think highly of me]—if you get what I am saying *[metalingual,* a comment designed to make sure the student reads me properly].

Student: I appreciate it more than you can know; I was so concerned *[emotive].* And don't worry *[conative,* an assurance designed to set my mind at rest regarding the upcoming teacher evaluations]. I'll remember your kindness as the semester continues [possibly *emotive* of the student's relief; possibly *contextual,* a statement about how she will act when my name comes up for tenure; possibly *conative,* a statement designed to continue making me feel better—it all depends on how it is said].

My imaginary conversation illustrates the many ways that words can take on meaning. What is noteworthy right away is the realization that poetry and prose are just a very rough dichotomy into which to force meaning—poetry is just one of the six ways that Jakobson divides up language. When we say that *Avinu Malkeinu* can be taken as poetry, we are just beginning our analysis. Were we to finish the task, we would have to analyze each sentence, and sometimes even each fragment of each sentence, and decide what it is meant to do; and often we would still be uncertain, because it would depend on the mind-set that the author and the worshipers bring to it.

No one has ever done this for liturgy, possibly because the task is so enormous. But just knowing that it could be done reveals the error of seeing prayer only as poetry or as prose. To be sure, identifying prayer as poetry goes a long way in opening us up to find meaning below the surface, but we also need to understand when the lines of prayer mean

- to make a statement about the way things are (contextual);
- to express our own feelings (emotive);
- to influence God to act a certain way (conative); or
- to check in with God (or with the other worshipers) to say that we are present (phatic), and
- that we are all on message using the same understanding of language (metalingual).

We may do any or all of the above through prose or, with heightened attention to the linguistic code itself, through the device that we call "poetry."

And in fact, things are not even as simple as all that! Quite regularly we use conative language (to influence others) when we have little chance of doing so and want mostly to be emotive—to express to those others how we feel about things. At times, also, it is not clear who the receiver of our messages is. Suppose I say to my wife, "Children should be more helpful to their parents!" It sounds straightforward enough at first, but if I say it out loud while those very children are sitting in front of us waiting for their parents to finish putting the dishes in the dishwasher so they can be served dessert, I may actually be addressing them, not their mother—letting them know how I feel (emotive) and making them feel contrite enough to help (conative).

Most important, perhaps, when it comes to prayer, we regularly use language as if to influence God (conative) with no necessary expectation that God will listen. In that case, we speak *optatively*—that is, we express hope for a certain outcome without actually anticipating it.

All of which brings us back to *Avinu Malkeinu*. What in the world does this prayer of prayers really mean?

It should be evident now that it might mean a whole lot of things! We already saw that to some extent, it is poetry, but we now see that beyond just "thickening language" or being "organized violence committed on ordinary speech," poetry is a form of meaning that derives its force from drawing attention to the very way it says what it says—the linguistic code itself (in technical terms)—which is to say, by using such literary devices as metaphor, alliteration, and parsimony of language. When it comes to poetry, the primal error is imagining that words are chosen for their normal prosaic meaning, when instead they are selected to satisfy linguistic considerations: the acrostic they make, the rhythm they establish, the metaphor they introduce, and so forth.

The repetitive use of the phrase *avinu malkeinu*, then, may have little or nothing to do with an original authorial intent to emphasize any particular theological depth implicit in these two words. Rather, the Talmud had recorded the memory of a drought in which Rabbi Akiva had addressed God as *avinu malkeinu* and successfully brought rain (see section entitled "Avinu Malkeinu, Once Again: How a Theology of Sin Gained the Upper Hand"); that precedent was viewed as prototypically effective; so as time went on, Rabbi Akiva's short prayer was expanded into an ever-growing litany, with *avinu malkeinu* as the repetitive refrain. But poetry invites interpretation, and the very fact that the litany began with the same two words meant that ever after, Jewish interpreters would find secondary meaning in them. The many essays in this volume testify to the great range of that meaning. What began as a poetic device thus ended as language that still draws commentaries, both favorable and unfavorable.

But *avinu malkeinu* is not just poetic; it is also *emotive*—a statement about how we feel as we stand before God, aware of our failings. It is not all that different from a patient who learns he has cancer. Although he generally calls his doctor by her first name, this time he looks her in the face and says, "But Doctor..."—because it is her medical skills that matter most at this moment of truth.

At the same time, addressing God as *avinu malkeinu* can be *conative*—an attempt to influence God to hear our prayer. We regularly alter our address to make the right impression; Jews who felt the gravity of the Days of Awe as *Yom Hazikaron* and *Yom Hadin* ("The Day of Remembering" and "The Day of Judgment") devised titles for God to fit the occasion. In the patriarchal culture of late antiquity (and even beyond), fathers and kings enjoyed the right to rule their respective domains (family and realm) the way a judge does a courtroom. It should not surprise us to find Rabbi Akiva (and then later Jewish tradition, following his precedent) addressing God as father and king.

Calling the repeated use of *avinu malkeinu* emotive or conative does not vitiate its role as poetry. Nor does it have any necessary bearing on the feminist critique that objects to the masculine language *especially because* it is the fallback imagery to express our insecurity (emotive) or hope to influence the divine (conative). But it does add a deeper appreciation of just how these two words should be read: rather than assert that God actually is a father and king, they may more likely just reflect our own sense of inadequacy (emotive) before a parent whom we choose to petition and even to placate (conative).

Philosophy Weighs In

These linguistic considerations of the way liturgy takes on meaning should be supplemented by a philosophical one. One of the great philosophical icons of the twentieth century was Ludwig Wittgenstein, the son of a German industrialist who was slated to continue his father's business, but who found his way to Cambridge University in England and impressed two of its greatest philosophers (Bertrand Russell and G.E. Moore) with his brilliance. In his later years, he came to believe that language should not be judged by what it means so much as by what it does. He likened language to the contents of a toolbox—we learn as children how to use linguistic tools to accomplish different ends. Sometimes we make statements of fact (true or false, the contextual meaning that we looked at above); sometimes we express how we feel (emotive), try to influence those to whom we speak (conative), or perform any of the other linguistic functions that we have already looked at. But language does other things too: it may promise, hope, question, doubt, or engage in playful repartee. We run into problems when we misunderstand the goal of any particular utterance.

Think also, said Wittgenstein, of language as a set of games. Misunderstandings arise when we do not recognize what game other people are playing: when (for instance) we think they are telling us a truth, but they mean only to tell us how they feel; or when they are participating in a ritual instead of an ordinary conversation—because rituals have their own peculiar ways in which language works, their own favorite set of linguistic tools.

As a kind of ritual, Jewish prayer has its own language games that are just part of the way Jewish liturgy works. Instead of toasts, for example, we have blessings: not "Raise a glass to...," but "God bless you with...." At toast time, no one refuses to "raise a glass" to "long life and happiness" on the grounds that they aren't thirsty or because the bride and groom already know how their guests feel, so why bother repeating it! Toasting is just part of the wedding game. Similarly, when we say, for those who are ill, "Blessed is God who heals the sick," it is inappropriate for people to opt out because they don't believe in God or have the experience of God not healing other people who were sick with the same malady last year. Invoking blessings is a language game that has nothing to do with belief in God or the likelihood that God will respond to what we ask. Objecting to God-language in a blessing because "I don't believe in God" is a case of mistaking language games.

A particularly trenchant example comes from the *Birkat Hamazon* (Blessing after Meals, which we looked at above); it ends by citing several

Psalm verses. Now, "citing Scripture" is itself a language game that Jewish liturgy often plays. The point isn't whether you believe in what gets cited. The point is simply to root the hope expressed by the blessing in a biblical context—the way a speaker quotes Shakespeare, not for the literal truth of what Shakespeare said, but for the imagery he offers and the connectivity to the greatness he represents. A keynote speaker at a conference arguing for a more compassionate nation concludes by saying, "'The quality of mercy is not strained; it droppeth as the gentle rain from heaven upon the earth beneath'—let us revel in the possibility of harvesting the mercy that comes naturally from God but goes to waste if we do not collect it and disburse it in everything we do." No one interrupts to remind the speaker that the atheists present do not believe in God or that mercy doesn't really fall from heaven. Everyone knows that quoting is part of the "speaking game." It adds artistry to what would otherwise be a dull lecture telling everyone what they already know—they probably came in the first place because they already believed in what the speaker was likely to say. So the *Birkat Hamazon* cites Psalms the way speakers cite Shakespeare.

One such citation is Psalm 37:25, which reads, "I have been young and now have grown old, but I have never seen the righteous abandoned while their children beg for food." Worshipers regularly balk at this patent untruth;

they say it under their breath or skip it altogether. But they misunderstand the game. Surely even the psalmist who wrote it knew it wasn't true. The citation was never intended as a statement of fact.

It is actually not all that different from the rest of the prayer—the last line of the first paragraph, for example, which concludes, "Blessed are You, who feeds all"—another untruth actually. Why, sometimes, are "the righteous abandoned while their children beg for food" if not precisely because God *doesn't* feed *all*? At least, not sufficiently; and not yet.

If we judge the *Birkat Hamazon* by the standards of "true or false," the entire thing is patently untrue. But that judgment confuses language games. The point of the prayer is not to state a fact; it is to express hope.

The same meals that end with the *Birkat Hamazon* begin with *Hamotzi,* the prayer over bread, which thanks God for "bringing forth bread from the earth," and the Talmud says of this verse, "God doesn't already bring forth bread from the earth, but in the *future* God will do so," a reference to the Rabbinic legend that described the Garden of Eden as a place where even bread grew wild on trees, so that no one had to work to make it. The whole point of Jewish mealtime liturgy is to bracket our own eating with hopeful prayers that someday bread will be as easy to obtain as it was in the Garden of Eden, and then the righteous will not be abandoned while their children beg for food. We say *Amen* whether or not we believe in an actual Garden of Eden, bread growing on trees, or the existence of a God who will feed the whole world someday. *Amen* to a blessing is like *L'chayim* or "Cheers" to a toast. The *Birkat Hamazon* plays an overall language game of hope—it is not about "true or false." It is intended, in technical terms, to be *optative,* "the grammatical mood for expressing hope."

The High Holy Day liturgy too does more than make statements of fact (although it does that some of the time). The decision to attend is tantamount to agreeing to participate in a language game (actually, a whole set of games) where the usual rules of speech no longer hold and to open ourselves to language that otherwise we would find questionable. Any given line in *Avinu Malkeinu* may be contextual, emotive, poetic, or conative (as we saw above), but it also may be the proper linguistic move in some other game such as expressing irony, community identity, or personal hope.

When Liturgy Hurts

Regardless of all these consideration, however, the God of *Avinu Malkeinu is* named "father" and "king," and a great number of people find that troubling. The many ways these two words take on meaning and the reason they arose historically do not minimize the fact that many women (and many men too) find it difficult, if not impossible, to relate to God in either one of these two roles. So the question remains: what do we do about liturgy when it actually hurts?

Liturgical content can attract change either because we judge it untrue or because it causes pain. If liturgy is merely untrue by modern standards, we can more easily invoke the many ways by which liturgy takes on meaning (as I have here) to explain away the discrepancy between the liturgy and what we take to be truth in a scientific era. Many people find it hard to believe, for instance, that (from the *Amidah*) "God resurrects the dead" or that (from the liturgy surrounding the reading of Torah) "this is the Torah that Moses put before the children of Israel, dictated by God and transcribed by Moses."[11] But they may say it anyway, explaining it away as metaphoric, symbolic, open to interpretation, halakhically required, or just the language game of affirming continuity with the past. The possibility that liturgy causes pain, however, is a different matter altogether. Sometimes liturgy *should* prove unsettling—we do not expunge the prophets to protect unscrupulous profiteers from critique. But liturgy should not gratuitously, inadvertently, or wrongly cause pain to the very people it is supposed to comfort. We should at least be clear about the *kind* of problem we face.

To the extent that worshipers may associate kings with the absolute monarchs who once exercised royal power unwisely and even cruelly, it is self-evidently "untrue" that God is a king. But Rabbinic tradition knew this: it regularly differentiated the divine king from "kings of flesh and blood," who fell short of the ideal standard that God represents. By now, moreover, we have abandoned royalty as the standard by which to measure God altogether. Even constitutional monarchs whom we admire and even love are just constitutional. Then, too, in a post-Freudian era, calling God "father" is at best a demotion from whatever God might be. These are, however, mere matters of truth or falsity. They are more easily handled than the propensity of the very same terms to cause pain.

It is probably true that absolute monarchy is such a distant reality for most of us that addressing God as king can hardly cause much pain anymore. God as father, however—and, by extension, God as the very masculine king—does inflict damage on many who have experienced abusive fathers or who suffer from what is still a patriarchal culture where women lack equality. The last fifty years have seen a great number of instances where hurtful liturgies have been properly emended—frequently despite the well-meaning protestations of people who enjoy the old familiar terms and do not appreciate the hurt they cause to others.

The best example for Jews may come from Christian liturgy where centuries-old content has been expunged because of the anti-Semitism that it supported. The Good Friday service of the venerable *Book of Common Prayer* once asked God to "have mercy upon all Jews, infidels, and heretics; and take away from them all ignorance, hardness of heart, and contempt of thy word." In 1928, that language became, "Have mercy on all who know thee not as thou art revealed in the Gospel of thy Son"—something of an improvement, although hardly what Jews would have preferred. That language is still in place, although Anglicans still struggle with it, knowing that Jews may find it hurtful.

In this instance, the people being hurt are not the worshipers themselves, but a parallel problem arises when they are, and that is the case with very many Jews who are expected to name God as "our father, our king." Many commentaries in this book address that vexing issue, but a solution that is satisfactory to all has yet to be determined.

At the very least, however, we should see liturgical questions as the complicated issues they are. Liturgy can comfort but also hurt; it tells truths but also promises, hopes, emotes, and does any number of others things that still await analysis. Naming is itself a language game, and it may be that when we think we are doing the naming (with *avinu malkeinu* or with the other metaphors contained in liturgical poetry—like *Ki*

Hinei Kachomer, included here) we are also engaging in any number of other linguistic pursuits, the sum total of which make us the amazingly verbal creatures that we are.

PART II
The Liturgy

Editor's Introduction to Avinu Malkeinu

Rabbi Lawrence A. Hoffman, PhD

Avinu Malkeinu has come down to us in many versions, each one known generally as a *minhag* (plural: *minhagim*), meaning "custom" or, more technically, "rite." Historically, these rites are associated with specific geographic centers where Jews have lived through the centuries, and where they have developed their own specific liturgical customs and prayer books. The most obvious and best-known examples are *Minhag Ashkenaz* (Jews from "Germany"—actually, all of central and northern Europe) and *Minhag Sepharad* (Jews from "Spain"—the entire Iberian Peninsula, really). But these very broad designations are often subdivided—*Minhag Ashkenaz*, for instance, occurs as *Minhag Rinus* ("the Rhineland Rite," as it developed originally in the Rhineland and then elsewhere in Germany) and *Minhag Polin* ("the Polish Rite," the way the Rhineland Rite was further developed by German Jews who moved to Poland in the sixteenth century and beyond). There are others as well: *Minhag Italia* ("the Italian Rite"), for instance.

Of the many versions in which *Avinu Malkeinu* occurs, we chose as our baseline the one that occurs in *Minhag Polin*, because it has the greatest number of lines and is, in that sense, the most complete. It is also the best-known version, found ubiquitously in Israel, Europe, and the Americas, where immigrants from Eastern Europe came in such large numbers with the Great Migration that began in 1881. The other rites that we include here have many of those same verses but may also omit (or add) others; they may also include them but with somewhat different wording or spelling; and they may rearrange even the verses that they have in common, so that the same verse may appear near the beginning of one rite but in the middle or end of another.

In what follows:
- We number the lines of the baseline Polish Rite in the order in which they appear (from 1 to 44).
- To facilitate comparison, we then number the lines of the other rites, so as to accord with the baseline numbering system.
- When lines differ somewhat in *wording*, they get the baseline number of the verse they approximate, but with a letter added, to indicate they are essentially the same, with small variations—11a or 14b, for example, are variations of 11 or 14.
- We also add letters when new lines are *thematically* related to lines in the baseline version. A line in *Seder Rav Amram*, for

instance, reads, "Write us in the book of memory." We number this 22a to connect it with our baseline verse 22, "Write us in the book of merit."

- Finally, for new lines that have no connection whatever to the baseline version, we add letters according to the place where they occur. *Machzor Vitry*, for instance, says, "Do not let sin and transgression interrupt our prayer." We number this 41a simply because in *Machzor Vitry* it follows line 41 (we could not number it 42, because 42 already exists).

We then insert all versions of all lines into the baseline version to come up with a composite, and for each lettered verse, we stipulate the rite from which it is taken. A line with just a number is thus the baseline *Minhag Polin*. A line with a number and letter has the name of the rite or rites from which it is taken written in parentheses.

In some rites, the text differs somewhat from Rosh Hashanah to Yom Kippur. The former tends to ask God to "write us" into the book of good life, for example, while the latter may ask God to "seal us" in that book. Similarly, the Yom Kippur *Avinu Malkeinu* sometimes emphasizes the theme of sin and pardon. The very earliest version of *Avinu Malkeinu* (*Seder Rav Amram*, ninth century), for example, begins by acknowledging, "We have sinned before You." Ashkenazi Jews say that on both Rosh Hashanah and Yom Kippur, but Yemenite and Sephardi Jews say it only on Yom Kippur; the current Yemenite *machzor* even prints it in bold type to make it stand out as a perspective that ought to govern the Yom Kippur recital of all the lines that follow. For comparison purposes, we provide the Rosh Hashanah, not the Yom Kippur, versions here.

Appendix A provides full accounts of each rite separately, so as to show the order in which the lines appear. We provide only the English there, but the numbering and lettering system is the same so that readers can easily compare these appendix lines with the original Hebrew, which occurs here.

Appendix B and Rabbi April Peters' overview of modern translations of *Avinu Malkeinu* (available as a free download at www.jewishlights.com) provide other, more modern variations on the liturgy that we provide here as our "official" traditional text.

Translator's Introduction to Avinu Malkeinu

Dr. Joel M. Hoffman

Dr. Joel M. Hoffman lectures around the globe on popular and scholarly topics spanning history, Hebrew, prayer, and Jewish continuity. He has served on the faculties of Brandeis University in Waltham, Massachusetts, and Hebrew Union College – Jewish Institute of Religion in New York. He is author of *And God Said: How Translations Conceal the Bible's Original Meaning* and *In the Beginning: A Short History of the Hebrew Language*, and has written for the international *Jerusalem Post*. He contributed to all ten volumes of the *My People's Prayer Book: Traditional Prayers, Modern Commentaries* series, winner of the National Jewish Book Award; to *My People's Passover Haggadah: Traditional Texts, Modern Commentaries*; and to *Who by Fire, Who by Water—Un'taneh Tokef*, *We Have Sinned: Sin and Confession in Judaism—Ashamnu and Al Chet*, *May God Remember: Memory and Memorializing in Judaism—Yizkor*, and *All the World: Universalism, Particularism and the High Holy Days* (all Jewish Lights).

Avinu Malkeinu centers around the double metaphor created by the opening words of each line, translated here as "our father" and "our king." However, the literal translations "father" and "king" are not our only options, nor are they entirely accurate. Other possibilities include "parent" for "father" and "monarch" or "sovereign" for "king."

We have two issues to keep in mind when making these choices: gender and general imagery.

In terms of gender, the first Hebrew word, *av*, is potentially gender neutral. This is why we translate the plural of that word as "ancestors" in the *Amidah*, not "fathers."

More importantly, though, the word here refers to the *role* of a father in a family. In this sense, the English "father" is also potentially gender neutral. A single-parent mother may have to be both father and mother to her children, for instance. Though we might disagree about what exactly that means, or whether it's true, that sentence is neither contradictory nor ungrammatical. So "father" matches up with *av* in this sense.

The English word "parent," of course, is also gender neutral. But that word is too broad. And the power of imagery comes from its specificity. So even though all fathers are parents, to use "parent" instead of "father" would diminish the impact of the words, just as their impact would be further diminished by using "family member" instead of "father," even though all fathers are family members. So in terms of gender, we stick with "father."

However, we have no reason to believe that the role of ancient fathers was the same as the role of modern ones. What if fatherhood in antiquity represented strictness and, in modernity, sustenance? If so, "father" in modern English would not convey what *av* did hundreds of years ago. For that matter, "father" means different things to different people, depending in no small part on their own upbringing.

In this regard, though, we have no better option. And, at least, both "father" and *av* convey a range of significantly overlapping images.

The same issues arise regarding "king" for *melekh*, but the imagery mismatch is more severe. "Monarch" isn't better than "king," but neither of those modern words conveys the impact of the ancient king, who was in some ways like our modern kings, in other ways closer to mayors and other ruling officials; and in some regards the ancient king was like a modern dictator, who could be beneficent or cruel.

Additionally, the modern word "king" often refers to a powerless figurehead of a modern democracy (certainly not what the Hebrew intended) or, worse, a fictitious character like King Arthur.

Still—as with "father"—we have no better option. So we opt for "our father, our king," noting that, though imperfect as a translation, the other options are worse.

Avinu Malkeinu

A NEW AND ANNOTATED TRANSLATION

Dr. Joel M. Hoffman

¹Our father, our king, we have sinned before You. ²Our father, our king, we have no king other than You. ³Our father, our king, act with us for the sake of your name. ³ᵃ(*Machzor Vitry*) Our father, our king, act kindly with us for the sake of your name.

¹ אָבִינוּ מַלְכֵּנוּ, חָטָאנוּ לְפָנֶיךָ.
² אָבִינוּ מַלְכֵּנוּ, אֵין לָנוּ מֶלֶךְ אֶלָּא אַתָּה.
³ אָבִינוּ מַלְכֵּנוּ, עֲשֵׂה עִמָּנוּ לְמַעַן שְׁמֶךָ.
³ᵃ אָבִינוּ מַלְכֵּנוּ, עֲשֵׂה עִמָּנוּ חֶסֶד לְמַעַן שְׁמֶךָ.

¹ *Our father, our king:* See Translator's Introduction.

¹ *Before You:* Or, "against You." Prepositions like "before" and "against" are notoriously difficult to translate. The English "against" suggests that God is the object of our sins, while "before" suggests instead that God witnesses them. By analogy, we can imagine contradicting someone or contradicting God. In the first case, we speak out "before God"; in the second, "against God." As nearly as we can tell, the Hebrew, like our English, means that our sins are before God. However, the context suggests that a sin before God is also a sin against God.

³ *Act with us for the sake of your name*: Commonly, "treat us well for your name's sake," but though the Hebrew implies good treatment, it doesn't actually specify how God should act, so we leave our English translation similarly ambiguous. The point is that we may be undeserving of good treatment, so we ask for treatment not based on our own merit, but rather in accord with God's name.

⁴Our father, our king, grant us a good ⁴ᵃ(*Seder Rav Amram*) Our father, our king, grant us good new decrees. ⁴ᵇ(*Machzor Roma*) Our father, our king, grant us good new tidings. ⁵Our father, our king, cancel all burdensome decrees against us.

⁴ אָבִינוּ מַלְכֵּנוּ, חַדֵּשׁ עָלֵינוּ שָׁנָה טוֹבָה.
⁴ᵃ אָבִינוּ מַלְכֵּנוּ, חַדֵּשׁ עָלֵינוּ גְּזֵרוֹת טוֹבוֹת.
⁴ᵇ אָבִינוּ מַלְכֵּנוּ, חַדֵּשׁ עָלֵינוּ בְּשׂוֹרוֹת טוֹבוֹת.
⁵ אָבִינוּ מַלְכֵּנוּ, בַּטֵּל מֵעָלֵינוּ כָּל גְּזֵרוֹת קָשׁוֹת.

The Hebrew here, from Jeremiah 14:7, leaves out both the premise (that we are undeserving) and the implication (that our treatment will be better once God's name is taken into account), so our English leaves them both out, too.

As for "your name," better would be just "You," but that would leave us with ungrammatical English. (Even the more common translation falls apart once the word "name" is taken out, because the English "treat us well for your sake" implies a threat that the Hebrew does not.)

[4] *Grant us a good new year:* Commonly, "renew for us a good year," but that's not generally how we use the word "renew" in English. Another possibility is "Renew us with a good year."

[4a] *Grant us good new decrees:* Like line 4, this line starts with the Hebrew verb for "(re)new." To make the lines match in English the way they do in Hebrew, we translate them similarly. In isolation, another possibility here would run along the lines of "renew us with good decrees."

[4b] *Grant us good new tidings:* Again, like verse 4, this line starts with the Hebrew "(re)new," and again we move the concept of "new" out of the verb and into the object, for "good new tidings." The phrase "good tidings" also appears in the *Havdalah* liturgy, where Elijah the Prophet brings us, literally, "good tidings, salvations, and comforts." We find the "salvations and comforts" in line 20a.

[5] *Cancel:* Or, "abolish," "annul," and so forth. We choose "cancel" here because the same Hebrew word appears in line b with "plans" as the object, and we want a verb that works well in English both times.

⁵ᵃ אָבִינוּ מַלְכֵּנוּ, בַּטֵּל מֵעָלֵינוּ כָּל גְּזֵרוֹת קָשׁוֹת וְרָעוֹת.
⁵ᵇ אָבִינוּ מַלְכֵּנוּ, בַּטֵּל מִמֶּנּוּ גְּזֵרוֹת קָשׁוֹת.
⁶ אָבִינוּ מַלְכֵּנוּ, בַּטֵּל מַחְשְׁבוֹת שׂוֹנְאֵינוּ.
⁶ᵃ אָבִינוּ מַלְכֵּנוּ, קַלְקֵל מַחְשְׁבוֹת שׂוֹנְאֵינוּ.
⁶ᵇ אָבִינוּ מַלְכֵּנוּ, בַּטֵּל מִמֶּנּוּ מַחְשְׁבוֹת שׂוֹנְאֵינוּ.
⁷ אָבִינוּ מַלְכֵּנוּ, הָפֵר עֲצַת אוֹיְבֵינוּ.

⁵ᵃ(*Minhag Yemen* and *Minhag Sepharad*) Our father, our king, cancel all burdensome and evil decrees against us.
⁵ᵇ(*Seder Rav Amram* and *Machzor Roma*) Our father, our king, cancel all our burdensome decrees.
⁶Our father, our king, cancel the plans of those who hate us.
⁶ᵃ(*Machzor Vitry*) Our father, our king, spoil the plans of those who hate us.
⁶ᵇ(*Seder Rav Amram*) Our father, our king, cancel the plans against us of those who hate us.
⁷Our father, our king, disrupt the schemes of those who are our enemies.

⁵ᵇ *Our burdensome decrees:* The Hebrew here is closer to the main text than our English translation would indicate. The only difference is the choice of preposition in Hebrew—*mei'aleinu* versus *mimenu*.

⁶ᵇ *Plans against us:* We add "against us" in English to reflect the added word in Hebrew. Unfortunately, the resulting English is convoluted while the original Hebrew is not.

More generally, our English is an attempt to capture the similarities and variations among different Hebrew lines and different textual traditions. Usually we can do so without sacrificing too much in the way on English style. This line and 7b below are notable exceptions.

⁷ *Schemes:* Or, just "plans," but we have already used that English word for a different one in Hebrew. (In North America, a "scheme" denotes something untoward. In British English, "scheme," like the Hebrew here, is neutral.)

⁷ *Those who are our enemies:* Or, just "our enemies," but the Hebrew here—literally, "our enemies"—matches the literal "our haters" in the previous line. Because we used "those who..." there, we want to use the same English pattern here.

⁷ᵃ(*Minhag Yemen*) Our father, our king, disrupt the schemes of all those who are our enemies.
⁷ᵇ(*Machzor Vitry*) Our father, our king, disrupt the schemes against us of those who are our enemies.
⁸Our father, our king, put an end to every one of our adversaries and foes.
⁸ᵃ(*Machzor Vitry* and *Minhag Lubavitch*) Our father, our king, put an end to every one of our adversaries and foes.
⁹Our father, our king, shut the mouths of our adversaries and accusers.
⁹ᵃ(*Machzor Vitry*) Our father, our king, shut the mouths of our enemies and accusers.
⁹ᵇ(*Machzor Vitry*) Our father, our king, side with those who teach our merits.
⁹ᶜ(*Minhag Lubavitch*) Our father, our king, shut the mouths of our adversaries and accusers.

⁷ᵃ אָבִינוּ מַלְכֵּנוּ, הָפֵר עֲצַת כָּל אוֹיְבֵינוּ.
⁷ᵇ אָבִינוּ מַלְכֵּנוּ, הָפֵר עֲצַת אוֹיְבֵינוּ מֵעָלֵינוּ.
⁸ אָבִינוּ מַלְכֵּנוּ, כַּלֵּה כָּל צַר וּמַשְׂטִין מֵעָלֵינוּ.
⁸ᵃ אָבִינוּ מַלְכֵּנוּ, כַּלֵּה כָּל צַר וּמַסְטִין מֵעָלֵינוּ.
⁹ אָבִינוּ מַלְכֵּנוּ, סְתֹם פִּיּוֹת מַשְׂטִינֵינוּ וּמְקַטְרְגֵינוּ.
⁹ᵃ אָבִינוּ מַלְכֵּנוּ, סְתוֹם פִּיּוֹת צוֹרְרֵינוּ וּמְקַטְרְגֵינוּ.
⁹ᵇ אָבִינוּ מַלְכֵּנוּ, תַּסְכִּים עִם מְלַמְּדֵי זְכוּתֵינוּ.
⁹ᶜ אָבִינוּ מַלְכֵּנוּ, סְתוֹם מַסְטִינֵינוּ וּמְקַטְרְגֵינוּ.

⁷ᵇ *Schemes against us:* As with 6b, we add "against us" to indicate how this line differs from the main text, even though the resulting translation is awkward.

⁸ᵃ *Adversaries:* This is the same word for "adversaries" that we find in verse 8, but here in *Machzor Vitry* it is spelled differently, with a *samech* instead of the usual *sin*. The meaning doesn't change, so the English translation is the same as the main text.

⁹ᶜ *Adversaries:* Again, the only difference between this word here and in the main text is the spelling.

¹⁰ Our father, our king, put an end to pestilence, war, famine, captivity, destruction, sin, and extermination among the people of your covenant. ¹⁰ᵃ(*Minhag Yemen*) Our father, our king, put an end to pestilence, war, famine, captivity, pillage, destruction, plague, Satan, evil inclination, and bad diseases from among the people of your covenant. ¹⁰ᵇ(*Seder Rav Amram*) Our father, our king, put an end to pestilence, war, famine, and destruction among the people of your covenant. ¹⁰ᶜ(*Machzor Vitry, Minhag Sepharad,* and *Machzor Roma*) Our father, our king, put an end to pestilence, war, famine, captivity, destruction, and plague among the people of your covenant. ¹⁰ᵈ(*Minhag Lubavitch*) Our father, our king, put an end to pestilence, war, famine, captivity, and destruction among the people of your covenant. ¹¹Our father, our king, prevent the plague among your heritage. ¹¹ᵃ(*Seder Rav Amram* and *Machzor Roma*) Our father, our king, stop the plague from your heritage.

¹⁰ אָבִינוּ מַלְכֵּנוּ, כַּלֵּה דֶּבֶר וְחֶרֶב וְרָעָב, וּשְׁבִי וּמַשְׁחִית וְעָוֹן וּשְׁמַד, מִבְּנֵי בְרִיתֶךָ.
¹⁰ᵃ אָבִינוּ מַלְכֵּנוּ, כַּלֵּה דֶּבֶר וְחֶרֶב וְרָעָב וּשְׁבִי וּבִזָּה וּמַשְׁחִית וּמַגֵּפָה וְשָׂטָן וְיֵצֶר רָע וָחֳלָאִים רָעִים מִבְּנֵי בְרִיתֶךָ.
¹⁰ᵇ אָבִינוּ מַלְכֵּנוּ, כַּלֵּה דֶּבֶר וְחֶרֶב וְרָעָב וּמַשְׁחִית מִבְּנֵי בְרִיתֶךָ.
¹⁰ᶜ אָבִינוּ מַלְכֵּנוּ, כַּלֵּה דֶּבֶר וְחֶרֶב וְרָעָב וּשְׁבִי וּמַשְׁחִית וּמַגֵּפָה מִבְּנֵי בְרִיתֶךָ.
¹⁰ᵈ אָבִינוּ מַלְכֵּנוּ, כַּלֵּה דֶּבֶר וְחֶרֶב וְרָעָב וּשְׁבִי וּמַשְׁחִית מִבְּנֵי בְרִיתֶךָ.
¹¹ אָבִינוּ מַלְכֵּנוּ, מְנַע מַגֵּפָה מִנַּחֲלָתֶךָ.
¹¹ᵃ אָבִינוּ מַלְכֵּנוּ, עֲצוֹר מַגֵּפָה מִנַּחֲלָתֶךָ.

¹⁰ *War*: Hebrew, "sword." But "put an end to sword" isn't English.

¹⁰ *Famine*: Or, "hunger."

¹⁰ *Extermination*: Or, the less specific "destruction." The Hebrew word takes on a variety of meanings—including even "conversion"—in various time periods and dialects.

[11] **Heritage:** That is, Israel.

[12]Our father, our king, forgive and pardon all our sins.
[12a]*(Machzor Vitry)* Our father, our king, pardon and forgive all our sins.
[12b]*(Seder Rav Amram* and *Machzor Roma)* Our father, our king, forgive and pardon our sins.
[13]Our father, our king, erase and remove our sins and our transgressions from your sight.
[13a]*(Machzor Vitry, Seder Rav Amram, Minhag Rinus,* and *Minhag Polin)* Our father, our king, erase and remove our sins from your sight.
[14]Our father, our king, in your great mercy erase all of our note of debt.
[14a]*(Machzor Roma)* Our father, our king, erase our note of debt.
[14b]*(Seder Rav Amram)* Our father, our king, erase our notes of debt.
[15]Our father, our king, place us again before You in perfect repentance.

[12] אָבִינוּ מַלְכֵּנוּ, סְלַח וּמְחַל לְכָל עֲוֹנוֹתֵינוּ.
[12a] אָבִינוּ מַלְכֵּנוּ, מְחוֹל וּסְלַח לְכָל עֲוֹנוֹתֵינוּ.
[12b] אָבִינוּ מַלְכֵּנוּ, סְלַח וּמְחַל לַעֲוֹנוֹתֵינוּ.
[13] אָבִינוּ מַלְכֵּנוּ, מְחֵה וְהַעֲבֵר פְּשָׁעֵינוּ וְחַטֹּאתֵינוּ מִנֶּגֶד עֵינֶיךָ.
[13a] אָבִינוּ מַלְכֵּנוּ, מְחֵה וְהַעֲבֵר פְּשָׁעֵינוּ מִנֶּגֶד עֵינֶיךָ.
[14] אָבִינוּ מַלְכֵּנוּ, מְחוֹק בְּרַחֲמֶיךָ הָרַבִּים כָּל שִׁטְרֵי חוֹבוֹתֵינוּ.
[14a] אָבִינוּ מַלְכֵּנוּ, מְחוֹק שְׁטַר חוֹבוֹתֵינוּ.
[14b] אָבִינוּ מַלְכֵּנוּ, מְחוֹק שִׁטְרֵי חוֹבוֹתֵינוּ.
[15] אָבִינוּ מַלְכֵּנוּ, הַחֲזִירֵנוּ בִּתְשׁוּבָה שְׁלֵמָה לְפָנֶיךָ.

[13] **Sins ... transgressions:** Here we have two Hebrew words for "sin," so we use two different English words. In line 12, above, we saw a third Hebrew word. In general, we do not have enough English synonyms or near synonyms to represent the many Hebrew words for "sin."

[14] **Erase:** Or, "cancel."

[14] **Debt:** A metaphor for sin.

[15] **Place us again before You:** Or, "bring us back," but we want to use the phrase "before

You" here in English to mirror the Hebrew, which repeats a phrase from line 1.

¹⁶Our father, our king, send perfect healing to those among your people who are ill.

^{16a}(*Machzor Vitry*) Our father, our king, send perfect healing to all those among your people who are ill.

¹⁷Our father, our king, tear up the evil sentence decreed against us.

^{17a}(*Seder Rav Amram*) Our father, our king, tear up for us the sentence decreed against us.

¹⁸Our father, our king, remember us favorably before You.

^{18a}(*Minhag Sepharad* and *Minhag Yemen*) Our father, our king, remember us favorably before You.

¹⁹Our father, our king, write us in the book of good life.

^{19a}(*Machzor Roma*) Our father, our king, write us in the book of life.

^{19b}(*Seder Rav Amram*) Our father, our king, write us in the book of life.

¹⁶ אָבִינוּ מַלְכֵּנוּ, שְׁלַח רְפוּאָה שְׁלֵמָה לְחוֹלֵי עַמֶּךָ.

^{16a} אָבִינוּ מַלְכֵּנוּ, שְׁלַח רְפוּאָה שְׁלֵמָה לְכָל חוֹלֵי עַמֶּךָ.

¹⁷ אָבִינוּ מַלְכֵּנוּ, קְרַע רֹעַ גְּזַר דִּינֵנוּ.

^{17a} אָבִינוּ מַלְכֵּנוּ, קְרַע לָנוּ גְּזַר דִּינֵנוּ.

¹⁸ אָבִינוּ מַלְכֵּנוּ, זָכְרֵנוּ בְּזִכָּרוֹן טוֹב לְפָנֶיךָ.

^{18a} אָבִינוּ מַלְכֵּנוּ, זָכְרֵנוּ בְּזִכָּרוֹן טוֹב מִלְּפָנֶיךָ.

¹⁹ אָבִינוּ מַלְכֵּנוּ, כָּתְבֵנוּ בְּסֵפֶר חַיִּים טוֹבִים.

^{19a} אָבִינוּ מַלְכֵּנוּ, כָּתְבֵנוּ בְּסֵפֶר הַחַיִּים.

^{19b} אָבִינוּ מַלְכֵּנוּ, כָּתְבֵנוּ בְּסֵפֶר חַיִּים.

¹⁷ *Evil:* The Hebrew grammar here is curious, with "evil" appearing as a noun before the word "sentence," not—as is more common—as an adjective after it. This nuance doesn't appear to change the meaning, but the grammatical construction is interesting (at least to people who find curious grammatical constructions interesting).

[18] *Before You:* Again, we add this phrase only to echo the way the Hebrew matches the opening line.

[18a] *Before you:* Hebrew, "from before you."

[19] *Write:* Or, the fancier "inscribe."

[19a] *The book:* Throughout the text, we translate the literal "write us in a book" into English as "write us in *the* book." Here we actually have "the book" in Hebrew.

[20] Our father, our king, write us in the book of redemption and salvation.
[20a] *(Machzor Roma)* Our father, our king, write us in the book of salvation and comfort.
[20b] *(Machzor Vitry)* Our father, our king, write us in the book of salvation and redemption.
[21] Our father, our king, write us in the book of livelihood and sustenance.
[22] Our father, our king, write us in the book of merit.
[22a] *(Seder Rav Amram)* Our father, our king, write us in the book of memory.
[22b] *(Machzor Vitry)* Our father, our king, write us in the book of peace.
[22c] *(Machzor Vitry)* Our father, our king, write us in the book of sustaining food.

[20] אָבִינוּ מַלְכֵּנוּ, כָּתְבֵנוּ בְּסֵפֶר גְּאֻלָּה וִישׁוּעָה.
[20a] אָבִינוּ מַלְכֵּנוּ, כָּתְבֵנוּ בְּסֵפֶר יְשׁוּעוֹת וְנֶחָמוֹת.
[20b] אָבִינוּ מַלְכֵּנוּ, כָּתְבֵנוּ בְּסֵפֶר יְשׁוּעָה וּגְאֻלָּה.
[21] אָבִינוּ מַלְכֵּנוּ, כָּתְבֵנוּ בְּסֵפֶר פַּרְנָסָה וְכַלְכָּלָה.
[22] אָבִינוּ מַלְכֵּנוּ, כָּתְבֵנוּ בְּסֵפֶר זְכֻיּוֹת.
[22a] אָבִינוּ מַלְכֵּנוּ, כָּתְבֵנוּ בְּסֵפֶר זִכָּרוֹן.
[22b] אָבִינוּ מַלְכֵּנוּ, כָּתְבֵנוּ בְּסֵפֶר שָׁלוֹם.
[22c] אָבִינוּ מַלְכֵּנוּ, כָּתְבֵנוּ בְּסֵפֶר מְזוֹנוֹת.

[19b] *The book:* Unlike in 19a, here we have the literal "a book" in Hebrew. The meaning doesn't change, so the translations in 19a and

here in 19b are identical. The Hebrew is very subtly different.

²⁰ᵃ *Salvation and comfort:* Literally, "salvations and comforts," a phrase that we also find in the *Havdalah* liturgy, where Elijah the Prophet brings us "good tidings, salvations, and comforts." See note 4b.

²¹ *Sustenance:* That is, financial well-being.

²² *Merit:* Hebrew, "merits," reflecting a notion that merits offset sins, in much the way that deposits now offset withdrawals at a bank.

²²ᵃ *Memory:* Or, "remembrance."

²²ᶜ *Sustaining food:* Or, just "food."

²³ אָבִינוּ מַלְכֵּנוּ, כָּתְבֵנוּ בְּסֵפֶר סְלִיחָה וּמְחִילָה.
²³ᵃ אָבִינוּ מַלְכֵּנוּ, כָּתְבֵנוּ בְּסֵפֶר מְחִילָה וּסְלִיחָה וְכַפָּרָה.
²³ᵇ אָבִינוּ מַלְכֵּנוּ, כָּתְבֵנוּ בְּסֵפֶר סְלִיחָה וּמְחִילָה וְכַפָּרָה.
²⁴ אָבִינוּ מַלְכֵּנוּ, הַצְמַח לָנוּ יְשׁוּעָה בְּקָרוֹב.
²⁵ אָבִינוּ מַלְכֵּנוּ, הָרֵם קֶרֶן יִשְׂרָאֵל עַמֶּךָ.
²⁶ אָבִינוּ מַלְכֵּנוּ, הָרֵם קֶרֶן מְשִׁיחֶךָ.
²⁶ᵃ אָבִינוּ מַלְכֵּנוּ, וְהָרֵם קֶרֶן מְשִׁיחֶךָ.
²⁶ᵇ אָבִינוּ מַלְכֵּנוּ, הָרֵם קֶרֶן מִזְבְּחֶךָ.

²³Our father, our king, write us in the book of forgiveness and pardon.
²³ᵃ(*Minhag Yemen*) Our father, our king, write us in the book of forgiveness and pardon and atonement.
²³ᵇ(*Machzor Roma*) Our father, our king, write us in the book of pardon and forgiveness and atonement.
²⁴Our father, our king, cause salvation to flourish for us soon.
²⁵Our father, our king, give strength to your people Israel.
²⁶Our father, our king, give strength to your messiah.
²⁶ᵃ(*Minhag Yemen*) Our father, our king, and give strength to your messiah.
²⁶ᵇ(*Machzor Vitry* and *Minhag Sepharad*) Our father, our king, give strength to your altar.

²³ᵃ Atonement: We use this English word because the Hebrew here, *kapara,* is similar to the Hebrew in *Yom Kippur* that gives us the "day of atonement," even though it is an odd word choice. English differs from Hebrew in that God forgives and pardons us but doesn't "atone us."

²⁵ Give strength to: Literally, "raise the horn of," a common metaphor in Hebrew.

²⁶ᵃ And give strength: The effect here is to combine line 26 closely with 25, as though 26 is the second half of 25: "Give strength to your people Israel ... and give strength to your messiah."

²⁷Our father, our king, fill our hands from among your blessings.
²⁸Our father, our king, fill our storehouses with plenty.
²⁹Our father, our king, hear our voice; have compassion and mercy on us.
²⁹ᵃ(*Machzor Roma*) Our father, our king, hear our voice and have compassion and mercy on us.
³⁰Our father, our king, accept our prayer with mercy and favor.
³¹Our father, our king, open the gates of heaven to our prayer.
³²Our father, our king, do not return us empty-handed from before You.
³²ᵃ(*Machzor Roma, Minhag Sepharad,* and *Minhag Yemen*) Our father, our king, do not return us empty-handed from before You.

²⁷ אָבִינוּ מַלְכֵּנוּ, מַלֵּא יָדֵינוּ מִבִּרְכוֹתֶיךָ.
²⁸ אָבִינוּ מַלְכֵּנוּ, מַלֵּא אֲסָמֵינוּ שָׂבָע.
²⁹ אָבִינוּ מַלְכֵּנוּ, שְׁמַע קוֹלֵנוּ, חוּס וְרַחֵם עָלֵינוּ.
²⁹ᵃ אָבִינוּ מַלְכֵּנוּ, שְׁמַע קוֹלֵנוּ וְחוּס וְרַחֵם עָלֵינוּ.
³⁰ אָבִינוּ מַלְכֵּנוּ, קַבֵּל בְּרַחֲמִים וּבְרָצוֹן אֶת תְּפִלָּתֵנוּ.
³¹ אָבִינוּ מַלְכֵּנוּ, פְּתַח שַׁעֲרֵי שָׁמַיִם לִתְפִלָּתֵנוּ.
³² אָבִינוּ מַלְכֵּנוּ, נָא אַל תְּשִׁיבֵנוּ רֵיקָם מִלְּפָנֶיךָ.
³²ᵃ אָבִינוּ מַלְכֵּנוּ, אַל תְּשִׁיבֵנוּ רֵיקָם מִלְּפָנֶיךָ.

²⁷ *From among your blessings:* Others, "with your blessings." But the Hebrew paints a picture of God's blessings, only some of which are used to fill our hands.

²⁹ *Compassion and mercy:* Two reasonable English representations of two Hebrew words, though we don't know the exact nuances of the Hebrew. (Also, the Hebrew offers two verbs, not nouns, but it is in general a mistake to focus on parts of speech.)

³¹ *Gates of heaven:* Or, "gates of the sky."

³² *Before You:* Yet again (see lines 15 and 18), we use "before You" instead of a more mellifluous option (like "your presence") to reinforce the verbal connection between this line and the opening one.

³³Our father, our king, remember that we are but dust.
³⁴Our father, our king, may this hour be an hour of mercy and a time of favor before You.
³⁴ᵃ(*Machzor Vitry*) Our father, our king, may this hour and every hour be favorable and an hour of your mercy before You.
³⁵Our father, our king, have compassion on us and on our children.

³³ אָבִינוּ מַלְכֵּנוּ, זְכוֹר כִּי עָפָר אֲנָחְנוּ.
³⁴ אָבִינוּ מַלְכֵּנוּ, תְּהֵא הַשָּׁעָה הַזֹּאת שְׁעַת רַחֲמִים וְעֵת רָצוֹן מִלְּפָנֶיךָ.
³⁴ᵃ אָבִינוּ מַלְכֵּנוּ, תְּהֵא הַשָּׁעָה הַזֹּאת וְכָל שָׁעָה רְצוֹן שָׁעָה רַחֲמֶיךָ מִלְּפָנֶיךָ.
³⁵ אָבִינוּ מַלְכֵּנוּ, חֲמוֹל עָלֵינוּ וְעַל עוֹלָלֵינוּ וְטַפֵּנוּ.

³³ *But dust:* Better would be "dirt," but the Hebrew line matches Genesis 18:27 ("I [Abraham] am but dust and ashes"); Genesis 2:7, where

God creates the first man from the dust of the earth; and other lines as well. In all of those places, "dirt" is a better translation for the Hebrew *afar*, but because "dust" is so well known, we use that (mis)translation here too, to help the English reader connect this line to the related biblical passages. (The modifier "but" in "but dust" here comes from the Hebrew word order.)

[34] *May this hour:* That is, "it is hoped that this hour be...." This is an expression of desire, not uncertainty. The translation "let this hour..." is tempting, but the Hebrew, perhaps surprisingly, doesn't ask God to make this hour into anything; rather, it expresses a more amorphous hope that the hour somehow be(come) something.

[34a] *Be favorable and an hour of mercy:* The Hebrew here looks erroneous, with "hour" and "hour of" confused in the text. The original reads, "may this hour and every hour be favor and an hour mercy before you." Another possible emendation reads, "may this hour and every hour of favor be...."

[35] *Compassion:* This is not the same word for "compassion" that we saw in line 29, above, but we have run out of English synonyms.

[35] *Children:* The Hebrew has two words for "children" here. Some translations translate them both ("children and infants," for instance). We prefer not to introduce awkward English.

³⁶ אָבִינוּ מַלְכֵּנוּ, עֲשֵׂה לְמַעַן הֲרוּגִים עַל שֵׁם קָדְשֶׁךָ.
³⁷ אָבִינוּ מַלְכֵּנוּ, עֲשֵׂה לְמַעַן טְבוּחִים עַל יִחוּדֶךָ.
³⁸ אָבִינוּ מַלְכֵּנוּ, עֲשֵׂה לְמַעַן בָּאֵי בָאֵשׁ וּבַמַּיִם עַל קִדּוּשׁ שְׁמֶךָ.
³⁹ אָבִינוּ מַלְכֵּנוּ, נְקוֹם נִקְמַת דַּם עֲבָדֶיךָ הַשָּׁפוּךְ.
⁴⁰ אָבִינוּ מַלְכֵּנוּ, עֲשֵׂה לְמַעַנְךָ אִם לֹא לְמַעֲנֵנוּ.
⁴⁰ᵃ אָבִינוּ מַלְכֵּנוּ, עֲשֵׂה לְמַעַנְךָ וְלֹא לְמַעֲנֵנוּ.
⁴¹ אָבִינוּ מַלְכֵּנוּ, עֲשֵׂה לְמַעַנְךָ וְהוֹשִׁיעֵנוּ.
⁴¹ᵃ אָבִינוּ מַלְכֵּנוּ, נָא אַל יְעַכֵּב חֵטְא וְעָוֹן אֶת תְּפִילָּתֵינוּ.
⁴² אָבִינוּ מַלְכֵּנוּ, עֲשֵׂה לְמַעַן רַחֲמֶיךָ הָרַבִּים.
⁴²ᵃ אָבִינוּ מַלְכֵּנוּ, עֲשֵׂה לְמַעַן רַחֲמֶיךָ הָרַבִּים וְרַחֵם עָלֵינוּ.

³⁶Our father, our king, act for the sake of those killed for your holy name.
³⁷Our father, our king, act for the sake of those slaughtered for your oneness.
³⁸Our father, our king, act for the sake of those who go through fire and water for your holy name.
³⁹Our father, our king, avenge the spilled blood of your servants.
⁴⁰Our father, our king, act for your sake if not for our sake.
⁴⁰ᵃ(Seder Rav Amram and Machzor Roma) Our father, our king, act for your sake and not for our sake.
⁴¹Our father, our king, act for your sake and save us.
⁴¹ᵃ(Machzor Vitry) Our father, our king, do not let sin and transgression interrupt our prayer.
⁴²Our father, our king, act for the sake of your great compassion.
⁴²ᵃ(Seder Rav Amram) Our father, our king, act for the sake of your great compassion and have compassion on us.

³⁶ *Act:* Or (here and below), "do this."

³⁶ *Those killed:* Others, "those who were killed." But the Hebrew is tenseless.

⁴¹ᵃ *Interrupt:* Or, "delay."

⁴²ᵇ(*Machzor Roma*) Our father, our king, act for the sake of your great compassion and your enormous love and have compassion on us.
⁴³Our father, our king, act for the sake of your great, mighty, and revered name by which we are called.
⁴³ᵃ(*Seder Rav Amram*) Our father, our king, act for the sake of your great name.
⁴³ᵇ(*Machzor Vitry*) Our father, our king, act for the sake of your great and revered name by which we are called.
⁴³ᶜ(*Machzor Roma*) Our father, our king, act for the sake of your great, mighty, and revered name.
⁴⁴Our father, our king, be gracious to us and answer us, for we have no merit; act justly and lovingly with us and save us.
⁴⁴ᵃ(*Machzor Vitry*) Our father, our king, be gracious to us and answer us, for we have no justice or love; act with us for the sake of your name and save us.

⁴²ᵇ אָבִינוּ מַלְכֵּנוּ, עֲשֵׂה לְמַעַן רַחֲמֶיךָ הָרַבִּים וַחֲסָדֶךָ הַגְּדוֹלִים וְרַחֵם עָלֵינוּ וְהוֹשִׁיעֵנוּ.
⁴³ אָבִינוּ מַלְכֵּנוּ, עֲשֵׂה לְמַעַן שִׁמְךָ הַגָּדוֹל הַגִּבּוֹר וְהַנּוֹרָא שֶׁנִּקְרָא עָלֵינוּ.
⁴³ᵃ אָבִינוּ מַלְכֵּנוּ, עֲשֵׂה לְמַעַן שִׁמְךָ הַגָּדוֹל.
⁴³ᵇ אָבִינוּ מַלְכֵּנוּ, עֲשֵׂה לְמַעַן שִׁמְךָ הַגָּדוֹל וְהַנּוֹרָא שֶׁנִּקְרָא עָלֵינוּ.
⁴³ᶜ אָבִינוּ מַלְכֵּנוּ, עֲשֵׂה לְמַעַן שִׁמְךָ הַגָּדוֹל הַגִּבּוֹר וְהַנּוֹרָא.
⁴⁴ אָבִינוּ מַלְכֵּנוּ, חָנֵּנוּ וַעֲנֵנוּ, כִּי אֵין בָּנוּ מַעֲשִׂים; עֲשֵׂה עִמָּנוּ צְדָקָה וָחֶסֶד וְהוֹשִׁיעֵנוּ.
⁴⁴ᵃ אָבִינוּ מַלְכֵּנוּ, חָנֵּנוּ וַעֲנֵנוּ, כִּי אֵין בָּנוּ צְדָקָה וָחֶסֶד עֲשֵׂה עִמָּנוּ לְמַעַן שְׁמֶךָ וְהוֹשִׁיעֵנוּ.

⁴²ᵇ *Enormous*: Or "great"—literally, "big" in Hebrew—but we have already used "great" for another Hebrew word.

⁴³ *Great, mighty, and revered*: Hebrew, *hagadol, hagibor, v'hanora*, matching the qualities ascribed to God in the *Avot*, the first prayer of the *Amidah*—itself based on Deuteronomy 10:17.

Translator's Introduction to Ki Hinei Kachomer

Dr. Joel M. Hoffman

Ki Hinei Kachomer is rhyming, rhythmic poetry. The four lines of the first stanza rhyme with each other. In the following stanzas, the first three lines rhyme, and the fourth line repeats the last line of the first stanza, thereby returning to that rhyme. The rhythm is loose tetrameter: four strong beats to a line, with various weak syllables around them.

In addition, the structure of each stanza is identical, literally:

> For, behold, like A in the hand of the B,
> At will, C'ing, and at will, D'ing,
> So are we in your hand, E (modified by F).
> Look at the covenant, and do not turn to the accuser.

The stanzas differ in their choice of A, B, C, D, E, and F. For instance, the first stanza offers "clay," "potter," "expand," "contract," "guardian," and "love," which combine into the following:

> For behold, like clay in the hand of the potter,
> At will, expanding it, and at will, contracting it,
> So are we in your hand, guardian of love.
> Look at the covenant, and do not turn to the accuser.

The Hebrew, of course, rhymes in tetrameter. In addition, wordplays permeate the original text. The words for "potter" and "accuser" share a root, and the word for "guardian" is nearly homophonous with the words for "potter" and "accuser." And the phrase "guardian of love" is taken from the thirteen attributes of God as listed in Exodus 34:6–7.

Much of the poem's power comes from the mixture of strict structure and innovative vocabulary: the shift in verse 3 from a material (like clay or stone) to a tool (like an ax or a ship's steering wheel) and then back, the rhyming epithets for God (e.g., guardian of love, supporter of the poor and impoverished), and more.

Additionally, the poem in Hebrew reads like a challenge: "Can you think of a word that rhymes with B and is the opposite of C?"—for instance, in the first verse, a word that rhymes with "potter" and is the opposite of "expanding."

A poetic translation of the first three verses that re-creates some of these key elements might run along the lines of the following:

[1] Like clay in the hand of the potter,
Mixing together the earth and the water,
So are we in your hand, loving author,
Look at the covenant, and avoid the source of horror.

[2] Like stones in the hand of the carver,
Who keeps some nearby and others farther,
So are we in your hand, life-giving father,
Look at the covenant, and avoid the source of horror.

[3] Like an ax in the hand of the blacksmith,
Inserting and removing iron sticks,
So are we in your hand, supporter of the impoverished,
Look at the covenant, and avoid the source of horror.

But to make the rhymes (almost) work, we obviously have to stray pretty far from what some of the words mean. For "expanding ... contracting," we have instead "earth ... water." So in general, we have no way to capture the rhythm, rhyme, nuance, wordplay, and meaning of the original Hebrew in English.

In large part, a rhyming translation that strays from the literal meaning of the words does more to capture the original text than a translation that takes the opposite approach, because the point of the poem is the clever choice of rhyming words. But eventually we run out of rhyming words in English, and a rhyming version ends up as an almost-rhyming but silly-sounding poem that does not do justice to the original.

So, recognizing that it is a poor representation of the Hebrew but still perhaps the best we can do, we revert to a literal translation of the Hebrew that ignores the rhymes and allusions.

Ki Hinei Kachomer

A NEW AND ANNOTATED TRANSLATION

Dr. Joel M. Hoffman

[1] For behold, like clay in the hand of the potter,
At will expanding it and at will contracting it,
So are we in your hand, guardian of love.
Look at the covenant, and do not turn to the accuser.

[1] כִּי הִנֵּה כַחֹמֶר בְּיַד הַיּוֹצֵר,
בִּרְצוֹתוֹ מַרְחִיב וּבִרְצוֹתוֹ מְקַצֵּר,
כֵּן אֲנַחְנוּ בְּיָדְךָ חֶסֶד נוֹצֵר,
לַבְּרִית הַבֵּט וְאַל תֵּפֶן לַיֵּצֶר.

[1] *Guardian of love:* After Exodus 34:6–7, where "guardian of love" is one of the attributes of God. The Hebrew words here are reversed ("of love, the guardian") in a way that is poetic in Hebrew but ungrammatical in English.

[1] *Accuser:* Literally, "source" or "inclination." The intent is clearly "evil inclination" or "source of evil."

²For behold, like stone in the hand of the carver,
At will seizing it and at will shattering it,
So are we in your hand, giver of life and death.
Look at the covenant, and do not turn to the accuser.
³For behold, like an ax in the hand of the blacksmith,
At will bringing it near the light and at will moving it away,
So are we in your hand, supporter of the poor and impoverished.
Look at the covenant, and do not turn to the accuser.

² כִּי הִנֵּה כָּאֶבֶן בְּיַד הַמְסַתֵּת,
בִּרְצוֹתוֹ אוֹחֵז וּבִרְצוֹתוֹ מְכַתֵּת,
כֵּן אֲנַחְנוּ בְּיָדְךָ מְחַיֶּה וּמְמוֹתֵת,
לַבְּרִית הַבֵּט וְאַל תֵּפֶן לַיֵּצֶר.
³ כִּי הִנֵּה כַּגַּרְזֶן בְּיַד הֶחָרָשׁ,
בִּרְצוֹתוֹ דִּבֵּק לָאוּר וּבִרְצוֹתוֹ פֵּרַשׁ, כֵּן אֲנַחְנוּ בְּיָדְךָ תּוֹמֵךְ עָנִי וָרָשׁ, לַבְּרִית הַבֵּט וְאַל תֵּפֶן לַיֵּצֶר.

² *Shattering:* Or, "pounding." The rare Hebrew word here *(m'khateit)* demonstrates perfectly the way the poem challenges the reader, as explained in the Translator's Introduction. Here, the challenge is, what rhymes with *m'sateit* ("carver") and is roughly the opposite of "seizing"?

² *Giver of life and death:* Or, "sustainer and killer."

³ *Like an ax:* The Hebrew imagery shifts here from materials to the tools used to work on the materials. Our English does the same.

³ *Light:* That is, fire. (Here the poetic structure of the poem would have allowed for the Hebrew word for "fire." The choice of "light" instead was driven by other artistic considerations.) The Hebrew provides "bringing

it nearer the light and bringing it further away." The "light" is fire.

⁴For behold, like a wheel in the hand of a sailor,
At will holding it and at will letting it go,
So are we in your hand, God who is good and forgiving.
Look at the covenant, and do not turn to the accuser.
⁵For behold, like glass in the hand of the glazier,
At will shaping it and at will melting it,
So are we in your hand, forgiver of arrogance and error.
Look at the covenant, and do not turn to the accuser.

⁴ כִּי הִנֵּה כַּהֶגֶה בְּיַד הַמַּלָּח,
בִּרְצוֹתוֹ אוֹחֵז וּבִרְצוֹתוֹ שִׁלַּח,
כֵּן אֲנַחְנוּ בְיָדְךָ אֵל טוֹב וְסַלָּח,
לַבְּרִית הַבֵּט וְאַל תֵּפֶן לַיֵּצֶר.
⁵ כִּי הִנֵּה כַּזְּכוּכִית בְּיַד הַמְזַגֵּג,
בִּרְצוֹתוֹ חוֹגֵג וּבִרְצוֹתוֹ מְמוֹגֵג,
כֵּן אֲנַחְנוּ בְיָדְךָ מַעֲבִיר זָדוֹן וְשׁוֹגֵג,
לַבְּרִית הַבֵּט וְאַל תֵּפֶן לַיֵּצֶר.

⁴ *A wheel:* Or, "the helm."

⁵ *Shaping:* The Hebrew is from the root for "wheel," as if to suggest "carving or shaping with a wheel."

⁵ *Forgiver:* Hebrew, *ma'avir*, literally, "causing to pass." This verb lies at the center of *Un'taneh Tokef.* (See *Prayers of Awe, Who by Fire, Who by Water—Un'taneh Tokef,* pp.98–102.)

⁶For behold, like cloth in the hand of the draper,
At will straightening it and at will misaligning it,
So are we in your hand, God who acts with jealousy and vengeance.
Look at the covenant, and do not turn to the accuser.
⁷For behold, like silver in the hand of the metalsmith,
At will purifying it and at will adulterating it,
So are we in your hand, creator of healing for wounds.
Look at the covenant, and do not turn to the accuser.

⁶ כִּי הִנֵּה כַּיְרִיעָה בְּיַד הָרוֹקֵם,
בִּרְצוֹתוֹ מְיַשֵּׁר וּבִרְצוֹתוֹ מְעַקֵּם,
כֵּן אֲנַחְנוּ בְּיָדְךָ אֵל קַנָּא וְנוֹקֵם,
לַבְּרִית הַבֵּט וְאַל תֵּפֶן לַיֵּצֶר.
⁷ כִּי הִנֵּה כַּכֶּסֶף בְּיַד הַצּוֹרֵף,
בִּרְצוֹתוֹ מְסַגְסֵג וּבִרְצוֹתוֹ מְצָרֵף,
כֵּן אֲנַחְנוּ בְּיָדְךָ מַמְצִיא לְמָזוֹר תֶּרֶף,
לַבְּרִית הַבֵּט וְאַל תֵּפֶן לַיֵּצֶר.

⁶ *God who acts with jealousy and vengeance:* Or, "God who is jealous and vengeful." The Hebrew leans more toward what God does and less in the direction of what God is.

PART III
Avinu Malkeinu

PART III

Avinu Malkeinu

The Music

The Music of Avinu Malkeinu

Gordon Dale, MA

Gordon Dale, MA, is a PhD student in ethnomusicology at the Graduate Center, the City University of New York, and holds an MA in ethnomusicology from Tufts University. He is a Mellon Doctoral Student Fellow at the Committee for the Study of Religion and currently focuses his studies on music and modernity in contemporary *Haredi* Jewish life. He teaches at Brooklyn College and the Debbie Friedman School of Sacred Music at Hebrew Union College – Jewish Institute of Religion.

Jews refer to God in many ways: "the name" *(hashem)*, for example, or "the Merciful One" *(harachaman)*. Some names are mystical (kabbalists discuss *Ein Sof*, "That which is without end"); while others are aspirational (the prophet Gideon writes on his altar that God is *shalom)*; or even downright anthropomorphic, as *avinu malkeinu* ("our father, our king") itself. Unlike so many of God's names, *avinu malkeinu* has become central to the High Holy Days and has thereby become not just a way we speak of God but also a way we express God's reality in communal song.

Many composers have set *Avinu Malkeinu* to music, but one particular melody is so popular that it is simply the default in many Ashkenazi synagogues, although its popularity extends beyond that too. The origin of this melody is unknown. Unable to provide an author's name, anthologies of Jewish song frequently list the piece simply as "traditional," and a tradition it certainly is. One cantor confided to me that while there are many other melodies for *Avinu Malkeinu* that he would love to select during High Holy Day services, his congregation would revolt if he denied them the opportunity to hear and sing this one.

There is good reason for the melody's broad appeal. It is simple enough that even a "religiously unmusical" person can catch on to it after just a few repeats, and the range is well within most people's capability. Additionally, the significance of the prayer imbues the melody with importance. Those of us who were raised hearing it invest it with a great deal of personal meaning. The experience of singing it surrounded by a congregation of voices blending together is a deeply moving event, embodying the essence of the High Holy Day ethos and message. As we plead to *our* father, *our* king, it is only fitting that we join together and lift our collective voices as brothers and sisters, all under the dominion of the God whom the song acknowledges. The opportunity to melt into a collective through song can be a powerful reminder of the connection shared by Jews and the unity toward which we strive.

Another reason, I believe, that the "traditional" melody is so well loved is that it simply sounds Jewish. Western music is largely built on an octave of clearly distinguishable notes along a certain scale of intervals. Much music of Jewish prayer works instead with modes, larger tonal patterns that change depending on the liturgical occasion. *Avinu Malkeinu* is composed in the musical mode known as *Ahavah Rabbah* or *Freygish,* the same mode that gives *Hava Nagilah* its Jewishness. In *Avinu Malkeinu,* the characteristic sound of *Ahavah Rabbah* can be heard in the descending melody of the word *malkeinu (mal-KAY-AY-AY NOO);* sing it to yourself—you'll hear it. In musical terms, we refer to this mode as having a flat two and an augmented second between the second and third scale degrees. Nonmusicians might just call it "Jewish."

Thinking beyond the technical aspects of the melody's construction, one notices that this melody so beautifully expresses the pleading nature of *Avinu Malkeinu's* text. This is more than a song; it is a prayer. It raises our words up to our father who sits upon his throne. For many Jews, this melody gloriously captures the essence of the High Holy Days.

There is something wonderful about the accessibility of *Avinu Malkeinu.* This call to a parent is universal—we all have parents and know what it is to appeal to them; we may not all have kings anymore, but the idea of monarchy is at least an aspect of the divine that we can easily comprehend. Perhaps that is why many popular musicians have chosen to record the piece. Phish, the hippie jam band, frequently performs its own funky, odd-meter, almost Latin-jazz rendition of the traditional melody, with harmonized vocals singing the Hebrew text. Barbra Streisand's 1997 album *Higher Ground* concludes with a moving rendition of Max Janowski's popular setting—a setting still especially popular in Reform congregations, where it is an annual cantorial favorite. Janowski composed especially with choral performance in mind, so Streisand's recording, complete with choir and full orchestra, truly does elevate the listeners. In 2001, Mogwai, a popular Scottish hard-rock band, released its own epic twenty-minute piece titled "My Father, My King," with a sticker on the album cover that described it as "two parts serenity, one part death metal." The band, which is not generally considered a religious ensemble, based the composition on the traditional *Avinu Malkeinu* melody and would perform the entire piece in all of its cacophonous glory at many of its shows.

Other singers too have recorded renditions of *Avinu Malkeinu*. Many of these musicians are not particularly religious and only minimally engaged with Judaism, yet nonetheless felt it important to associate themselves with this prayer—and for good reason: they saw *Avinu*

Malkeinu as an ideal expression of Jewishness. Its beautiful simplicity is so easy to relate to; yet it is so endlessly deep, a ready symbol to many worshipers. Musicians, some of whom have little else on which to pin their Jewish identities, have chosen *Avinu Malkeinu* to represent their spiritual and cultural heritage.

And yet, for many Jewish communities, *Avinu Malkeinu* is a time for pure recitation, not for singing. With the notable exception of Chabad, nearly all Hasidic sects recite it without a melody. Orthodox Sephardi friends have also told me that the idea of singing this prayer is strange to them. Most *yeshivish* (Lithuanian Orthodox) shuls also daven *Avinu Malkeinu* with no musical component. When I asked a respected Orthodox rabbi why his congregation does not sing it, he thought for a moment, then raised his hands to the sky, and cried out, "*Avinu malkeinu, s'lach um'chal l'chol avonoseinu!* [Our father, our king, forgive and pardon all of our iniquities!] To sing this? It just doesn't go!"

A Hasidic friend echoed this sentiment. He considered it inappropriate to sing during a section of the prayer service where we beg God to forgive all of the many sins that we have committed. However, he told me, if you pay attention to a skilled cantor, someone who really knows how to pray, you will hear the voice inflected a bit differently for each of the verses. Strictly speaking, then, this is not a melody in such congregations, but each verse is powerful enough in its own right as to cause the *chazzan* to respond to it in a slightly different way. I love the way this interpretation ascribes such formidable agency to the prayer's words. In this Hasidic mind, the text of *Avinu Malkeinu* is so strong that it influences its own recitation!

While some Jewish authorities avoid music because of *Avinu Malkeinu's* magnitude, others do just the opposite—they insist on singing because of the suspicion that the timing of *Avinu Malkeinu* within the service makes it a particularly auspicious occasion for song. Leading up to the High Holy Days this past year, a friend reminded me of the Rabbinic teaching that on Rosh Hashanah, *hasatan* (the character who appears in Job and causes Job his distress; literally, "the *satan*," or "the adversary") tries to prosecute us for our sins. One of the ways to confuse *hasatan* and thwart his efforts is to sing joyously during *Avinu Malkeinu*. It is as if we are laughing while crying out, as if our song will give the impression that we have nothing to fear on this momentous occasion, so *hasatan* need not even attempt to argue against us. In addition, he added, by singing *Avinu Malkeinu*, we actually convert our sins into *mitzvot*. The Talmud (Yoma 86b) suggests that *t'shuvah* ("repentance") has the power to retroactively convert transgressions into merits. So too, music can transform the very nature of a sin, converting it into a mark of virtue in our judgment on Yom Kippur.

Avinu Malkeinu, we see, attracts not just musical composition but musical imagination as well: we project much onto its melodies, which become symbols in their own right. In this way, the music of *Avinu Malkeinu* transcends the synagogue and even the High Holy Days themselves. It serves as an important connection to Jewish identity, to the Jewish community, and to the Jewish religion itself.

Who's Your Daddy?

Chazzan Danny Maseng

Chazzan Danny Maseng has served as cantor and music director of Temple Israel of Hollywood in California and is patron artist of the Abraham Geiger School of Cantorial Arts in Berlin, Germany. The critically acclaimed off-Broadway one-man show *Wasting Time with Harry Davidowitz* and the innovative theatrical concert *Soul on Fire* have earned Danny accolades. A book about the luminaries of Israeli songwriting is in the works, and a novel titled *Apollonia* has just been completed. Danny is an internationally known composer of contemporary liturgical and synagogue music, performs extensively on stage, television, and film, and has been the guest of the Jerusalem Symphony Orchestra.

My father did not believe in God. I, on the other hand, have been God-obsessed since I was seven years old, and that obsession has never abated, even as it has morphed over the years. This obsession with God has driven me to search, plead, draw near, escape, return, hide, and return again and again to the path. I have done so as a thoroughly flawed, imperfect human being; I have done so with a clueless passion that will not let go of me. I am a failed, but determined detective.

And yet, in spite of all my failures, I am not bereft of lessons. These lessons have etched themselves in my soul and in my heart and have shaped my artistic/religious life and journey. If I have learned anything along my torturous path, it is that abstraction is the enemy of the heart and that tangible, specific imagery is the friend of the spirit and the imagination. To attain something pure and essential that goes beyond the empirical, one must begin from the personal, visceral core, from one's very foundation.

My father was a great man: a hero, an exceptionally gifted pilot, a poet, a bird-watcher, and an amateur archaeologist. My father was also extraordinarily remote, aloof, and inaccessible. My father was not a loving, compassionate father, but he was a just, wise, and powerful father, always teaching lessons that will not fade and are still with me day by day: when I rise and when I sleep, when I write, and when I compose. My father was surely with me as I composed my *Avinu Malkeinu,* seventeen years after his passing.

When I was asked to write a new score for *Avinu Malkeinu* for Central Synagogue in New York, I was given a wish list: the piece should be accessible, it should be a dialogue between the cantor and the congregation, and it should include the original Hebrew and the English translation. Other than that, I was on my own.

What is accessible? How do you compose accessible music?

I was delighted by the challenge, because there are no abstractions and no ambiguities in *Avinu Malkeinu,* just straightforward pleading to a father and king—the very stuff to drive liberal, enlightened, educated North American Jews crazy. *Avinu Malkeinu* is as anthropomorphic a piece of liturgy as one could find. How gender specific, how concrete a prayer—just the prayer to turn off any ambivalent Jew from ever praying to God.

"Anthropomorphism" is a word I feared from childhood. It whispered of forbidden intentions, tainted theology, pagan animism, and plain, flat primitivism. I, who was raised by "enlightened," educated Jews, knew better than to succumb to "anthropomorphism"—a dreaded virus spread by ignorant, superstitious "shtetl" Jews who still viewed God as a king, a ruler, in spite of the agonizing evidence of the post-pogrom, post-Holocaust experience that had obliterated any such notions of an almighty, omnipresent, all-knowing, all-compassionate God.

Walt Disney, my parents' bête noire, was an anthropomorphist writ large, and we, aesthetes that we were, were repulsed by his pagan animism. His Bambi, Donald Duck, and Dumbo were, to us, all artificial superimpositions of human traits on God's creatures. In my parents' minds, all anthropomorphisms, whether applied to animals, plants, or objects—let alone to the ever-disappearing God—were to be shunned and reviled. Pitied, mostly. The God in whom my daddy thoroughly disbelieved was to remain ethereal and elusive, unattainable—certainly indescribable. God, to whom my father rarely alluded, was to remain mute.

So why, in spite of my father's discouragement, did I love *Avinu Malkeinu* above all other prayers? Why was I drawn as a child to the synagogue on Rosh Hashanah and Yom Kippur to stand like an inept grasshopper among the black-clad giants of my sweaty, male congregation of self-assured autocrats, to hear the pleading cries of *Avinu Malkeinu?* How could I delight in the pleas of the feebleminded multitudes, sung with a ferocity I had never before, nor since, encountered? What was really at play here?

Harav Avraham Yitzchak Kook, in his *Lights of Holiness,* has this to say about anthropomorphism: "It is foolishness, this fear of utilizing anthropomorphic similes in the study of the secret teachings of the Torah."[1] It is "foolishness," according to the great sage, because we know full well that God cannot be defined by any image—anthropomorphic or abstract. God, ultimately, is completely beyond the grasp of humanity; completely beyond description.

Anthropomorphism is, therefore, the very best tool with which to begin grappling with our ever-elusive God precisely because it is so obviously flawed.

To paraphrase Harav Kook, the source of human suffering is in infantile attachments to concepts of God.[2] To actually fix God to any concept—abstract or anthropomorphic—is idolatry in the eyes of the great thinker. All names of God, all conceptions of God, must be understood as mere illusory stepping-stones, rungs on Jacob's ladder, advancing us higher and higher, deeper and deeper toward our ultimate goal—knowledge of the One.

Most Jews I know are filled with ambivalence and doubt about the very idea of God, and the one remedy I know for these maladies is music. Play it, sing it, listen to it with enough commitment and passion, and all doubts—indeed, all thoughts—are obliterated. Instead, what takes over is experience. Past and future all melt into an overwhelming present, free of any concrete thought, free of speculation and cleverness. Music is the language of the heart, the color of the soul. Music, while definitely requiring intelligence to compose, to perform well, and to analyze, is first and foremost emotional and experiential.

Here lay the assembling instructions for my new project: Write a piece of music that can reach the heart quickly, that can move and uplift, that can be easily learned upon first hearing it. Write a piece that will sound familiar, as though recalling an ancient melody you have always known, even though it is completely new. Write a piece of music that can be hopeful and pleading, joyful and sad, and write this piece addressing it directly to a specific person—my father, my king, my daddy.

I knew immediately that if the music would be directed in such a human way, it would help elevate those who sang it and those who listened to it to a place beyond the words, and that, in a nutshell, is the sole purpose of liturgical music—to take the liturgy beyond words and beyond concepts. If I were to succeed in composing this piece, it would have to leave the singer and the listener in a transformed emotional state.

Anyone who has ever had the experience of hearing good music—liturgical or not—knows well the transformative power of that experience. As a composer, I go through an even more intense experience, since I am both the creator and the receiver, both the performer and the listener, both the architect and the critic. It is an exhausting and exhilarating process, always on the brink of total failure and always in full awareness of the probable futility of the entire endeavor. I am reaching for an intangible goal using very fragile tools.

Come to think of it—that's prayer: reaching for the intangible, using well-worn forms with no assurances. That is the whole point of *Avinu Malkeinu:* turning to a completely unknown God as though to a father, a king, believing, somehow, that it will succeed. Who's your daddy? If that language doesn't work for you, try mother and queen, try lover and beloved; but whatever you try, make it simple, concrete, intimate, and totally personal, because our personal experience is all we really know, if we know anything at all. And it makes no difference if our personal experience has been joyful or sad, complicated or straightforward, tragic or redemptive. Any and all of these experiences speak directly to our connection with God.

The authors of *Avinu Malkeinu* chose these images because these were the ones that spoke to them most viscerally, and I composed my music with my ever-present father in mind because that is the image that speaks to me most viscerally.

I had always been unsure of my father's love for me, just as I have always been unsure of God's love for me. When I was seventeen years old, I told my daddy that I would love him in spite of my uncertainty, and I would become more ferocious and tenacious with my love the less certain I became. I have kept that same promise with God.

Twenty-four years after my father's passing I still love him in spite of my lingering uncertainty of his love. It is with that in mind that I composed my *Avinu Malkeinu,* and it is with that in mind that I ask you to hear it and sing it: drown your thoughts in music; obliterate your questions and doubts with the sound of your voice; destroy even the last vestige of belief you may have, any faith you may profess, because even they are, ultimately, obstacles.

May the music of my soul and the meditations of my heart be acceptable before you.[3]

PART IV
Precursors, Foundations, and Parallels

Biblical Precursors

FATHER, KING, POTTER

Dr. Marc Zvi Brettler

Dr. Marc Zvi Brettler is the Bernice and Morton Professor of Judaic Studies at Duke University. He contributed to all volumes of the *My People's Prayer Book: Traditional Prayers, Modern Commentaries* series, winner of the National Jewish Book Award; and to *My People's Passover Haggadah: Traditional Texts, Modern Commentaries; Who by Fire, Who by Water—Un'taneh Tokef; All These Vows—Kol Nidre;* and *We Have Sinned: Sin and Confession in Judaism—Ashamnu and Al Chet* (all Jewish Lights). He is coeditor of *The Jewish Annotated New Testament* and *The Jewish Study Bible,* which won the National Jewish Book Award; coauthor of *The Bible and the Believer;* and author of *How to Read the Jewish Bible,* among other books and articles. He has also been interviewed on National Public Radio's *Fresh Air* by Terry Gross.

The image of God as father is familiar to all of us, if not from Jewish sources, then from the New Testament's Lord's Prayer, which begins, "Our Father who art in heaven." This familiarity, however, does not make it less problematic to our gender-sensitive ears, a problem that also pertains to the image of "God as king." By contrast, in our highly industrial and even post-industrial age, we are likely to find the image of "God as potter" simply bizarre. But all these terms—God as father, king, and potter—are borrowed from the Bible, even though their liturgical use is quite independent from the Bible. This is because Judaism developed and changed over time, remaining biblically based but no longer biblical.

Avinu Malkeinu combines an uncommon biblical image of God (as father) with a common one (as king). Both are strictly hierarchical—in the biblical period, the father had such tremendous power over his children that one law even permits parents to have their rebellious boys put to death (Deuteronomy 21:18–21). The biblical notion of parental honor was even more stringent than that found in other ancient Near Eastern cultures. For example, in the Babylonian Laws of Hammurabi, the child who hits his father has his hand cut off (law 195), while the comparable offense in the Bible is punished by death (Exodus 21:15). Honoring parents was viewed as central enough to be included in the Decalogue itself (Exodus 20:12; Deuteronomy 5:16) as well as other law collections. The king too was powerful, so much so that just cursing him was a capital crime (cf. 1 Kings 21:10–13; Ecclesiastes 10:20). Thus, both "father" and "king" reflect human subservience to the same sort of powerful being, in this case the most powerful of all: God.

These images are metaphoric, however—God was not understood to be a literal father or a real king; God lacked many of the standard attributes of fathers or kings. As a father, God had no real children and did not reproduce sexually with a wife. Only in a metaphor can God have been "the father of orphans" (Psalm 68:6), a phrase that, taken literally, is an oxymoron. As king, God had no father from whom to inherit the throne, nor a crown-prince who would inherit it from God. Unlike a human king, God reigned from the days of yore (Psalm 10:16) without ever being anointed. Yet God was understood to share enough features with fathers and kings that God could usefully be likened to them. These metaphors became even more important as they continued into the Rabbinic period.[1]

The Bible inherited these divine metaphors from the ancient Near Eastern world at large, where deities were regularly depicted as fathers and kings. But there, the image was sometimes different: older non-Israelite deities could be the literal fathers of other deities, and powerful deities could be declared kings of a pantheon.

God as "father," however, is relatively rare in the Bible: God is called "father" fewer than ten times there, in fact—quite a surprise, since God is regularly depicted as "father" in the surrounding ancient cultures and shows up regularly as "father" in Israelite names. Such names typically combine two parts—a noun with God's name (or some surrogate for that name), followed by an adjective depicting a divine attribute. Over twenty different names use *av/ab*, "father" (meaning God), as the first element—for example, Abshalom ("father is peace"), Abner ("father is light"), and Abidan ("father is a judge"). The identification of God as a father comes through especially clearly in the names Aviel ("father is God") and Aviya or Abihu, which mean "Yahweh is father." The name Abimelekh, meaning "father is king," brings together the two ideas of our prayer *Avinu Malkeinu*.

Only these texts explicitly call God Israel's father:

- Deuteronomy 32:6: Do you thus requite Adonai, O dull and witless people? Is not He the father who created you, fashioned you and made you endure!
- Isaiah 63:16: Surely You are our father.... You, O Adonai, are our father; from of old, your name is "our redeemer."
- Isaiah 64:7: But now, O Adonai, You are our father; we are the clay, and you are the potter, we are all the work of your hands.
- Jeremiah 3:19: I had resolved to adopt you as my child, and I gave you a desirable land—the fairest heritage of all the nations;

and I thought you would surely call Me "father," and never cease to be loyal to Me.
- Jeremiah 31:9: They shall come with weeping, and with compassion will I guide them.... For I am ever a father to Israel, Ephraim is my first-born.
- Malachi 1:6: A son should honor his father, and a slave his master. Now if I am a father, where is the honor due Me?

In addition, Malachi 2:10 views God as the father of all humanity: "Have we not all one father? Did not one God create us?" Other texts assume the image of father, even though they do not explicitly say it—for example, Exodus 4:22, "Then you shall say to Pharaoh, 'Thus says Adonai: Israel is my first-born son'" (see also Numbers 11:12, Hosea 11:1, and Proverbs 3:12). The paucity of "fatherly" references to God in the Bible and the complete absence of "God the father" in any prayers or psalms there suggest some discomfort with the parental image in the biblical period; this changed by the Rabbinic period, however, when we find many parables comparing God to a father.

Given that biblical Israel was a patriarchal or certainly a male-favoring society, where men, including fathers, had more power than women, including mothers, it is not surprising that the Bible never calls God "mother"—although a handful of verses in the later part of Isaiah depict God as a woman (cf. Isaiah 42:14, 45:10, 46:3–4,

49:15, 66:13). In fact, even though we often associate compassion with mothers—and so does the Bible in many cases—Psalm 103:13 states, "As a father has compassion for his children, so Adonai has compassion for those who fear Him." The fact that the Bible here deliberately disassociates God from being a mother highlights the Bible's discomfort with the idea.

The image of God as king is found very commonly in biblical texts, mostly poetic, and ranging from among the earliest in the canon (Exodus 15:18, "Adonai will reign for ever and ever!") to the latest (Daniel 4:34). God's kingship is also reflected in a small number of personal names, such as Elimelekh ("*El* is king") and Abimelekh ("father is king," noted above). Although this metaphor hardly resonates with us, it was effective in ancient Near Eastern cultures, where gods were modeled after the most powerful human, the king. This pervasive idea explains, for example, why God in the Bible (and later in Rabbinic literature) is depicted with a group of advisors, a semi-divine cabinet (see esp., 1 Kings 22:19–23 and Job 1–2). God takes on many royal attributes throughout the Bible, even when not explicitly called "king."

God, however, is more fair and powerful than the typical human monarch. Thus, Psalms 93, 95–99, which depict God as king, picture universal joy at God's arrival (e.g., 97:1), because God is more powerful than any human king and fundamentally fair as well (e.g., 99:4)—in contrast to merely human monarchs. As much as the metaphor "God is king" helps describe God, therefore, it does not confine God to the attributes and abilities of human royalty. Similarly, Jeremiah 31:9 describes God as an ideal father, though the idealization of the role is much more prevalent in "God as king."

Kingship was especially well suited to describe the many roles that God was expected to play. Like human kings, God is wise (e.g., Isaiah 31:2), wealthy (e.g., Haggai 2:7–8), and strong (Psalm 24:8). Like kings also, God judges—but with ideal fairness (e.g., Psalm 96:13). Like ancient kings who engaged in building projects, God created the world. God sits on a throne (e.g., Psalm 47:9), just as human kings do, and God's subjects bow to God (Psalm 95:6). Even human coronation is projected onto God, who is acclaimed with much noise (e.g., Psalm 98:7–8)—not unlike human kings, such as King Saul (1 Samuel 10:24–25). Unlike the rare image of "God as father," "God as king" appears often in prayers and psalms, especially in Psalms 29, 47, and 93–99, which explicitly describe the entailments of God's kingship. This metaphor continues in the Rabbinic period and later—modified, of course, to accord with changing notions of royalty in different times and places.

Avinu Malkeinu's combination of "father" and "king" reinforce each other in emphasizing a hierarchical relationship with Israel, the subservient partner. Yet, the images are not identical—unlike fathers, who could enjoy intimacy with their children, kings had impersonal relationships with their subjects. The combination of the two images thus highlights divine love on one hand (father) and power on the other (king).

Avinu Malkeinu draws on the Bible in style as well. It sometimes features couplets in typical biblical parallelism, where adjacent lines composed with the same form say almost the same thing—for example:

> [6] Our father, our king, cancel the plans of those who hate us.
>
> [7] Our father, our king, disrupt the schemes of those who are our enemies.
>
> [27] Our father, our king, fill our hands from among your blessings.
>
> [28] Our father, our king, fill our storehouses with plenty.

Sometimes too, the couplets are expanded—for example:

> [36] Our father, our king, act for the sake of those killed for your holy name.
>
> [37] Our father, our king, act for the sake of those slaughtered for your oneness.

[38] Our father, our king, act for the sake of those who go through fire and water for your holy name.

The prayer is also filled with other biblical phrases, alongside many post-biblical ones as well, naturally. Being written in a "book of livelihood and sustenance," for instance (line 21), or heavens with gates that need to be opened for prayers to enter (line 31) are not biblical. But the central idea (from lines 19–23) of various "books" of destiny is implied in the Bible about ten times (e.g., Exodus 32:32–33, Isaiah 4:3, Daniel 12:1) and is based on a Mesopotamian model of tablets of destiny, which portray the fates of individuals. It is unclear if the reference to "the book of life" in Psalm 69:29 refers to such a heavenly book of life or just to an earthly register of citizens, but in early post-biblical literature, including the Dead Sea Scrolls, the book of life is used in the sense found here, and two New Testament books refer to "the roll of the living" (Philippians 4:3; Revelation 3:5, 13:8; cf. Luke 10:20; Hebrews 12:23).

The prayer as a whole also follows the biblical style of petitions. They customarily begin with an invocation (like our *avinu malkeinu*); then continue with requests (or better yet, demands), couched in the imperative; and then offer a motivation for why these should be heard. The specific invocation *avinu malkeinu* is not biblical, and some of the petitions are couched in non-biblical language, but most of the motives attributed to God are found in the Bible, including the ideas that God should act for the sake of God's name (= reputation; see Ezekiel 36:22) and God's *chesed,* "loving-kindness."

The poem *Ki Hinei Kachomer* is based on Jeremiah 18:1–12, where (as an object lesson) the prophet is asked to watch a skilled potter fashioning and refashioning clay into whatever shape he pleases. The symbolism becomes clear as the passage unfolds:

> Then the word of Adonai came to me: O House of Israel, can I not deal with you like this potter?—says Adonai. Just like clay in the hands of the potter, so are you in my hands, O House of Israel! At one moment I may decree that a nation or a kingdom shall be uprooted and pulled down and destroyed; but if that nation against which I made the decree turns back from its wickedness, I change my mind concerning the punishment I planned to bring on it. (Jeremiah 18:5–8)

This passage, especially verse 6, is the basis of our poem, which likens God to the potter and Israel to inanimate clay that God can shape however God wishes. God is thus the master potter, as (elsewhere) God is the superlative king. Jeremiah's image of clay does not seem to refer to Genesis 2:7, where people are created from "the dust *[afar,* not *chomer]* of the earth," but for the author of the *piyyut*, these two biblical images (dust and clay) are likely conflated, so that God becomes the potter of both Israel as a whole and of individual beings in particular.

This initial picture of God as potter is expanded with other biblical imagery. God as "guardian of love" (line 1) can be found in Exodus 34:7; and God's "looking at the covenant [*b'rit*]" (line 1) is a direct quotation from Psalm 74:20. The image immediately following, "do not turn to the accuser," is not biblical, however, and even in the Bible, the reason God "looks" at the covenant is uncertain; is this *b'rit* imagined as written down in heaven?

Six other paragraphs in a similar form follow. They too contain biblical and post-biblical imagery. For example, Psalm 139:15 depicts God as a "draper" (line 6), and several times (e.g., Isaiah 1:25, Jeremiah 9:6, Zechariah 13:9) God appears as a metalsmith (line 7), although never in passages as detailed as Jeremiah 18, where the potter image derives. Overall, the poet has started with a biblical image of potter, but not satisfied with God as potter alone, has added other ones to it, making God literally into the jack of all crafts, *the* master craftsman.

To some, the multiplicity of metaphors used to describe God in a single composition—whether just father and king (as in *Avinu Malkeinu*) or potter, carver, blacksmith, sailor, glazier, draper, and metalsmith (as in *Ki Hinei Kachomer*)—may be surprising. Can't one single image suffice? How can God be all of these contradictory things? Yet the use of conflicting imagery is common when describing anything that is complex. Love, for example, may be compared to a journey ("crossroads"), a physical force ("sparks"), a sport ("he fell for her, hook, line, and sinker"), or even a disease ("lovesickness").[2] If used together literally, these are contradictions, but when used figuratively, they complement each other, suggesting the complexity of what they seek to describe. Similarly, in the Bible, God may be a brave male warrior (Isaiah 42:13) and in the very next verse (42:14) a woman in labor! These two images enhance one another, rather than cancel each other out.

So it is with liturgical images generally and our two poems *(Avinu Malkeinu* and *Ki Hinei Kachomer)* in particular. No single metaphor can encompass God, especially as God is experienced on the High Holy Days, when different people will be attracted to different images, so that no single image suffices. So building upon and supplementing the Bible, these poems offer many metaphors for God. In addition to making God more powerful and godlike (unlike any human), this multiplicity makes God more approachable rather than abstract and ultimately makes prayer possible.

What goes for the past is true today as well. No single image is sufficient to contain God. When worried about Israel's security, we might highlight God as warrior; when concerned about the world's injustices, we might call upon God as ultimate and righteous judge. As occasions shift, so do the primary images we call upon. At times, new images arise—like God as mother. Similarly, the meaning of old images changes as their basis in reality is altered; with the experience of different types of kings, for example, the meaning of "God as king" changed.

As most of us imagine God, the biblical metaphors of king, father, or potter are distant and difficult to appreciate. We may appreciate God as parent or friend. But (for Americans anyway) "God as king" presents challenges, because it cannot easily be transformed into "God as president." (God cannot be impeached, for instance, and God has ruled longer than even FDR!) The biblical metaphors in our prayers help us understand our ancestors' understanding of God, which we may then have to "translate" into new metaphors for our own times.

Father or King

A VIEW FROM THE PSALMS

Rabbi Jonathan Magonet, PhD

Rabbi Jonathan Magonet, PhD, is emeritus professor of Bible at Leo Baeck College in London, where he was principal (president) from 1985 to 2005. He is coeditor of three volumes of *Forms of Prayer* (the prayer books of the British Movement for Reform Judaism) and editor of the eighth edition of *Daily, Sabbath and Occasional Prayers*. He is editor of the journal *European Judaism*. He contributed to *Who by Fire, Who by Water—Un'taneh Tokef*, *All These Vows—Kol Nidre*, *We Have Sinned: Sin and Confession in Judaism—Ashamnu and Al Chet*, *May God Remember: Memory and Memorializing in Judaism—Yizkor*, and *All the World: Universalism, Particularism and the High Holy Days* (all Jewish Lights).

The combination of *avinu*, "our father," and *malkeinu*, "our king," is so familiar from the High Holy Day liturgy that it is easy to take it for granted. Yet each suggests a different relationship with God, and both can be found in the Hebrew Bible. In particular, two biblical psalms (103 and 145) explore these themes, and they are actually linked together by their common quotation of a biblical passage that itself plays a significant role in the High Holy Days: Exodus 34:6–7, the "thirteen attributes of God." Both psalms cite those attributes.

Psalm 103 cites the order exactly as it is given in Exodus: (1) *rachum v'* (2) *chanun Adonai,* (3) *erekh apayim v'* (4) *rav chased,* "(1) loving and (2) gracious is Adonai, (3) long suffering and (4) great in faithful love" (v. 8). Psalm 145, however, is an alphabetic acrostic, and the author reverses the order of the first two attributes ([1] *rachum v'*[2] *chanun*) so as to get the proper initial letter to introduce the verse—a *chet,* in this case (from[2] *chanun*), the eighth letter of the Hebrew alphabet for what turns out to be the eighth verse of the psalm. He also substitutes *g'dol* for *rav* (the two words both mean "great"). But otherwise, it is the same: (2) *chanun v'* (1) *rachum Adonai,* (3) *erekh apayim u'* (4) *g'dol chased.* Both cut short the original sentence from Exodus, however, by omitting the last word *ve'* (5) *emet,* "and (5) truth." This omission gives special prominence to what now becomes the last word, *chesed,* the "faithful love" that binds together the partners in a covenant.

Psalm 145 is a particularly familiar psalm in Jewish liturgy, appearing three times daily—among other things, as an introduction to the afternoon service *(Minchah).* Its focus on the theme of God as *melekh,* "king," is announced in the opening verse, "I will exalt You, my God and *king,*" and is reinforced by the three central verses, 11–13, each of which includes some use of *malkhut*, "kingdom" or "kingship":

> [11] They shall talk of the majesty of your kingship and speak of your might,
> [12] to make his mighty acts known among men, and the majestic glory of his kingship.
> [13] Your kingship is an eternal kingship; your dominion is for all generations.

Since this is an alphabetic acrostic, it may be that the author was playing a little game by selecting kingship verses for the geographic center of his psalm. The three verses in question (11–13) correspond to the Hebrew letters *kaf, lamed,* and *mem,* which, in reverse order, spell *MeLeKH,* "king"!

The psalm is actually very formally organized using a concentric or (technically) a "chiastic" structure, which is to say, a focal idea at the psalm's very center with parallel treatments of it leading up to that center and then, in reverse order, leading away from it. In form, it is something like a palindrome, a word that spells the same thing forward and backward (like the Hebrew name AVIVA).

In the case of Psalm 145, the opening three verses and the last one contain the verbs "to bless" and "to praise," the word *shem,* "name," and the concluding phrase *l'olam va'ed,* "forever and ever"—thereby "bracketing" the psalm with praise of God. We have already noted that the three central verses (11–13) speak of God's kingdom, so they form the thematic heart of the psalm, to which the earlier verses (4–10) lead and from which the later verses (14–20) return.[1]

The pattern looks like this:
- A1. 1–3: I praise God.
- B1. 4–7: All generations speak of God's deeds.
- C1. 8–9: God's attribute of love and compassion.
- D1. 10: All God's works offer praise (what people do for God).
- E. 11–13: God's kingship.
- D2. 14–16: God helps the fallen and provides sustenance
- C2. 17: God's attribute of righteousness.
- B2. 18–20: God is near to all who call.
- A2. 21: I and all flesh, shall praise God.

Psalm 145 thus defines our relationship with God as the ideal king. We acknowledge God, who conversely provides us with our needs. The praise that the psalmist, "I," offers at the beginning (v. 1) becomes a universal praise by "I and all flesh" at the end.

The psalm works on a material level, speaking of gifts given by God. But the quotation from Exodus sets these blessings in the context of the covenant, sealed by *chesed*, the faithful love that transcends the generations. The formal elements of the psalm—the alphabetic acrostic and balanced structure—underscore the stability, logic, and security of this relationship.[2]

Psalm 103 is less formally constructed, perhaps also as a reflection of its different intent. Instead of Psalm 145's emphasis on the material benefits that flow from the covenant, it focuses on the spiritual nature of the covenantal relationship itself. Most striking is the way it explores the continuation of the passage in Exodus 34:7, *Nosei avon vafesha v'chata'ah*, literally, God "lifts away" (i.e., forgives) "habitual wrongdoing, downright rebellion, and failings."[3] Each of these three terms has its own individual meaning, but together they depict a comprehensive state of human error, with the promise that all manner of wrong will be forgiven (on condition, of course, that the individual engages in true repentance). Psalm 103:10–12 uses all three terms but extends God's willingness to forgive considerably further than in Exodus, through the repetitive use of the emphatic word *lo*, "not!" at the start of the sentences:

> [10] *Not* for all time does God accuse,
> *not* forever remain angry,
> *not* as our failings [*chata'ah*] deserve has God dealt with us,
> *not* treated us as our wrongdoing [*avon*] required.

> ¹¹"For as the heavens are high above the earth,
> so great is God's love for those who fear Him,
> ¹²As east is far from west,
> so far has God removed our rebellion *(pesha)* from us.

Just as Psalm 145 established the theme of kingship at the outset, so here in Psalm 103 the psalmist sets his theme of divine forgiveness, describing God as one who "pardons all your wrongdoing *[avon],* and heals all your suffering" (v. 3). Moreover, God "crowns you with *chesed v'rachamim"* (v. 4), thus anticipating the key terms of the Exodus passage to be quoted in verse 8.

What seals this generous willingness of God to forgive is verse 13, which introduces a totally new dimension to the picture:

> ¹³As a father *[av]* has compassion *[k'rachem]* for his children,
> so Adonai has compassion *[richam]* for those who fear Him.

Instead of the detached king of Psalm 145, the God of Psalm 103 is a father who loves his children and will go, literally, to the very end of heaven and earth to forgive them. The mixed fatherly emotions of anger and tenderness are beautifully captured by Jeremiah (31:20):

> Ephraim is a dear son to Me.
> A child that is dandled.
> Whenever I would turn against him,
> My thoughts would dwell on him still.
> That is why my heart yearns for him.
> I will surely have compassion [*racheim arachamenu*] on him.

For Psalm 103, in verse 15, that compassion translates into God's awareness of the transience of our lives:

> [15] Man's days are like those of grass;
> he blooms like a flower of the field.
> A wind passes by and he is no more.

Yet God's *chesed*, the faithful love of the covenant, already promised to Moses to last for a "thousand generations" (Exodus 34:7), is reaffirmed, "for all eternity."

Both of these psalms are reflections on the Exodus passage that addresses God's compassion—the thirteen attributes, that is—but specifically the way in which God responds to Israel's sins. In Psalm 145, God is king to a subject people—the very model for *malkeinu*. In Psalm 103, God is a father for his children, the very model for *avinu*.

Given the prominence of the thirteen attributes in the High Holy Day period and their centrality in both psalms, it is possible that these two contrasting texts and images influenced the liturgical author who first put them together as *Avinu Malkeinu*. Both perspectives are elegantly reflected in the opening confession that is also an appeal: "Our father, our king, we have sinned before You."

Why "Our Father"?

Dr. Annette M. Boeckler

Dr. Annette M. Boeckler is senior lecturer for liturgy at Leo Baeck College in London and manager of its library. She studied theology, Jewish studies, and Ancient Near Eastern Studies in Germany and Switzerland and *chazzanut* both privately (with Cantor Marcel Lang, z"l, and Cantor Jeremy Burko) and at the Levisson Instituut in Amsterdam. She contributed to *All These Vows—Kol Nidre, We Have Sinned: Sin and Confession in Judaism—Ashamnu and Al Chet, May God Remember: Memory and Memorializing in Judaism—Yizkor,* and *All the World: Universalism, Particularism and the High Holy Days* (all Jewish Lights).

"No tree of the field was yet on earth and no herb of the field had yet sprouted, for Adonai, God had not sent rain upon the earth" (Genesis 2:5). "Why?" asks the medieval commentator Rashi. "Because there was no human to work the soil, and no one who could recognize the goodness of rain. When Adam came and realized rain's necessity for the world, he prayed for it and it fell, and the trees and the variety of vegetation sprouted."

Rain became a metaphor for dependency on God, because "the land to which you come ...

is not like the land of Egypt from where you left, where you would plant your seed and water it yourself like a vegetable garden. The land to which you cross over ... drinks water by the rain of the heavens" (Deuteronomy 11:10–11). With the Exodus came realization of our dependency on God: as God had provided freedom, so too God would provide water. Drought was a sign of God withholding rain as a consequence of human sin.

Hence the origin of *Avinu Malkeinu*, which the Talmud (Ta'anit 25b) traces to a fast day. The standard twenty-four benedictions prescribed for fasts were recited by Rabbi Eliezer ben Hyrcanus, without success; then Rabbi Akiva stepped forth and said, "*Avinu, malkeinu,* our father, our king, we have no king other than You. Our father, our king, for your sake, have mercy upon us!" And the rain fell.

But what do we mean by "father"?

Our understanding of words depends on the personal past experience to which those words have been applied. You know what "love" is—because you know what it is for you, but is it the same for you as it is for me? We talk and listen from different horizons of understanding. Language is an art, after all, and art inevitably attracts diverse interpretations. Paintings, music, poetry, and the ordinary words of conversation speak differently to each of us because our associations are different.

Several Jewish prayers—not only *Avinu Malkeinu*—address God as "father," and for a long time the meaning of this address seemed undisputed. In modern times, however, with family roles no longer fixed and our consciousness of family relations more enhanced, we have begun to see that the role of "father" varies from family to family—and even (within the same family) from child to child. Many children grow up without a father; several more suffer traumatic experiences with their fathers. How, then, can we continue to call God "father"—knowing, as we do, that the term may evoke images that do not fit Israel's ideal and that were not intended by the prayer to begin with?

The image of God as father *(av)* in ancient times is connected to the parallel view of God as king *(melekh)* because Semitic languages do not limit "father" to the family.[1] The Hebrew *av* can also mean "ancestor," "teacher," "leader," and "expert." When a god in the environment of ancient Israel was called "father," the intended definition depended on the specific character of the god in question. For example, the Mesopotamian god of the sky, Anu, was father as begetter of other gods—the highest divine authority, unapproachable by humans, and producer of all inferior gods. The moon god, Sin, was father as creator of life specifically on earth, because he had created life by dewdrops in the night. The sun god, Shamash, was the warrant of justice, in charge of overseeing the rights of the weak and vulnerable in society. The Babylonian god Marduk, to whom incantations for healing were addressed, was father because of his mercy toward human beings and his caring, healing powers.[2]

So, too, the biblical idea of God's fatherhood must be understood with reference to God's specific role for Israel: the father who redeemed us from Egypt. This specific role, however, derives from the legal responsibility of a father in antiquity (the *pater familias*) to redeem a family member from bondage. "You are our father," says Isaiah (63:16). "From of old, your name is 'Our Redeemer.'" God thinks, "They are my people, children who will not play false," so "He became their deliverer" (63:8). God cannot allow Israel's sins to have the last word in relegating Israel into perpetual exile—God must redeem his child, by obligation.

The just-mentioned Isaiah passage, however, comes from the second half of the book, Deutero-Isaiah, as it is called, the section composed by an otherwise unknown prophet from Babylonian exile. It therefore stands rather at the end of the biblical development of the "God-as-father" image. Originally the idea belonged to kingship language. Ancient Near Eastern kings were seen as sons of gods—making the god, literally, a divine father. Earthly kings were like sons doing their father's business, hence stand-in fathers, as it were, for their own heavenly father above and due the same respect themselves down here below.

Israel debated the legitimacy of such a human king, as we see from the books of Samuel. To be victorious against new enemies, especially the Philistines, who had mastered the new technology of iron weaponry, Israel needed a warrior king. But God was already Israel's savior king, the opposition argued. We should trust only in God, not in human replicas. In the end, the pro-monarchical party wins: God gives them, reluctantly, first Saul and then David.

Following ancient Near Eastern precedent, David took on the role of being God's son, according to God's words in Psalm 2:6–7: "I have installed my king on Zion, my holy mountain.... You are my son, I have fathered you this day."[3] The prophetic writings modify that claim, creating a distinctively Israelite theology that associates God's fatherhood with forgiveness, redemption, and eternal faithfulness. The prophet Nathan tells David:

> Adonai declares to you ... When your days are done and you lie with your fathers, I will raise up your offspring after you, one of your own issue, and I will establish his kingship.... I will be a father to him, and he shall be a son to Me. When he does wrong, I will chastise him ... but I will never withdraw my favor from him. (2 Samuel 7:11–15)

The father-son relationship is here defined by education rather than an automatic transmission of heavenly power to the king on earth.

A younger poetic version of this oracle—written, very likely, in the time of exile when Israel no longer had a king, land, or temple—can be found in Psalm 89:27–33. Here it is not David's physical son Solomon who will (according to God's words) "forsake my teaching ... violate my laws and not observe my commandments" (vv. 31–32), but David's "sons" (plural), meaning the people of Israel. What was said about the king is now applied to the people he once ruled. The psalm describes Israel's story, reinforcing the saving role that is God's alone and pleading, therefore, that God not abandon his people: "O my Lord, where is your steadfast love of old, which You swore to David in your faithfulness?" (Psalm 89:50).

In the book of Jeremiah, the image of God as father is expressly democratized to include not just kings but all of Israel. When there would no longer be a human king in Israel, God's kingship remains—and thus his fatherhood as well:

> They shall come with weeping,
> and with compassion will I guide them.
> I will lead them to streams of water,
> by a level road where they will not stumble.

> For I am ever a father to Israel,
> Ephraim is my first-born. (Jeremiah 31:9)

The Torah too calls the people of Israel God's "son." As ancient Near Eastern kings became divine sons by their coronation, so did Israel in the moment it became God's people. God tells Moses:

> Say to Pharaoh, "Thus says Adonai: Israel is my first-born son. I have said to you, 'Let my son go, that he may worship Me,' yet you refuse to let him go. Now I will slay your first-born son." (Exodus 4:22–23)

God is the ultimate king but also the ultimate father, redeeming a son from bondage.

The third part of the prophet Isaiah (chapters 56–66) universalizes the image of God as father by declaring the blood lineage from Abraham to be less important than the fact of being children of God:

> Surely You are our father,
> because Abraham no longer knows us
> and Israel cannot recognize us [they are dead, mere history].
> You, O Adonai, are our father;
> from of old, your name is "Our Redeemer."
> (Isaiah 63:16)

What follows is an intense and lengthy plea for God's help (Isaiah 63–64):

> You have hidden your face from us,
> and made us melt because of our iniquities.
> But now, O Adonai, You are our father;
> we are the clay, and You are the potter,
> we are all the work of your hands.
> Be not implacably angry, O Adonai.
> Do not remember iniquity forever.
> Oh, look down to Your people, to us all!
> (Isaiah 64:6–8)

As father, God redeems his child from disaster, despite that child's sins; and as father also, God is the being that forms us—the way a potter forms life out of clay.

Other biblical texts—from the late biblical period, when Persia had conquered Babylonia and allowed Jews to return home to the land whence they had been exiled—take up the same God-as-father image but focus on the human side of the relationship. *Parashat Ha'azinu*, usually read on Shabbat Shuvah between Rosh Hashanah and Yom Kippur, asks rhetorically, "Do you thus repay Adonai, O dull and witless people? Is not He the father who created you, fashioned you and made you endure!" (Deuteronomy 32:6). One of the last biblical prophets, Malachi, puts it even more forcefully: "A son should honor his father, and a slave his master. Now if I am a father, where is the honor due Me?" (1:6).

Malachi depicts the carelessness of the priests in the Second Temple. God will not automatically be father to all of Israel, but only to those who prove worthy of being God's sons:

> And on the day that I am preparing, said Adonai of hosts, they shall be my treasured possession; I will be tender toward them as a man is tender toward a son who ministers to him. And you shall come to see the difference between the righteous and the wicked, between those who served God [and thus behaved as sons] and those who did not. (Malachi 3:17–18)

In the end, then, only our own behavior will define whether God is our father or not. God's fatherhood is conditional. In this line of thinking, the very late biblical books of Chronicles cite Nathan's earlier oracle to David, emphasizing Solomon's ideal kingly piety:

> It will be your son Solomon who will build my House and my courts, for I have chosen him to be a son to Me, and I will be a father to him. I will establish his kingdom forever, if [!!] he keeps firmly to the observance of my commandments and rules as he does now. (1 Chronicles 28:6–7)

This conditional fatherhood is also expressed in the psalm that Progressive Jews associate with Yom Kippur, Psalm 103 *(Barachi nafshi et Adonai)*: "As a father has compassion for his children, so Adonai has compassion for those who fear Him" (v. 13)—but only "for those who fear Him," note! The Rabbinic story about Rabbi Akiva and Rabbi Eliezer is interpreted by the Talmud along these lines. A divine voice *(bat kol)* explains Rabbi Akiva's successful *Avinu Malkeinu,* by saying, "It was not because one sage was greater than that one, but because one is merciful, the other is not" (Ta'anit 25b). The power of *Avinu Malkeinu* lies not in its words but in the character of the *chazzan /chazzanit.*

Another verse from Malachi became prominent in the nineteenth century—inscribed, in fact, above the entrance door of the Temple in Seesen in 1810, the very place where Israel Jacobson first experimented with liturgical reform. It can also be seen above the famous scene of the Yom Kippur service in Metz during the Franco-Prussian War in 1870: "Have we not all one father? Did not one God create us?" (Malachi 2:10). Nineteenth-century Jews loved the verse for its apparent universalism. In its biblical context, the meaning is less certain, however, because it continues with the question "Why then do we break faith with one another?" and chastises the ways Malachi's contemporaries deal with their mixed marriages. But Jews in the 1800s saw the single verse they chose as a sign of Judaism's positive attitude toward the Enlightenment ideals of universal reason and harmony.

Why today should we still address God as "our father"? It cannot be simply the many meanings that have accrued over time, most of which worshipers today can hardly be expected to know. The poetic language of prayer does not come with its theological history as background. It is judged instead by its relationship to the contemporary experience of the worshipers. As we saw above, however, language itself is an art—all the more so language in service of liturgy, which is a further art in and of itself. Liturgical appreciation is more aesthetic than academic. For many, *Avinu Malkeinu* has become a mantra, where the words are experienced as a set of sounds, not of meaning; emotion, not understanding. The significance of *Avinu Malkeinu* is the fact that we hear an "a," an "i," and a "u," arranged to familiar and anticipated music, not that we actually call God a "father." The familiar sounds evoke feelings of togetherness, memories of years gone by, reflections about the future—the very stuff of the High Holy Days.

Some, however, do focus on the meaning of the words, especially those who have little emotional history with the liturgy. Their experience makes us wonder whether we can still call God "father" nowadays. We know too much about real-life fathers to automatically associate them with such beneficent functions as forgiving sins, redeeming family members from bondage, or causing it to rain. And they are, after all, so masculine—in an era that seeks female models as well as male. To avoid severe misunderstandings, which can even damage people's relationship with God,[4] we rightly search for images that express today the ancient intended meanings: that God is *per se* the One who provides freedom, the source of life itself, and the proper object of trust because God is the guarantor of care and goodness and all that we hold dear.

Prayer and Character

THE STORY BEHIND *AVINU MALKEINU*

Rabbi Elie Kaunfer, DHL

Rabbi Elie Kaunfer, DHL, is cofounder and executive director of Mechon Hadar (www.mechonhadar.org). He holds a doctorate in liturgy and is the author of *Empowered Judaism: What Independent Minyanim Can Teach Us about Building Vibrant Jewish Communities.* He is a contributor to *Who by Fire, Who by Water—Un'taneh Tokef, All These Vows—Kol Nidre, We Have Sinned: Sin and Confession in Judaism—Ashamnu and Al Chet,* and *All the World: Universalism, Particularism and the High Holy Days* (all Jewish Lights). *Newsweek* named him one of fifty top rabbis in America.

What can we learn about a prayer by focusing on the people behind it—the character of the poets who wrote the prayers, or the leaders of prayer who conduct our services with their words? Many prayers in the siddur are anonymous, and the process of composing the prayer is lost to history. However, our tradition identifies a few prayers with a particular author, and an even smaller subset of prayers—including *Avinu Malkeinu*—in which the story of their composition is told. Already a "favorite" prayer of the High Holy Day season, *Avinu Malkeinu* becomes even more fascinating if we look at the circumstances under which it was written.

Avinu Malkeinu is usually traced to a story in the Talmud—actually, one of two stories that themselves are part of a larger series of stories about public fasts in times of drought:

> Our rabbis taught:
> A story: Rabbi Eliezer declared thirteen fasts on the public, but no rain fell.

תלמוד בבלי מסכת תענית
דף כה עמוד ב

At the end [of the fast], the people started to leave. He said to them: "Have you prepared graves for yourselves?" All the people burst into tears, and the rain fell.	תנו רבנן מעשה ברבי אליעזר שגזר שלש עשרה תעניות על הצבור ולא ירדו גשמים. באחרונה התחילו הצבור לצאת. אמר להם: תקנתם קברים לעצמכם? געו כל העם בבכיה, וירדו גשמים.
Another story: Rabbi Eliezer led the *Amidah* [lit., he went down before the ark] and said twenty-four blessings [the usual eighteen plus six additional blessings for public fasts], but was not answered. Rabbi Akiva led after him, and said: "Our father, our king, [we have sinned before You. Our father, our king]¹ we have no king other than You. Our father, our king, [for your sake]² have mercy upon us." And the rain fell. The rabbis shouted/complained. A heavenly voice came out and said: "Not that this one is greater than that one. "Rather this one passes over his character traits [*ma'avir al midotav*] and this one does not." (Talmud, Ta'anit, 25b)	שוב מעשה ברבי אליעזר שירד לפני התיבה ואמר עשרים וארבע ברכות ולא נענה. ירד רבי עקיבא אחריו, ואמר: אבינו מלכנו [חטאנו לפניך. אבינו מלכנו] אין לנו מלך אלא אתה. אבינו מלכנו (למענך) רחם עלינו, וירדו גשמים. הוו מרנני רבנן. יצתה בת קול ואמרה: לא מפני שזה גדול מזה, אלא שזה מעביר על מידותיו, וזה אינו מעביר על מדותיו.

There are a number of striking aspects to these two stories, not the least being the immediate uncertainty about what the key phrase *ma'avir al midotav* means. We will return to this all-important point later. But for the time being, we should look at the stories more generally.

First, Rabbi Eliezer seems to be following the Rabbinic rules of how to end a drought, as laid down by the Mishnah, but without success. In the first story, he declares a series of public fasts (cf. Mishnah Ta'anit 1:4–7, 2:6–7), to no avail. In the second story, he leads a special *Amidah* (cf. Mishnah Ta'anit 2:2–4), also to no effect. It is only when Rabbi Akiva deviates from the prescribed formula that the rain actually comes.

Second, it is human behavior itself—and spontaneous behavior at that—that seems most effective at bringing the rain. In the first story, the people burst into tears, a mini-rainstorm, as it were, which causes the rain to come from above. In the second story, Rabbi Akiva recites a prayer—presumably invented on the spot—that unleashes the rain. But the coda to the story informs us that it is not because of Rabbi Akiva's greatness relative to Rabbi Eliezer, but rather because he "passes over his character traits" *(ma'avir al midotav)*—an enigmatic explanation that, as I say, deserves its own "unpacking" later.

Finally, Rabbi Eliezer, the appointed leader in both of the stories, is presumably the most fitting person to lead the people out of distress. Elsewhere, the Mishnah explains, "[During a drought] they appoint as leader for the *Amidah* [lit., they bring down before the ark] an experienced elder.... So that his heart should be entirely dedicated to the prayer" (Mishnah Ta'anit 2:2). Rabbi Eliezer is presumably just such a man.

But surprisingly, in neither episode is Rabbi Eliezer the one to bring the rain. In the first story, one might argue (at best) that his harsh words caused the people to cry and indirectly brought the rain. It is not clear, however, if that was his intention or if, alternatively, just by chance his remark moved the people to tears, solving the problem. In any event, it was certainly not his prayer that did the job; he doesn't even pray at all.

In the second story, by contrast, prayer is central, but it too leaves us with the basic question of why Rabbi Eliezer fails at the task while Rabbi Akiva succeeds. What is their relationship to each other? Is the story about prayer or character? And if character, as it seems, what is this enigmatic character trait (*ma'avir al midotav* = "passing over his difficult [?] character aspects") that Akiva possesses but Eliezer does not? And is it important that Akiva uses the language of "father" and "king" in his short plea? Presumably, that does matter—the story is careful to cite it—but if so, why?

Another Version of the Story

Fortunately, we have yet another version of the story regarding Rabbi Eliezer and Rabbi Akiva—this time in the Jerusalem, not the Babylonian, Talmud—with some important differences.

Rabbi Eliezer declared a fast, but no rain fell. Rabbi Akiva declared a fast, and the rain fell. [Rabbi Akiva] entered and said before them: "I will explain it in a parable. What is it like? Like a king who had two daughters. "One was brazen [*chutzpadik*] and one was proper. When the brazen one wanted to enter before [the king], he would say: 'Give her what she wants, so that she may go away.' "When the proper one [wanted to] enter before him, he was patient, because he liked hearing her pleas." Is it permissible to say this [could this really be the reason behind Rabbi Akiva's success and Rabbi Eliezer's failure]? [Rabbi Akiva said it] to prevent blaspheming the house of Rabbi Eliezer [that is, he gave an explanation that saved R. Eliezer from being maligned]. (Jerusalem Talmud, Ta'anit 3:4)	תלמוד ירושלמי מסכת תענית פרק ג דף סו טור ג — טור ד/ה"א רבי ליעזר עבד תעני ולא איתנחת מיטרא עבד רבי עקיבה תעני ונחת מיטרא עאל ואמר קומיהון אמשול לכם משל: למה הדבר דומה? למלך שהיו לו שתי בנות אחת חצופה ואחת כשירה אימת דהות בעייא ההיא חציפתא עלת קומוי הוה אמר יבון לה מה דהיא בעייא ותיזיל לה ואימת דהות ההיא כשירתא עלת קומוי הוה מאריך רוחיה מתחמד מישמוע שועתה ואית שרי מימור כן? אלא שלא לחלל שם שמים בי רבי אליעזר

This version of the story has nothing to do with prayer. It is simply Rabbi Eliezer's fast versus Rabbi Akiva's. In both versions, the implicit criticism of Rabbi Eliezer (who fails at his task) is mitigated: in the Babylonian Talmud (Bavli), a heavenly voice lauds Rabbi Akiva for passing over his *midot* (character traits); in the Jerusalem Talmud (Yerushalmi), Rabbi Akiva himself provides the explanation in terms of the parable of two daughters.

While no prayer at all (so no *Avinu Malkeinu*, in particular) is present in the Yerushalmi account, God nonetheless appears as a father and a king in its parable; and strikingly, the father/king is relating to two daughters, rather than two sons. If we transpose the understanding of the Yerushalmi onto the Bavli, we would say that the Bavli version gives voice to the "brazen" *(chutzpadik)* daughter—Rabbi Akiva—and the "proper" daughter—Rabbi Eliezer—through prayer. The "lengthened pleas" of the fitting daughter become the "long *Amidah*" of Rabbi Eliezer, to no effect. And we understand *Avinu Malkeinu* in a new light: the daring plea of a daughter who is known to be bold, bordering on rude. What is commonly assumed to be the utterance of a penitent (male) worshiper becomes a brazen appeal from a (female) princess.

Rabbi Eliezer and Rabbi Akiva: The Background

Rabbi Eliezer and Rabbi Akiva have a deep and complex relationship that extends well before and after this scene with the drought. Rabbi Akiva is Rabbi Eliezer's prized student (Sanhedrin 68a, 101a). But like many student-teacher relationships, theirs too is fraught with conflict. Rabbi Eliezer complains that Rabbi Akiva hasn't learn enough from him (Sanhedrin 68a), but he also doesn't fully grasp just how much Rabbi Akiva actually has gained from his teaching (Pesachim 69a). Rabbi Eliezer treats Rabbi Akiva harshly, predicting his violent death without mercy (Sanhedrin 101a, Pesachim 69a), yet Rabbi Akiva sees Rabbi Eliezer as an ongoing father figure who is readily approachable.

Rabbi Akiva and Rabbi Eliezer also play contrasting roles when it comes to water—relevant for the drought imagery. In our own Bavli story here, it is noteworthy that Rabbi Eliezer spurs the assembled crowd to paroxysms of weeping following the thirteen fasts, but not a tear drops from his eyes. In similar fashion, Eliezer is compared elsewhere (Mishnah Avot 2:8) to a cistern that does not lose a drop—that is, in light of these sources, a vessel that never releases its water but simply holds it in.

According to one account in the Bavli (Bava Metzia 59b), even when Rabbi Eliezer cries, the tears are destructive rather than restorative. We are told that Rabbi Eliezer is banned from the academy, at which time Rabbi Akiva bursts into tears; Eliezer also cries, but his tears damage the crops and soon become fire, which burns everything in his sight. On his deathbed, Rabbi Tarfon evaluates Rabbi Eliezer as "better than a drop of water," but the analogy does not impress Eliezer (Sanhedrin 101b). Rabbi Akiva, by contrast, releases liquid—when Rabbi Eliezer dies, Akiva beats himself until blood flows.

In sum, Rabbi Eliezer is "stopped up"—like the God who refuses to let the rain fall. Water flows from Rabbi Akiva, however, like the God who lets rain fall. Rabbi Akiva models the way he wants God to behave. His prayer becomes the focal point of the way we normally read the story, but the tale's deeper message is the efficacy of the prayer leader. The story of *Avinu Malkeinu* prompts us to ask: how does human character impact the force of prayer?

What more, then, can we learn about the character of Rabbi Eliezer on one hand and Rabbi Akiva on the other?

For one thing, Rabbi Eliezer is a mercurial personality who angers the authorities and acts angrily himself. At one point, Rabbi Eliezer is banned from the academy (Bava Metzia 59b; Jerusalem Talmud, Mo'ed Katan 3:1, 81c), and it is Rabbi Akiva who approaches him, "lest the world be destroyed" (Bava Metzia 59b). Eliezer is also accused of being a Christian (Tosefta, Chulin 2:24), and Akiva engages his teacher in the issue of his fascination with a forbidden teaching. When Rabbi Eliezer is on his deathbed, only Rabbi Akiva can calm him (Sanhedrin 68a).

In all these stories a common theme is struck. Rabbi Akiva is the understanding and compassionate friend who visits, counsels, and mollifies the harsher and more mercurial Rabbi Eliezer. This difference in character is mirrored in the two rabbis' styles of combating the drought. Rabbi Eliezer responds with all his typical harshness, even causing the people to cry; Rabbi Akiva, by contrast, intervenes with God the way he did with Rabbi Eliezer himself—using his innate empathy and understanding to evoke God's mercy and bring rain.

Rabbinic relations between student and teacher were much more profound than what we usually think of happening in a modern classroom. When Rabbi Eliezer dies, Rabbi Akiva cries out, "My father, my father," the very words used by the prophet Elisha upon seeing his teacher Elijah (another harsh character, at times) ascend into heaven at the time of his death (2 Kings 2:12). It is as if Rabbi Akiva redirects his feelings toward Rabbi Eliezer (and his skill at opening him up) to his prayerful stance before God. Rabbi Eliezer is "father," and God is "father." Rabbi Akiva's various experiences at softening Rabbi Eliezer reflect his ability to do the same with God when rain is required for Israel. This leads us to ask: how do we map our own relationships with authority figures (parental or otherwise) onto our relationship with God?

Ma'avir al Midotav—A Curious Phrase

As we saw above, Rabbi Akiva is described as *ma'avir al midotav*, an attribute to which I said we would return. What could that mean?

Although I rendered it "passes over his character traits," the meaning is by no means obvious.

The use of the word *ma'avir* (from the root *avar*, meaning "to pass") coupled with *midah* ("attribute"), however, points clearly to Exodus 33:19–34:7, where God tells Moses, "I will make all my goodness pass *[a'avir]* before you."[3] God then does indeed pass before Moses, as promised, calling out the thirteen divine attributes *(midot)* that the Rabbis associate with God's mercy (a possible literary link with the thirteen fasts). Rabbi Akiva, who shares some traits with Moses elsewhere (Menachot 29b), mirrors the actions of God. Both "pass" over their difficult *midot*—perhaps a reference to the harsher, more judgmental character traits that Rabbi Akiva (and God) is able to overcome but Eliezer cannot.

Rabbi Akiva therefore acts like God, or more precisely, like the God he wants to see in the world. But there is more. The character and actions of Rabbi Akiva and God interchange in more ways than one. The telltale verb *avar*, "to pass," is regularly used by the Rabbis to signify "passing before the ark," the equivalent of "going down before the ark" (in our story) and a description of leading prayer. The Rabbis therefore interpret God's passing before Moses as God's taking on the role of prayer leader—exactly what Rabbi Akiva will do during the drought.

> ויעבר ה' על פניו ויקרא
> אמר רבי יוחנן: אלמלא מקרא כתוב אי אפשר לאומרו, מלמד שנתעטף הקדוש ברוך הוא כשליח צבור, והראה לו למשה סדר תפלה. אמר לו: כל זמן שישראל חוטאין — יעשו לפני כסדר הזה, ואני מוחל להם
>
> "God passed before him and proclaimed" (Exodus 34:6). Rabbi Yochanan said: Were it not written in the Torah, one could not say this: The Holy One, Blessed be He, wrapped Himself in a *tallit* like one who leads prayer and showed Moses the order of this prayer. "Whenever Israel sins, let them recite this same order of prayer and I will forgive them." (Rosh Hashanah 17b)

The parallelism of human and divine action is not meant to lead to an equation of the two. Rather, Rabbi Akiva's human action on earth evokes similar action by God by unleashing the way God is *meant* to act: it allows God's mercy to overcome God's justice. God too must *ma'avir al midotav*. Indeed, in a daring passage in which the Rabbis describe God's own prayer, God prays for God's mercy to overcome God's *midot*: "May it be my will that my mercy will conquer my anger, and my mercies shall override my attributes, and I will behave with children through the attribute of mercy" (Berakhot 7a).

Ultimately, Rabbi Akiva's *Avinu Malkeinu* is not just a powerful turn of phrase that manages to work because of what the words objectively mean in their own right. They work because they reflect Akiva's own character, as observed in the relationship to his teacher (Rabbi Eliezer) and to God—both of whom, he calls "my father."

In what ways do we associate certain people with godlike status? How often do we confuse our conception of God as a transferred relationship with another father figure?

In the High Holy Day liturgy, *Avinu Malkeinu* arrives only at the end of the very long *Amidah*—a similar prayer to the one that Rabbi Eliezer performed but that did not work in bringing rain. When the normal channels of prayer are not effective, *Avinu Malkeinu* just might succeed. In our own prayer service, Rabbi Eliezer is followed by Rabbi Akiva, as it were. The "good" daughter croons on in prayer, but the "daring" daughter reminds the king of his all-important preference for mercy.

Avinu Malkeinu, then, is a prayer that allows us to reflect on our own relationships—with parents, with teachers, with God—and to strive to behave in ways that engender merciful action from the divine above.

Divine Epithets and Human Ambivalence

Rabbi Reuven Kimelman, PhD

Rabbi Reuven Kimelman, PhD, is professor of classical Judaica at Brandeis University in Waltham, Massachusetts. He is the author of *The Mystical Meaning of Lekha Dodi and Kabbalat Shabbat* and of the audio books *The Moral Meaning of the Bible* and *The Hidden Poetry of the Jewish Prayerbook*. He contributed to *Who by Fire, Who by Water—Un'taneh Tokef*, *All These Vows—Kol Nidre*, *We Have Sinned: Sin and Confession in Judaism—Ashamnu and Al Chet*, and *All the World: Universalism, Particularism and the High Holy Days*; and to the *My People's Prayer Book* volumes *P'sukei D'zimrah (Morning Psalms)* and *Kabbalat Shabbat (Welcoming Shabbat in the Synagogue)* (all Jewish Lights).

The more unnerving it is to address God, the greater the need for multiple metaphors. This explains why we revert to multiple liturgical metaphors when we stand before God as sovereign and judge on the High Holy Days. It is so hard to get the language right, and even when we get the language right, we find ourselves having to use more than a single formulation. Think of traditional liturgical poems such as

Ha'ochez b'yad midat mishpat ("He who holds the standard of justice"), *L'el Orekh Din* ("To the God who arbitrates judgment"), and *Atah Hu Eloheinu* ("You who are our God"), which all refer to God in twenty-two different ways, corresponding to the twenty-two letters of the Hebrew alphabet. Most illuminating is the liturgical form of *Ki Anu Amekha* ("For we are your people"). It provides twelve designations for us and twelve corresponding epithets for God. Each line has four words, two for us and two for God. The first three are as follows:

1. We-are your-people and-You-are our-God
2. We-are your-children and-You-are our-father
3. We-are your-servants and-you-are our-lord

The last three are as follows:

10. We-are your-cherished-ones and-You-are our-intimate-one
11. We-are your-people and-You-are our-king
12. We-are the-ones-You-have-spoken-forand-You-are-the-One-we-have-spoken-for.[1]

These various relationships between us and God show how liturgical metaphors are as much statements about us as about God. They work in tandem. In designating God X, we become Y. When God is addressed as father, we become children; when as lord, we become servants. Line 12 makes this point vividly. It develops a romantic metaphor used earlier in the poem ("We-are your-spouse and-You-are our-beloved") into a covenantal metaphor, thereby using marriage as a way of grasping the duo-directional nature of the partnership between God and Israel.

Note that "we are your people" in line 1 is repeated in line 11, except instead of "our God" we say "our king." But when we see ourselves as "your children," we revert to "our father." The two, father and king, are the dominant contrasting metaphors for the High Holy Days. The liturgy itself is sometimes unclear about which one of them to use, because of the deep ambivalence we have knowing we are both children of the divine father[2] (on the one hand) and subjects of a divine monarch (on the other). Thus after the blowing of the shofar, in the three parts of the *Musaf* service, we say:

> Today is the birth of humanity *[olam]*.[3] Today He will place under judgment all the creatures of the world. [We are not sure how we come] *whether as children or as servants.* If as children, have mercy upon us as a father has mercy on children; if as servants, our eyes look to You to grace us by issuing a positive verdict.

This commentary on our ambivalence of not knowing whether we are children or servants and whether we approach God as father or king harks back to Psalm 103:13–19, which begins with the image of a compassionate father and closes with that of a sovereign king:

¹³As a father has compassion for his children,
so Adonai has compassion for those who fear Him.
¹⁴For He knows our temptation;
mindful that we are dust.
¹⁵Man, his days are like those of grass;
he blooms like a flower of the field;
¹⁶a wind passes by and it is no more....
¹⁷But Adonai's kindness is for all eternity....
¹⁹Adonai has established His throne in heaven,
and his kingship rules over all.

This ambivalence is not unique to us. It is part of the human condition. Already before the Common Era (mid-second century BCE), *The Letter of Aristeas* quoted a Hellenistic Egyptian:

> They [the Jews] worship the same God—The lord and creator of all the universe, as all other men, as we ourselves, O king, though we call him by different names, such as Zeus or Dis. This name was very appropriately bestowed upon Him by our first ancestors, in order to signify that He through whom all things are endowed with life and come into being is necessarily the ruler and lord of all. (15–16)

And as for "father," the Jewish philosopher Philo (early first century CE) testifies, "He exists whom all Greeks and barbarians unanimously acknowledge, the supreme father of gods and men and the maker of the whole universe."[4] Philo often refers to God as father and king. In *On the Creation,* he calls God "father of the universe" (72), "father and ruler of all" (135), "maker and father" (7, 10, 21, 77), and "father and king" (144). At the end of the first century, Josephus claims that "the wisest of the Greeks learnt to adopt these conceptions of God from principles with which Moses supplied them."[5] Not much later, the pagan Dio Chrysostom designated Zeus as the "God who governs the universe" and who is "the common father and savior and guardian of mankind." According to him, Zeus "alone of the gods is entitled father and king.... He is addressed as king because of his dominion and power; as father ... on account of his solicitude for us and his kindness."[6] The famous statement of Plato, "All things center in the king of all, and are for his sake, and He is the cause of all that is good,"[7] was cited approvingly by Christian and pagan alike in the latter half of the second century.[8] In the same period, the philosopher Numenius of Apamea writes, "The first God abstains from every work and is the king."[9] About 180, Maximus of Tyre recognizes a universally accepted truth by Greeks and barbarians alike, namely, "There is only one God, king and father of all."[10]

This general religious reality also stands behind Tertullian's question, posed at the end of the second century, "Do you not grant, from general acceptance, that there is some being higher and more powerful, like an emperor of the world, of infinite power and majesty?"[11] Jews would readily have granted that, of course.

Even earlier evidence for this shared theological tradition comes from a dialogue between the church father Justin (who preached in Rome in the mid-second century) and Trypho (a reputed Jewish refugee from the Bar Kokhba war, 133–135CE, and a student of philosophy himself). "Don't the philosophers talk all the time about God," Trypho asks rhetorically, "and don't their enquiries always concern divine monarchy and providence?"[12] In the early third century too, a Christian philosopher, Marcus Minucius Felix, after summarizing various philosophical conceptions of God, concludes, "These opinions are pretty well identical with ours: we recognize God, and we also call Him father of all."[13]

We should not be surprised to find echoes of these views among the Rabbis, therefore, and indeed, Trypho's older contemporary and compatriot Rabbi Akiva balanced the kingship and fatherhood of God by praying, "Our father, our king, we have no king other than You" (Talmud, Ta'anit 25b). These two divine epithets do not appear together in the Bible or the Dead Sea Scrolls from Qumran,[14] but they do appear in the daily *Amidah* in Blessings 5 and 6 on repentance and forgiveness, showing just how deep the double epithet goes in Jewish tradition. That *Amidah* parallel is worth looking at in its own right.

Blessing 6 (on the theme of divine pardon) gives us a perfect parallelism. "Pardon," "father," and "sin" form one cluster of associations; "forgive," "king," and "rebellion" form another:

	a	b	c
1.	Pardon us [*s'lach lanu*]	our father	for we have sinned [*chatanu*].
2.	Forgive us [*m'chal lanu*]	our king	for we have rebelled [*pashanu*].

3. For You are a good and pardoning God.
4. Blessed are You, who abundantly pardons.

"Pardon" (from the root *salach*) is deployed for its distinctive biblical meaning of "reconcile" or "heal," indicating God's desire for reconciliation with people in order to maintain the relationship. It does not imply, however, the cancellation of punishment due—only its postponement or possibly its suspension.[15] A suspended sentence in a court of law is, in practice, cancellation, even if not in theory. In 1 Kings 8:50, both sin and rebellion are associated with *salach*. In Psalm 103:9–13, God is asked to remove both, "the way a father has mercy on his children." The formulation of the first strophe makes this point by designating the wrongdoing as sin *(chet)*, the term for the kind of inadvertent error we might ascribe to children. Appealing to God as father, we seek reconciliation as his children. The goal is not the eradication of the wrong through appropriate chastisement at the time, but the suspension of punishment that we might expect from loving fathers.

In the same vein, the specific point of the second strophe is made by designating the wrongdoing rebellion *(pesha)*, the term for deliberateness. Here, we appeal to God as king, seeking amnesty. Since we rebelled against God as king, we seek to expunge the wrong from the record. Indeed, an alternative version, which reworks Psalm 51:3b, reads, "Wipe out and remove our acts of rebellion from before your eyes, for many are your mercies."[16] The combining of the two *(chet* and *pesha)* is to convince us that whether we have sinned or rebelled, we can be assured that God as father (for the first) and as king (for the second)[17] will forgive and be reconciled to us[18] as God expresses God's graciousness by abundantly pardoning. An apocryphal book from somewhere between the second century BCE and the first century CE known as the *Prayer of Manasseh* states, "According to your great kindness You have promised repentance and forgiveness to those who have sinned against You.... For You, O Adonai, are the God of those who repent" (vv. 7, 13). Such a dynamic of forgiveness paves the way for the quest of redemption in our own *Amidah,* Blessing 7.

Having looked at Blessing 6 on pardon, we now need to examine Blessing 5, on repentance *(t'shuvah)*, the state of mind that leads us to seek pardon. Again we see father and king, in deliberate parallelism.

	a	b	c
1.	Bring us back	our father	to Your Torah.
2.	Draw us near	our king	to your service.

	a	c	b
3.	Lead us back	by complete repentance	to your presence.

4. Blessed are You who desires repentance.

The rhetoric of the blessing focuses on the theme of return. It is based on the parallel drawn by Nehemiah between "returning them to You" (Nehemiah 9:26) and "returning them to your Torah" (Nehemiah 9:29). Each strophe deals with an aspect of repentance. In the first strophe, which deals with the return to Torah, God is addressed as "our father"; in the second strophe, which deals with drawing near to God's service or worship, God is addressed as "our king." According to the third strophe, we must return to both Torah and worship to achieve complete repentance. In doing so we are restored to "your presence," as father and king.[19] Whether asking for forgiveness or seeking repentance, we approach God both as father and as king. We need both; neither can be reduced to the other. If this is the case in the daily *Amidah*, all the more so on the High Holy Days, when the need for multiple metaphors is felt so intensely.

Our Father, Our King

OLD AND NEW PARABLES

Dr. Wendy Zierler

Dr. Wendy Zierler is Sigmund Falk Professor of Modern Jewish Literature and Feminist Studies at Hebrew Union College – Jewish Institute of Religion, New York. She is editor with Rabbi Carole Balin, PhD, and translator of *To Tread on New Ground: The Selected Writings of Hava Shapiro* and *Behikansi atah* (Shapiro's collected writings, in the original/Hebrew). She is also author of *And Rachel Stole the Idols* and the feminist Haggadah commentary featured in *My People's Passover Haggadah: Traditional Texts, Modern Commentaries* (Jewish Lights), a finalist for the National Jewish Book Award. She contributed to *Who by Fire, Who by Water—Un'taneh Tokef*, *All These Vows—Kol Nidre*, *We Have Sinned: Sin and Confession in Judaism—Ashamnu and Al Chet*, *May God Remember: Memory and Memorializing in Judaism—Yizkor*, and *All the World: Universalism, Particularism and the High Holy Days* (all Jewish Lights).

People generally cite only part of the familiar Talmudic account on the origins of *Avinu Malkeinu*: during a drought, we hear that Rabbi Akiva recites, "Our father, our king, we have no king other than you. Our father, our king, for your sake have mercy upon us." Immediately, rain falls.

What goes less noticed is the fact that the story is told as a comparison account of Akiva and his teacher, Rabbi Eliezer. First Eliezer tries to bring rain by leading the congregation in twenty-four benedictions for fast days. When he fails and Akiva succeeds, a *bat kol* ("a heavenly voice") explains that unlike Eliezer, Akiva is *ma'avir al midotav*—that is, he is a forbearing person who forgives easily.

Elsewhere in the Talmud, also, Eliezer engages in a Rabbinic controversy that is informed by a *bat kol*: the famous debate on the kosher fitness of an oven (the oven of Akhnai) (Bava Metzia 58b). Here too Eliezer loses, but in this case, he himself summons a *bat kol* on his own behalf. It duly cries out, "Why do you dispute Rabbi Eliezer, with whom the halakhah always agrees?" But Rabbi Joshua ben Levi, Rabbi Akiva's teacher, objects, "The Torah is not in heaven!" (Deuteronomy 30:12)—that is, Jewish law follows majority rule, not some heavenly *bat kol*.

Given this story in Bava Metzia, we know better than to rely on a *bat kol*. Perhaps, then, the *bat kol*'s explanation regarding Akiva's character should not be awarded the final word. Perhaps the very words *Avinu Malkeinu* explain Akiva's success—the Talmud does, after all, go to the trouble of quoting them.

Calling God "father" and "king" implies that even powerful, *human* kings have families, to whom they pay special consideration; all the more so should the divine king respond to the people of Israel with patriarchal love and care. It is this earthly metaphorical claim on God that brings success.

Akiva did not invent the metaphors of father and king.[1] Rabbinic literature abounds in their use: a king who had a son who angered him and was banished; a king with a beloved bride who is abandoned and waits patiently for her husband's return.[2] Using such hackneyed imperial and patriarchal metaphors today might seem cliché, but for the Rabbis, they supplied a literary structure for the chaos of Jewish exile and suffering. Behind, or below, their conventional plots lie subversive ideas that enable and justify theological complaint.

In *Lamentations Rabbah* 3:2, for example, a king (God) marries a woman (the people of Israel), writes her a generous *ketubah,* and then abandons her for many years to travel the world. In his absence, the queen's neighbors taunt her over her missing husband and urge her to give up hope of his returning. When the king finally returns, the queen explains that the promises of her *ketubah* prevented her from being led astray by her taunters. So too, with the people of Israel, whom the nations mock in their exile. Whenever they read or study Torah, however, they are reminded of God's promises to make them numerous and never to abandon them. When redemption finally comes, and God (as it were) returns, the people will tell God that were it not for the promises of Torah, they would have abandoned their faith long ago. The lesson is, first, that redemption will indeed come, a reward for Jewish forbearance in the face of exilic suffering. At the same time, the analogy calls implicit attention to the seemingly needless and undeserved suffering of the people, their almost superhuman, incomprehensible fidelity in the face of it all.

This combination of consolation and complaint is especially evident in another parable of a king prompted by the description of Jerusalem as having become "like a widow" (Lamentations 1:1):

> To what can this be likened? To a king who becomes angry at his queen, even gives her a *get* [document of divorce] but then snatches it back from her, leaving her in a bind. If she attempts to marry someone else, the king asks her, "Where is your *get*?" But if she sues for alimony, the king claims that he has divorced her. So it is with Israel. If it is drawn to idolatry, God asks them, "Where is your bill of divorce?" [Isaiah 50:1]. But whenever they ask God to perform a miracle for them, God says, "I have already divorced you, as it is written, 'I cast her off and handed her a bill of divorce' [Jeremiah 3:8]."[3]

David Stern, an expert on these king parables, explains the irony in the phrase *k'almanah* ("like a widow"; Lamentations 1:1): "[Israel] is like a widow inasmuch as her husband might as well be dead ... but she is only 'like' a widow because, alas, her husband is not dead." The parable presents "a critique of God's treatment of Israel" while also serving "an apologetic end." By holding that "God refuses to release the Jews from their covenantal bond even *after* He has divorced them," it provides a rationale for Israel's ongoing misery.[4]

In this mixed sense, parables of God the father/king have continued to resonate even with modern Hebrew writers who no longer share the imperial context or the stalwart faith of the Rabbis. In his famous story *Hamitpachat* ("The Kerchief"), S.Y. Agnon (1888–1970) consciously marries the traditional king parable with the image of God as departed father to urge the youth of his day to carry on Jewish tradition, without, however, waiting around passively for heavenly redemption.

The story opens with the narrator—young Agnon himself—recounting his father's yearly business trips to a regional fair, leaving his mother, like Jerusalem, crying by the window. The narrator takes consolation, however, in that his mother, like the queen in the Lamentations parable, is only *like a* widow—her husband will eventually return.

Meanwhile, his father's absence affords the narrator an opportunity to pretend to be grown up. Lying in his father's bed, the boy stretches out his limbs, counts the days until his father's return, and fantasizes about the eventual coming of the messiah, the king. In the background of his imaginings is a tale of the messiah from the Talmud, Sanhedrin 98a, where Joshua ben Levi asks Elijah the prophet when the messiah will come and is told by Elijah to go ask the messiah himself.

"Where is he sitting?" asks Joshua.

"At the entrance to Rome."

"And by what sign may I recognize him?"

"He is sitting among the poor lepers: all of them untie and retie their bandages all at once, whereas he, the messiah, unties and reties each separately, thinking, should I be wanted to reveal myself as the messiah, I must not be delayed by needing to redo all my bandages."

With this tale in mind, the boy recalls: Sometimes I would laugh to myself when I thought of the consternation that would come about in the whole world when our just messiah would reveal himself. Only yesterday he was binding his wounds and his bruises, and today he's a king! Yesterday he sat among the beggars and they did not recognize him ... and now suddenly, the

Holy One, Blessed be He, has remembered the oath he swore to redeem Israel, and given him permission to reveal himself to the world.[5]

The boy narrator reveres this humble version of the messiah. Yet he remembers a dream in which a great bird carries him to Rome, where he averts his eyes from lepers gathered by the gates. Unlike the messiah of the story, he just cannot stare actual suffering in the face.

He is not alone, however, because later in the story, a beggar like the one depicted in the Talmud appears in town, and not one of the supposedly righteous adult members of the community looks kindly upon him or feeds him. The adults too are unwilling to confront intractable human misery. The world is clearly in deep need of repair, and no one is doing anything about it.

In the meantime, the boy's father returns from his business trip, bringing his mother a kerchief that seems to be endowed with sacred power, in that no matter how long it is worn, it remains forever clean without ever needing washing. On the day of his bar mitzvah, the mother ties this holy kerchief around her son's neck, a mark of his special status as bar mitzvah. On the way back from synagogue, the narrator happens upon the same despised beggar and gives him his mother's kerchief to bind his sores, an act of messianic compassion (borrowed from the Talmudic tale), as if the boy has internalized his bar mitzvah responsibility by deciding to play the role of the messiah—to redeem the world, at least in some small way—himself.

Significantly, his father is nowhere to be seen that day. When the boy returns home, we learn why. He finds his mother sitting by the window as if her husband is again away on business, but the slowed paces and hushed voices of those passing by the house imply that this is a house of mourning—the father is away not for business but forever. The mother, then, is no longer just *k'almanah*, "*as if* a widow." She is a widow for real, and the son, by extension, is a fatherless orphan. In the tragic absence of his earthly (and by symbolic extension, his *heavenly*) father, the boy has indeed grown up. As we saw from his giving away the kerchief, he is able now to face the suffering he could not abide in his dream. Significantly, he has decided to play an active redemptive role himself, rather than wait for divine intercession. The mother gazes at him with love, approving of his helping the beggar, and thereby effecting at least a small act of repair here on earth.

Significantly, this story was published against the backdrop of Hitler's ascent to power in Germany. It alludes to Rabbinic images of "our father, our king" but challenges them with subversive notions of earthbound self-reliance and (Zionist) activism.

Israeli poet Yehuda Amichai too ruminates on the difficulty of applying the metaphors of *avinu malkeinu* to the post-Holocaust context. We saw how Agnon's story upended the father/king metaphor by transforming the "as if" widow into an actual one. In Amichai's poem, both the father and the father's children have paradoxically perished and endured all at the same time.

> Our Father, Our King, what does a father do,
> whose children are orphaned when he is still alive. What does a father do
> whose children have died and he has become a bereaved father, forever and ever?[6]

Having scrutinized the *avinu* metaphor in light of the Holocaust, Amichai then deflates the *malkeinu* part of the prayer by imagining a Roman-emperor-type king, ruling over a "republic of pain" and cynically attempting to appease the people with "bread and circuses [*sha'ashu'im*], the bread of memory and the circuses of forgetting."[6] The word *sha'ashu'im* recalls yet another prayer in the Yom Kippur liturgy, which cites Jeremiah 31:20, where God the father fondly recalls Ephraim as a *yeled sha'ashu'im*, "a dear child," symbolic of Israel in the young heyday of its faith. Yet Amichai's poem concludes with a description of the descendants of this same *yeled sha'ashu'im*, harboring longings (*ga'agu'im*) for a better world—capped by the words *avinu malkeinu*. Some two thousand years later, the people of Amichai's imagining still return to Rabbi Akiva's liturgical formula, hoping that just as in the case of that early humble sage, the bereaved and seemingly absent father-king will actually heed their prayers, too.

Empowerment, Not Police

WHAT ARE WE TO DO WITH PROBLEMATIC LITURGICAL PASSAGES?

Rabbi Dalia Marx, PhD

Rabbi Dalia Marx, PhD, is a professor of liturgy and midrash at the Jerusalem campus of Hebrew Union College – Jewish Institute of Religion and teaches in various academic institutions in Israel and Europe. Rabbi Marx earned her doctorate at the Hebrew University in Jerusalem and her rabbinic ordination at HUC – JIR in Jerusalem and Cincinnati. She is the author of *When I Sleep and When I Wake: On Prayers between Dusk and Dawn* and *A Feminist Commentary on the Babylonian Talmud*, and coeditor of three books. She is involved in various research groups and is active in promoting progressive Judaism in Israel. Rabbi Marx contributed to *Who by Fire, Who by Water—Un'taneh Tokef*, *All These Vows—Kol Nidre*, *We Have Sinned: Sin and Confession in Judaism—Ashamnu and Al Chet*, *May God Remember: Memory and Memorializing in Judaism—Yizkor*, and *All the World: Universalism, Particularism and the High Holy Days* (all Jewish

Lights). She writes for academic journals and the Israeli press and is engaged in creating new liturgies and midrashim.

Avinu Malkeinu is one of the most beloved liturgical pieces of the High Holy Days, the very symbol of the Days of Awe and the spirit of the Jewish New Year. Its tune evokes ancient memories from long before we were born. The emotion in the synagogue mounts as the cantor sings the poem or chants it responsively with the congregation; and then the entire congregation joins together in the final verse, singing as one, expressing their collective yearning, apprehension, and profound hope.

Carried along by the wave of the haunting melody, we sometimes forget that *Avinu Malkeinu* contains some difficult challenges. Rabbi David A. Teutsch, PhD, writes:

> Perhaps more than any other prayer, *Avinu Malkeinu* invokes the image of a long-bearded king sitting in judgment upon his throne. How many are the ways that this image can trouble us! Some Jews are struggling to recover from the harsh judgment of parents or peers, or from harsh self-judgments. Some are struggling to escape from the transcendent imagery of God and replace it with the divine within. Some have trouble with the maleness in the image.[1]

In addition to this, *Avinu Malkeinu* is very long.[2] Yet, as Teutsch himself recognizes, "There is a powerful core of truth in the *Avinu*

Malkeinu that transcends the trouble of [its] imagery."[3] Even liberal prayer books include it,[4] usually altering the text to make it more acceptable for their communities.

How are we to react to discomforting, annoying, or troubling passages in our prayers? The need to confront difficult liturgical texts is fundamental to contemporary liberal Judaism. As it turns out, however, even though the challenges are contemporary, the solutions are frequently not modern at all.

Traditional Ways of Coping with Troubling Sacred Texts

Not only the liturgy but the Bible itself is the result of many centuries of creation and redaction, most of it so hidden from our eyes that we can only guess at the issues faced by its editors. For example, the stories about King David reveal indirect criticism of him, but only if we read between the lines. Rabbinic literature preserves controversies regarding certain biblical books that gained entry into the canon (e.g., Ecclesiastes and Esther) only with great difficulty, while other candidates for inclusion were passed over.[5]

Once the canon was in place, however, the Rabbis faced the further challenge of how to use it liturgically. Their approach is difficult to discern because there were still no written prayer books and the wording of prayers was not yet completely fixed. Instead, we will try to learn from the manner in which our ancestors dealt with another sacred text, the most sacred one, the Bible. Many of its parts—the five books of Torah, the Five Scrolls, many psalms and prophetic passages—are recited as part of our liturgy. Some of them contain parts that the Rabbis deemed difficult, and they were reluctant to include certain passages in public synagogue worship. They seem to have applied various approaches to dealing with troubling biblical texts when used liturgically. Below I list six of them:

1. *They replaced them:* The Rabbis could not change the actual text in the written Bible, but they could replace problematic phrases with laundered euphemisms when they were read aloud, as we see from a comment preserved by the Tosefta (third century CE):

    All offensive texts written in the Torah are to be read as praise: for example, "You shall betroth a wife, and another man shall ravish her *[yishgalenah]*" (Deuteronomy 28:30) is to be read aloud as "Shall lie with her *[yishkavenah]*." (Tosefta, Megillah 3:39)

    This bold approach records two versions of a text: the written one and an oral alternative. In most editions of the Hebrew Bible both versions appear: the "tainted" word—*k'tiv* ("as written")—appears within the text but without vowels; while a replacement that is to be read aloud—*k'rei* ("as read")—appears in the margin. The offensive word is retained in the text but is not said aloud in public.[6]

2. *They did not translate it:* During the Torah service in the ancient synagogue the weekly portion was read aloud first in Hebrew, the language of the Torah, and then in Aramaic translation, the spoken language of the time (this custom continued until the High Middle Ages, and is still practiced in some Yemenite synagogues). Again, the Tosefta provides the relevant rule:

> Some [biblical passages] are read and translated, [some are] read and not translated, [some are] neither read nor translated. (Tosefta, Megillah 3:31)

One of the examples given for a text that is read but not translated is the story about Reuven, who slept with Bilhah, his father Jacob's concubine (Genesis 35:22). This troubling story was heard in the sacred tongue that only educated members of the community understood. Its content remained unavailable for everyone else.

3. *They did not read it at all:* Sometimes the Rabbis specify texts that are "neither read nor translated." This was not possible with the Torah, the entirety of which had to be

publicly read in the course of the regular cycle.[7] The haftarah (prophetic) readings, however, were negotiable, and the Rabbis specified some passages that were not to be selected, such as the embarrassing story of King David and Bathsheba, the married woman he watched bathing and took for himself while her husband was off in battle, fighting for him (2 Samuel 11–12). The Rabbis were embarrassed by the utterly immoral conduct of the king of Israel and probably were uncomfortable with the sexual ethics expressed in it, so they ordered this story not to be read in the synagogue at all. The change here goes beyond being read differently. The text is so discomforting that it is removed from the public sphere completely.

4. *They explained it differently:* Another method employed by the Sages is reinterpretation, a strategy designed to remedy a portrait of biblical figures as flawed. A lengthy Gemara passage addresses several such cases, including Reuven and David:

Said Rabbi Shmuel bar Nachmani in the name of Rabbi Yonatan...: Whoever claims that Reuven sinned is mistaken ... [he just] disordered his father's bed and the Torah imputes [blame] to him as though he had slept with her [Bilhah].... Whoever claims that David sinned is mistaken ... David thought about doing the sinful act but didn't actually do it. (Talmud, Shabbat 55b–56b)

As we saw, the latter would never have arisen in synagogue services at all, but the former would have—at least for those who understood the Hebrew, but the same learned people who followed the reading in Hebrew might also know the Gemara's exonerating explanation of how to understand it.

5. *They juxtaposed it with other texts:* We have already seen how the Torah is read liturgically "cover to cover," while the haftarot were chosen selectively due to many considerations, generally because of their textual or thematic connection to the Torah reading they accompany. Alternatively, the haftarah elaborates on something that was mentioned in the Torah portion, or it provides a different perspective to the Torah reading. But sometimes the haftarah challenges the Torah portion that it follows! The traditional Torah reading for Yom Kippur, for example, is a detailed description of the high priest's service in the Tabernacle, including the slaughtering of the sacrificial offering and the sprinkling of the blood, and so forth (Leviticus 16).[8]

The Rabbis chose a prophetic reading in which Isaiah harshly criticizes the people's precise performance of these commandments as devoid of meaning, stressing the superiority of moral conduct over empty ritual (Isaiah 57:14–58:14). The haftarah may also deflect our attention away from a difficult text by concentrating on an altogether different aspect of the Torah portion in question. In any case, the haftarah creates a stimulating dialogue with the Torah, and each teaches something about the other.

6. *They dramatized the reading to make their discomfort clear to the listeners:* Some Torah passages promise blessing in return for meritorious conduct but also curses for going astray. Two portions in particular are known, therefore, as *B'rakhot uk'lalot* ("Blessings and Curses"): *B'chukotai* (Leviticus 26:14–43) and *Ki Tavo* (Deuteronomy 28:15–68). As part of Torah, they could not be skipped, but the Rabbis cringed at reading these threats in all their horrid detail. They therefore ruled that the curses be recited rapidly and in a whisper—a clear acknowledgment that the text is problematic.

A parallel tactic utilizes the musical tropes that are employed; these too influence the way the readings are heard and understood. Special musical tropes accompany the reading of the Five Scrolls that are read on fasts and festivals. All five of them have their own melodic style: a festive chant for Ruth (on Shavuot), Ecclesiastes (on Sukkot), and Song of Songs (on Pesach); a particularly joyous sound for Esther on Purim; a mournful trope for Lamentations (on Tisha B'av, the anniversary of the Temple's destruction). Interestingly, some verses in the scroll of Esther are recited in the sad trope of Lamentations—for example, the listing of the vessels used in the king's feast (Esther 1:7)—because traditionally they were believed to have been taken from the Jerusalem Temple.

These six traditional strategies deal with the public performance of difficult biblical texts. They call attention to problematic texts by replacing them or by not translating them, by refraining even from publicly reading them and by providing them with less difficult interpretations, by juxtaposing them with other texts and thus coloring their perception, or by using performative means to convey the challenges they contain. It seems that worshipers could not help but ask such things as why a particular verse was not translated, why the reader read rapidly through a section, in a whisper, and why a mournful trope was used.

It is enlightening to see that our ancestors did not seek easy solutions to the problems involved with reading the Bible publicly. Quite the contrary, they preserved the tension that they saw in the text, so that their reservations (and even their outright objections) were duly noted alongside the text within their worship.[9] In short, all these devices are used not only to present us with a more acceptable text but also to cause us to struggle with it, to reflect on it, and to engage with it.

All the above deal with the use of the Bible in services, not in prayer books themselves. Prayer books are different, since the Bible is considered a sacred and unchangeable writ that even the most radical reformers treated it as a closed canon beyond the possibility of actual modification. The Rabbis could experiment with what and how much of it to read in services, using the strategies reviewed above, but they could not change the text they had inherited. The liturgy, however, had never been completely canonized and closed to change. It emerged in authoritative forms only in the ninth century and, indeed in many circles, is still evolving. Prayer books are much more fluid and open than the Bible. Still, we can learn from the Rabbinic devices for dealing with difficult biblical language and apply them to the liturgy as well. Keeping them in mind, let us see how some contemporary liturgists have dealt with the *Avinu Malkeinu*.

Modern Liturgical Sensitivities

In the 1960s, Jakob Petuchowski created a list of the major concerns that have animated liturgical reform through the years:

1. Abbreviation of the traditional service
2. Use of the vernacular
3. Omission of angelology
4. Toning down of particularism
5. Omission of prayers for the ingathering of the exiles and the return to Zion
6. Omission of the prayers for the restoration of the sacrificial cult
7. Substitution of the "Messianic Age" and "Redemption" for a personal messiah
8. Substitution of spiritual immortality for physical resurrection
9. Provision of variety—psalms and prayers used in the traditional liturgy on a single occasion are distributed over various occasions
10. Addition of new prayers voicing contemporary concerns[10]

It is obvious even from a quick glance at this list that some of the issues are still relevant today in liberal liturgy, while others have become less so. Most striking perhaps is the fact that gender-related concerns are altogether absent from Petuchowski's list. Despite their ubiquitous presence today, the feminist critique entered liturgical discourse only in the late 1970s or early 1980s and became central only in the mid- to late 1990s.

To be sure, liberal Jewish theology already manifested some gender-related interest as early as nineteenth-century Germany, when the benediction thanking God "for not making me a woman" was omitted from the morning benedictions. Still, the search for gender-balanced language and for equal liturgical participation of women did not gain prominence until the last decades of the twentieth century. Only in the late 1970s and '80s did women gradually appear as religious leaders and equal prayer participants in non-Orthodox synagogues of North America, and later on in Israel.

Feminists were increasingly concerned that women's sensibility and experience be reflected in Jewish life. They hoped that women would be allowed to reshape the rabbinate and the cantorate rather than simply follow traditional male models. Most importantly, they sought to incorporate women's voices and thoughts into Jewish liturgy and into the interpretation of classical Jewish texts.[11]

This feminist critique generated its own list of concerns. Examples might easily come from North America, the United Kingdom, or elsewhere, but where possible I will make a point of drawing on illustrations from the exclusively Hebrew-language liturgies of Israel.

Inclusive Language When Referring to Worshipers

A Hebrew example appears in the early morning prayer that thanks God for restoring our souls: "I gratefully acknowledge...." The feminine form *(modah ani)* is juxtaposed to the male form *(modeh ani)*.[12]

The Addition of Representative Female Characters

Liberal prayer books regularly began adding the names of the matriarchs (Sarah, Rebecca, Leah, and Rachel) to the patriarchs (Abraham, Isaac, and Jacob) in the first blessing of the *Amidah*. Here is the version that appears in the 1991 Israeli edition of *Ha'avodah Shebalev* (my English translation in parentheses):

(Blessed are You, Adonai our God and God of our fathers *and mothers* God of Abraham, Isaac and Jacob, *God of Sarah, Rebecca, Rachel and Leah* ... Blessed are You, Adonai, shield of Abraham *and the One who remembers Sarah*.)[13]

בָּרוּךְ אַתָּה ה׳, אֱלֹהֵינוּ וֵאלֹהֵי אֲבוֹתֵינוּ וְאִימוֹתֵינוּ, אֱלֹהֵי אַבְרָהָם, יִצְחָק וְיַעֲקֹב אֱלֹהֵי שָׂרָה רִבְקָה, רָחֵל וְלֵאָה...
בָּרוּךְ אַתָּה ה׳, מָגֵן אַבְרָהָם וּפוֹקֵד שָׂרָה.

In the blessing for redemption *(G'ulah)*, following the *Sh'ma,* Miriam's name is often added to the name of Moses:

(Moses, Miriam and the children of Israel exclaimed a song to You with great joy, and they all said: "Who is like You among the might.")[14]

מֹשֶׁה, מִרְיָם וּבְנֵי יִשְׂרָאֵל לְךָ עָנוּ שִׁירָה בְּשִׂמְחָה רַבָּה, וְאָמְרוּ כֻלָּם: "מִי כָמֹכָה בָּאֵלִים ה', מִי כָּמֹכָה נֶאְדָּר בַּקֹּדֶשׁ נוֹרָא תְהִלּוֹת עֹשֵׂה פֶלֶא"

Reclaiming and Adapting Old Rituals or Creating Altogether New Rituals and New Ritual Opportunities

At stake here is the celebration of women's experience, something more or less absent altogether in traditional liturgies composed by men, for men.[15] Compared to the United States, Israeli liberal women have been somewhat slower to adopt rituals, prayers, and services created by and for women alone, but in recent years we have witnessed several. Some reclaim old female precedents; some adapt existing rituals to female experience; some innovate completely to address women's life events.[16]

Among the reclaimed rituals lost in the course of history and rediscovered now are Rosh Chodesh ("new moon") ceremonies, which premodern Judaism knew as a women's holiday. Among the adapted ceremonies are egalitarian weddings, baby-girl naming celebrations, and adult bat mitzvah ceremonies. Included in the newly created rituals are practices marking life passages such as first menstruation, the beginning of a spousal relationship, becoming pregnant, experiencing a miscarriage or an abortion, undergoing fertility treatments, recovering from illness, suffering abuse, going through a divorce, reaching menopause, and many more.[17]

Gender-Inclusive and Gender-Balanced Metaphors of God

The most radical and controversial issue involves changes related to addressing and describing God.[18] Despite the commonly accepted principle in the Jewish tradition that God has no body or physical image, we have no option but to draw on human imagination when referring to the divine. If all God's images are masculine (e.g., king, father, warrior, shepherd, judge), women are forced to approach God only from the perspective of being the excluded "other."[19] Feminists have therefore called for creative reformulation of the male-centered "God-language." In English (and to a lesser extent in other European languages) it is relatively easy to avoid referring to God in gendered language, since the pronoun *He* can be easily changed to *God* without any further syntactical changes in the sentence, but in Hebrew the task is far more difficult, because all nouns, verbs, and adjectives are gendered.[20]

Avinu Malkeinu typifies the problems feminists face. It is the quintessential High Holy Day statement of God as loving parent (with whom we may be intimate) and just ruler (who evokes awe and wonder). But it employs decidedly male-centered metaphors. No wonder, then, that *Avinu Malkeinu* has become a center of attention for contemporary liturgists and worshipers alike. Evidence of the growing interest in gender issues in the last few decades can be discerned from *Gates of Forgiveness,* a collection of meditations and *Selichot,* the penitential service in preparation for the Days of Awe, created by the North American Reform Movement. The 1980 edition reads:

> Our Father, our King, be gracious and answer us....[21]   אָבִינוּ מַלְכֵּנוּ, חָנֵּנוּ וַעֲנֵנוּ ...

The later edition, from 1993, changes both the Hebrew and the translation to gender-balanced language

> Our Father, our *Mother*, be gracious and answer us....[22]   אָבִינוּ אִמֵּינוּ[!], חָנֵּנוּ וַעֲנֵנוּ ...

The revised version sacrifices the king imagery *(malkeinu)* in favor of addressing both "our father" and "our mother." The Hebrew, however, proved more difficult to reconstruct. Given the need to have gendered grammar throughout the sentence, it retains masculine grammatical forms in what follows. University of Worcester professor Luke Devine explains, "Masculine imagery is tolerated [in Reform liturgy], but only (it seems) when it is immediately counterbalanced by feminine language."[23]

Let us now survey different approaches to *Avinu Malkeinu* in liberal liturgies as a test case for dealing with challenging texts.

No More Avinu?! No More Malkeinu?! Contemporary Treatments of the Poem

As mentioned above, *Avinu Malkeinu* is problematic in at least four aspects: length, gender, penitential rhetoric, and the images of God.

The North American Reform *machzor Gates of Repentance* (1978) contains a shortened version of *Avinu Malkeinu* and moves the penitential verse "We have sinned before You" from the beginning to a later point in the prayer, where it may not be quite as noticeable; but it does not seem to be disturbed either by the idea of kingship or by the masculine imagery—it simply translates, "Our Father, our King."[24] It thereby represents, along with the 1980 edition of *Gates of Forgiveness* (mentioned above), the era just before gender-related issues became central for editors of progressive liturgies. I will turn below to contemporary American Reform liturgy.

The editors of *Kavanat Halev*, the Israeli Reform *machzor* (1989), chose a multifaceted approach: they kept *Avinu Malkeinu* but coupled it with two more poems (reproduced in appendix B). The first is a short version of the Sephardi hymn *Eloheinu Shebashamayim* ("Our God in Heaven"), referring to God in a gender-neutral voice. The second is an offering composed especially for the *machzor* by Rabbi Yehoram Mazor, *Shekhinah M'kor Chayeinu* ("*Shekhinah, Source of Our Lives*"), which addresses God in feminine language and refers to God's caring and nurturing aspects. Prayer leaders can choose among the options. In addition, the alternatives are available for congregations who follow tradition in omitting *Avinu Malkeinu* on Shabbat.[25]

More recent progressive *machzorim*—those published after the era of *Gates of Repentance*—address the gender aspects of *Avinu Malkeinu*. The *machzor* of British Liberal Jews, *Machzor Ruach Chadashah* (2003), maintains the traditional Hebrew but provides a translation that tones down both the masculine and the royal imagery: "Our Creator, our Sovereign." In addition, it provides a supplication about the *Shekhinah*, the presence of God that is feminine both in nature and in grammar.[26] The draft of the new British Reform *machzor Forms of Prayer* (2014) includes four versions of the text. Two are shorter forms of the traditional text, and the third is the Sephardic penitential hymn *Eloheinu Shebashamayim* ("Our God in Heaven"), a gender-neutral text that appears in a shorter version in the Israeli Reform *machzor* (see appendix B). The last, and most innovative, version contains an alphabetic acrostic of God's many attributes. The author, Rabbi Paul Freedman, explains:

> In order to emphasize that *"avinu"* and *"malkeinu"* are but two of the varied images that we may use in speaking to and of God, the version offers a wider range of epithets based on biblical and rabbinic sources.
>
> The alphabetical acrostic reminds us that even this remains a limited selection. The acrostic structure begins with the two familiar masculine images but centers on the *Sh'khinah*, the feminine divine presence, dwelling, hidden in our midst.[27]

And indeed the line "God [= *Shekhinah*] who dwells among us, our Everpresent Hope, renew this year for us as a good year" is located in the middle of the poem and serves as an axis from which the entire text expands (see the entire poem in appendix B).

Let us now explore contemporary North American liturgies. The American Reconstructionist *machzor Kol Haneshamah* (1999) provides a commentary (cited above) by Rabbi David A. Teutsch, PhD, specifying the problematic nature of the poem. He concludes, however:

Despite these very real difficulties, there is a powerful core of truth in the *Avinu Malkeinu* that transcends the trouble many of us have with its imagery [...] chanting the *Avinu Malkeinu* reminds us of the standards by which we ought to judge ourselves.[28]

Kol Haneshamah then provides four alternatives. The first is the traditional Hebrew text with a gender-neutral translation:

אָבִינוּ מַלְכֵּנוּ חָטָאנוּ לְפָנֶיךָ

Our creator, our sovereign, we have done wrong in your presence.[29]

The second is *A Woman's Meditation* by Ruth Brin, which acknowledges the limitations of any image of God: "But I am a woman, not a slave, not a subject, not a child who longs for God as a father or mother.... God is far beyond what we can comprehend."[30] The third is an alternative version, which changes the first words in every stanza—for example:

מְקוֹרֵנוּ אֱלֹהֵינוּ חָטָאנוּ לְפָנֶיךָ

Our Source, our God, we have done wrong in your presence.[31]

Finally, *Kol Haneshamah* concedes, "Many other versions can be constructed to reflect different theological outlooks and ethical concerns."[32] It encourages the worshipers to create their own version by selecting a word from each column to create their own introductory phrase:

I	
Our mother	אִמֵּנוּ
Our God	אֱלֹהֵינוּ
Our source	מְקוֹרֵנוּ
Our creator (literally, father)	אָבִינוּ
Our presence	שְׁכִינָתֵנוּ
II	
Our queen	מַלְכָּתֵנוּ
In heaven	שֶׁבַּשָּׁמַיִם
Our crown	עֲטַרְתֵּנוּ
Our presence	שְׁכִינָתֵנוּ
Our sovereign[33]	מַלְכֵּנוּ

The creators of this *machzor* aimed to provide a rich liturgical language for a diverse audience with a spectrum of needs.

The American Conservative *Mahzor Lev Shalem* (2010) cites the entire traditional poem both in Hebrew and in English, but instead of an English translation, it simply transliterates the Hebrew *Avinu Malkeinu*. An accompanying commentary emphasizes the liturgical centrality of the poem and the paradox of describing God as close and caring on one hand and distant and transcendent on the other. The commentary acknowledges that the images of "father" and "sovereign" that were so central to our ancestors "may not have the same resonance for us" and offers an alternative version "featuring a variety of imagery" along with the idea that "its alphabetical listing conveys the idea that we grasp the ineffable God through an infinite number of images."[34]

Interestingly, *Mahzor Lev Shalem's* Israeli Conservative (Masorti) counterpart, *Machzor Pote'ach Sha'ar* (2013), offers no special treatment of *Avinu Malkeinu* and settles for the traditional text alone.

Mishkan HaNefesh, the new North American Reform *machzor* (still in process), provides a shorter version of the traditional *Avinu Malkeinu* and (like the Conservative *machzor*) transliterates the terms *avinu* and *malkeinu* rather than translates them. The translation appears only in a footnote.[35] Additionally, the Reform *machzor* provides a wide variety of alternative readings and meditations addressing God with various metaphors. The concluding service of Yom Kippur, for example, suggests a prayer called "Soul Sustainer, Source of Our Life." Other prayers use the transliterated terms *avinu* and *malkeinu* with altogether novel content (see an example in appendix B).

The Jewish Renewal Movement is known for its openness to creating new liturgies and to reshaping old ones. Unlike the Reform, Reconstructionist, and Conservative Movements, Renewal is not an organized movement with a single official liturgy; nonetheless, the Renewal *machzor* published in 2014 by Rabbi Burt Jacobson of Kehilla Community Synagogue (Oakland, California) can serve as one example of many. It provides four sets of repeating metaphors that are used throughout the text. After the traditional address (making it the only contemporary liberal version that explicitly translates *Avinu Malkeinu* as "Our Father, our King"), it adds, "Our Mother, our Queen," "Our Source and our Destiny," and "Our Guide and our Truth." In addition, the entire content of the prayer is recomposed primarily as requests for wisdom (see the full text in appendix B).

The liturgy of the only Israeli congregation affiliated with Jewish Renewal, Jerusalem's Nava Tehila, led by Rabbi Ruth Gan Kagan, provides the entire traditional text, but the address to the divine alternates between the traditional masculine *avinu malkeinu* and the feminine *imeinu shekhinateinu* ("our mother, our *Shekhinah*").[36]

In short, progressive liturgies today all recognize *Avinu Malkeinu* as necessary but offer a variety of solutions to the challenges it presents. Some offer commentaries, some prefer multiple versions or euphemistic translations that tone down the male-centered language of the text, some expand the liturgical imagery to include diverse addresses to God. Most provide several options—especially the Reconstructionist *Kol Haneshamah*, which is most explicit regarding the "do-it-yourself" opportunity for worshipers to create their own personal versions.

If we were to generalize from the specific question of *Avinu Malkeinu* to an overall understanding of the ways progressive Jews deal with difficult liturgical texts, we would find the various options captured in the following flow chart.

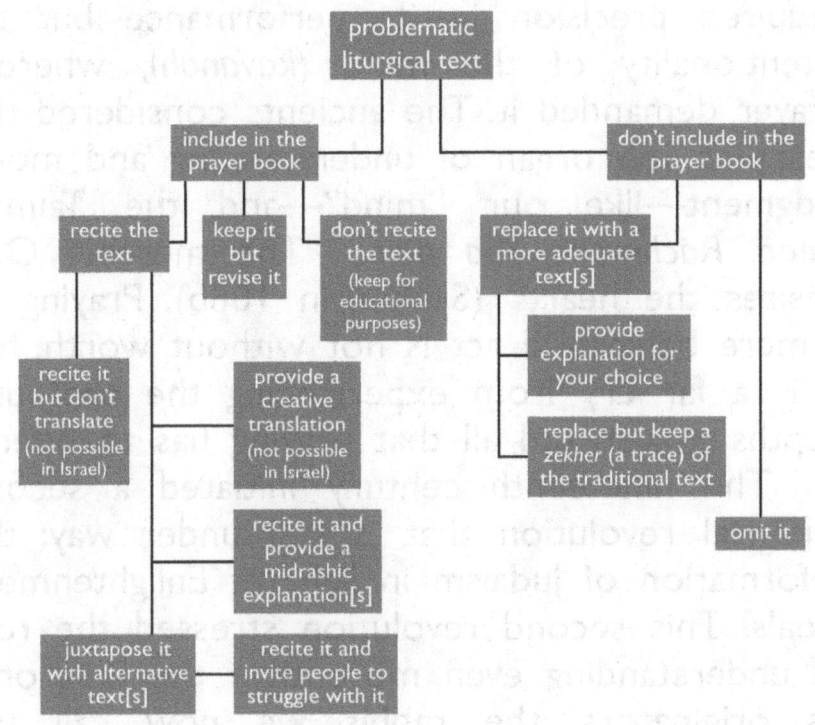

My preference is to be both as faithful to the traditional text and as creative as possible when it comes to our liturgy—I turn to this next.

A Balanced Approach to Difficult Liturgical Texts

The great Rabbinic revolution of the first centuries of the Common Era transformed sacrificial worship into prayer—in effect, in the absence of the Jerusalem Temple, a personal offering made directly to God without the mediation of priests and Levites. There was this further difference as well: sacrificial worship required precision in its performance but no intentionality of the mind *(kavanah)*, whereas prayer demanded it. The ancients considered the heart as the organ of understanding and moral judgment—like our "mind"—and the Talmud ruled, *Rachmana liba ba'ei*, "The merciful One desires the heart" (Sanhedrin 106b). Praying as a mere behavioral act is not without worth, but it is a far cry from experiencing the profound depths prayer and all that praying has to offer.

The nineteenth century initiated a second liturgical revolution that is still under way: the reformation of Judaism in light of Enlightenment ideals. This second revolution stressed the role of understanding even more than the first one. Its originators, the rabbis we now call the classical Reformers, maintained that Judaism is a rational set of concepts that Jewish liturgy formulated into a proclamation of faith.[37] Its prayers must, therefore, speak the truth!

Worshipers today are not as doctrinaire as the classical Reformers. They do not demand that the liturgy conform to strict theological concepts or have a quest for ultimate truths. Many yearn to find meaningful and touching prayer, prayer that provides a cozy sense of comfort and a sense of *meaning*.

There is something to be said for both claims. We hardly want to recite a liturgy that strains credulity, and it is not too much to expect that prayer should comfort us and not tax us further than the world already does. But taken to its extreme, the notion that we may do anything we like to the liturgy may be the epitome of self-indulgence; it retards the demand that human beings struggle with challenge. What we call creativity can sometimes actually be laziness of mind or an unwillingness to grapple with ideas that we find unpalatable.

Liturgical innovation may entail creating new texts and deleting old ones, but it should not deprive us of the opportunity to encounter ancient texts with fresh eyes. To be sure, there are offensive elements in our liturgy that we should not tolerate (blessing God for not creating the worshiper a woman or a gentile, for example). But sometimes we need to have more patience, to read our prayers as the Midrash reads the Torah, by questioning it but then enlarging its possibilities, deepening our understanding of what it says to us and living with the problematic aspects of it.

It is no easy matter deciding which of these two alternatives best fits any given case of liturgical concern. But that is precisely the task of liturgical editing: trying one's best to make that distinction and to make liturgical choices cognizant of the great responsibility inherent in this task for contemporary as well as past and future generations of Jews.

We Are Called Israel for a Reason—We Struggle!

Sometimes revealing the difficult aspects of our tradition is much more authentic, educational, stimulating, and engaging than suppressing them or covering them over with new words or a laundered translation. The "cleansed" text may be momentarily gratifying but lack the gravity and richness of a liturgy that is necessarily messy and unruly, given its centuries-long evolution. We can, of course, simply eliminate our difficult texts. But we might also include them for educational purposes (but not recite them aloud), add short explanations of the context in which they were composed, add substitutes side by side from which people may choose, or append an empowering commentary that adds new meaning to old words. As we saw above, all these methods were employed at one time or another by our ancestors.

True creativity is the skillful and artistic combination of old and new produced by trying to breathe new meaning into challenging texts instead of always dispensing with them. When it comes to gender questions, we should avoid the temptation to become gender police, who automatically replace every difficult image with an acceptable alternative. Sometimes acknowledging a difficulty and facing it is more honest, useful, and transformative than merely covering it over.

Now that we have become aware of the harsh inequities faced by women throughout the generations, we inevitably see the world through gender glasses. Politics, economics, family life, and religion—none of these will ever look the same again. In day-to-day affairs we remain wholeheartedly committed to uproot inequality and discrimination based on gender (and, of course, race, religion, class, and age as well). But the issue of gendered liturgical language, which is in and of itself symbolic speech, is more nuanced. Hebrew speakers are particularly aware of this because the Hebrew language of the prayer book is also the language of the street, and in Hebrew (as we saw) every noun, pronoun, verb, and adjective comes gendered as either masculine or feminine; Hebrew speakers know better than to think that we can aspire to total linguistic equality.[38] This is true, at least to some extent, of many European languages as well.

English, of course, is different. There we can indeed be more thorough in rendering language more egalitarian, but not without a cost, since English syntax does require the pronouns "him" or "his" when referring back to a gender-indefinite subject, and the various ways of circumventing that rule are not very satisfying. It is commonplace nowadays, for example, to substitute the plural third-person pronoun "their" even for a single subject, as in "A teacher should keep order in *their* classroom." But the practice is jarring. In some essays authors alternate "his" with "her," but that strategy is not easily applied to liturgy.

Consider the traditional sentence "May God quickly bring about his kingdom." We can change "kingdom" to "rule," but what do we do with "his"? We cannot say "their" obviously, nor can we easily render it "her" just because a few lines back we said "his." Many editors settle for repeating "God"—"May God quickly bring about God's kingdom"; but that is clumsy, at best. There are other solutions, too—I do not mean to exhaust them all—but I hope my point is clear. Even English does not easily allow complete eradication of non-egalitarian linguistic formulas, simply because it, too, is gendered to some extent.

For me, the mere fact that we acknowledge gender liturgical inequality is often sufficient. We hardly have to rewrite our entire prayer book, in a Soviet *Pravda* style that demands wholesale excision of every image we do not like. Do we really need (and can we really even achieve) systematic deletion of any use of the pronoun "He" or every reference to God as "father" or "king" in order to pledge allegiance to gender equality?

By analogy, I am reminded of my experience with some hostile Israeli interviewers who do not want to recognize me, a woman, as a rabbi and a scholarly authority. I insist that they publicly introduce me as "rabbi" and "professor" (much harder with the former than the latter), but once they have done so, they may just call me Dalia—I do not need them to repeat the titles again and again. So too, with liturgy: once we demonstrate allegiance to gender inclusivity we need not exercise it every time we encounter a noun or an adjective that might prove troubling. Retaining the traditional language does not necessarily vitiate our commitment to egalitarianism, and it may add depth to our liturgy by paying homage to our liturgical roots as well.

***

Our liturgy presents us with a rich and complicated literary world but only if we are open to a flexible understanding of liturgical metaphors. *Avinu Malkeinu* is the quintessential example. Although it is a difficult text for many (for all the reasons specified above), preserving it and struggling with it may take us to a palpable world of vivid imagery. It invites us to be symbolically present on that day in the drought-stricken Galilee when the usual liturgy did not produce rain and Rabbi Akiva arose to cry out, "*Avinu malkeinu*, we have sinned before You. *Avinu malkeinu*, we have no king other than You" (Talmud, Ta'anit 25b). It invites us to encounter countless generations of Jews turning brokenhearted to their heavenly father and king in times of trouble and despair, pleading for mercy. Its very familiarity opens a window onto a small rural community in Yemen, the first synagogues in the "New World," or an old Jewish community in the Old City of Jerusalem; it takes us by the hand to our own early childhood and our first shul experiences.

Our liturgy is like a precious and somewhat cryptic letter delivered to us from generations past. It is ours to own, to rework, to expand, or to change but, in any case, to cherish and to pass on with great care to our children.

The desire to impose theological consistency on our prayer books is not only inappropriate; it is also impossible. Liturgy is, by definition, an unruly and unsystematic construction, created over the course of two millennia and still being renewed by numerous people in various countries and cultures. We must not ignore or dissolve the liturgy's inconsistencies. Its very messiness is its strength; we must celebrate its diversity!

***

We must always move in two directions simultaneously: from and toward our tradition. In order to do so and to make truly informed choices, however, we need to be informed. Liberal Jews do not have the privilege of hiding behind statements like "This is what my grandfather always did," "This is what the rabbi says," or "This is what the *Shulchan Arukh* demands." We need to be learned enough to make reasonable choices and not run away from religious freedom; the freedom to deviate from such authorities forces us to confront responsibility. It defines the very Jewishness we treasure!

The liturgy is one of the important arenas in which Jews struggle to find meaning in their lives. We will not and cannot be gender blind. We cannot hope to achieve total gender balance or inclusion in the liturgy, but we must remain gender conscious and promote greater equality.

We are called "the people of Israel" after Jacob, our ancestor, who wrestled with an angel and was told, "Your name shall no more be called Jacob, but Israel; for you have striven with God and with men, and have prevailed" (Genesis 32:29).

Our very name teaches us that our tradition values struggle—not easy accommodation or acceptance, and certainly not a desire simply to *feel good*. The Jewish way is to grab on to difficult issues and deal with them; to avoid dogmatic thinking and to realize that if reality itself is messy and unruly, so too is our liturgy!

***

Feel-good Judaism may be pleasant and cozy, but when it is the primary consideration, it can also be boring and unengaging. Sometimes we want our prayer to be like our old worn slippers, comfortable and shaped to our feet. But occasionally we need to change into sneakers and run breathlessly for the extra mile. Sometimes, too, we want to wear our fancy and a-little-too-tight ballroom shoes and pray with elegance. And at other times still, we have to approach prayer in just our bare feet, willing to experience the liturgy just as it is with all that it has to offer, without barriers.[39]

Why We Say Things We Don't Believe

Rabbi Karyn D. Kedar

Rabbi Karyn D. Kedar teaches matters of the spirit to groups throughout the United States. She is senior rabbi at Congregation B'nai Jehoshua Beth Elohim in the Chicago area and the inspiring author of *The Bridge to Forgiveness: Stories and Prayers for Finding God and Restoring Wholeness;Our Dance with God: Finding Prayer, Perspective and Meaning in the Stories of Our Lives;* and *God Whispers: Stories of the Soul, Lessons of the Heart* (all Jewish Lights). She contributed to *Who by Fire, Who by Water—Un'taneh Tokef, All These Vows—Kol Nidre,* and *May God Remember: Memory and Memorializing in Judaism—Yizkor* (all Jewish Lights).

Words. They describe our dreams, fears, and aspirations, moments of darkness and moments of transcendence. Words shape perceptions. Words are the magical incantations that judge or nurture, defeat or elevate, experience. By our declaration, what happens is rendered as good, bad, frustrating, beautiful, affirming, difficult, loving, or confusing.

We say it is so, and so believe it to be true.

The poet, master of diction, lover of language, teaches us the power of literary convention for understanding what is ultimately indescribable, mysterious, and unknowable. In a universe complicated beyond comprehension, this the poet knows for certain: to be careful with our words. Careless or thoughtless expression leads to concepts that confuse, confound, and obscure.

Our struggle with God is so often linguistic. We use words about God that are limited, biased, chauvinistic, or even an affront to our sense of morality. How indignant is the sensitive soul when confronted with the God who abandons the good, punishes the world with flood, fire, and brimstone; permits genocide; or appears as angry, moody, and vindictive as a child. In so many ways our God-language has failed us.

So the Rabbis warn us not always to take literally what we hear and what we say. The midrash (Exodus Rabbah 29:1) insists that each of us "hears" the reality of God according to our strength:

> It is written, "Has a people ever heard the voice of God?" (Deuteronomy 4:33).... Rabbi Levi explained: Had it said "the voice of God is in *his* strength," the world would not be able to survive, but it says instead: the voice of God is in strength (Psalm 29:4)—that is, according to the strength of each individual, the young, the old, and the very small ones.

As metaphors become literal, our perception of God is weakened and our experience of God becomes limited. So we call upon the poets to teach us that metaphor is symbolic, that God is beyond reach and can only be understood in whispers of meaning and in pictures that are diverse and rich. God is father-*like* and mother-*like*, God is *like* a king—but in *actuality*, God is none of the above. And beyond the metaphor of gender, God is my light, *Adonai ori* (Psalm 27:1); and God is wind, *ru'ach elohim m'rachefet* (Genesis 1:2); and God is a silent whisper, *kol d'mamah dakah* (1 Kings 19:12); and God is the shadow beneath the wings, *b'tzeil k'nafekha* (Psalm 63:8).

When metaphor and simile are used consciously and deliberately, our understanding of all things hidden is elevated; and when we evoke paradox and irony in our personal narrative, the ineffable becomes a bit more accessible.

Once the eye is alert and the imagination awakened, we discover different types of metaphors:
- *Invisible metaphor:* The meaning of the metaphor and image is overt and yet somehow invisible to us, because the assumptions on which it depends have become habitual, making us blind to the obvious.
- *Hidden metaphor:* This is different from the invisible metaphor because its meaning is

unclear, hidden behind the fog of history. We catch a glimpse of what may once have been obvious but now is lost.
- *Mixed metaphor:* This is used clearly to confound. Since words cannot adequately, accurately, or effectively reflect the truth of God's nature, we mix conflicting imagery to arrive at a higher truth than either image alone can represent.

We shall see that *Avinu Malkeinu* is a mixed metaphor, but before going into its detail, we should look briefly at the other kinds of metaphor that inform our liturgy.

The Invisible Metaphor

For many centuries we have uttered the words "Blessed are You, Adonai our God, king of the universe." That has led to the tendency to believe in God as an actual king. The image of the king dominates our imagination. It has become for many of us the pictorial assumption, that if God were like something, "king" would be it. And so we have become blind to other possibilities. Yet, the defining myth of our own Jewish narrative uses an image of God that is nearly the complete opposite of king—the birthing mother:

> In the beginning God created the heaven and the earth. The earth was unformed, with darkness over the surface

of the deep and the spirit of God sweeping over the water. (Genesis 1:1–2)

The words used to describe pre-creation—unformed, dark, deep, the spirit of God, water—are a lovely and powerful description of the womb.

God said, "Let there be light"; and there was light. God saw that the light was good, and God separated the light from the darkness. God called the light Day, and the darkness She called Night. And there was evening and there was morning, a first day. (Genesis 1:3–5)

God births the world into being. And God saw the light as good. And so to be created in the image of God is to be a creative force for good, to birth into being a bit of the world that is filled with light and goodness.

Another image for God, similar to the birthing mother, is *el shaddai*, the God of nourishment. Having birthed the world into being, this God must now nourish us with love, protection, and an abiding presence. There seems to be a connection between *el shaddai* and the Hebrew word *shad*, meaning "breast." We know of Semitic fertility goddesses in the form of small statues with large breasts. *El shaddai*, the God of blessing, abundance, nourishment, and fertility, is known to our ancestors and is a part of the blessing Jacob gives his son Joseph:

By the God of your father, who helps you,

> *shaddai*, who blesses you,
> with blessings of heaven above,
> blessings of the deep that lies below,
> blessings of the breasts [*shadayim*] and of the womb
> [*rechem*].
> (Genesis 49:25)

Later, Rabbinic tradition rendered *shaddai* invisible by reinterpreting its meaning and turning the word into an acronym, rather than a metaphor. The three letters that make up *shaddai*—*shin dalet yod*—in the Rabbinic interpretation stand for *shomer d'latot yisrael*, "protector of the doors of Israel." As we enter and as we exit and see the word *shaddai* on the mezuzah, suddenly the God of nourishment and abundant blessing becomes invisible to the generations that follow.

The Hidden Metaphor

The power of the word, specifically, the name of God, was of central importance to the priests of the Second Temple. The name *YHVH* had extraordinary power and could only be uttered once a year, on Yom Kippur, in the court of the Holy of Holies by the high priest. This utterance of *YHVH* was a part of a confessional; and the people (understanding the delicate and fragile realities of life and death, forgiveness and sin, redemption and oblivion) respond, "Blessed be the name [of God] whose glorious kingdom is now and forever."

By the time this ritual was recorded in the Mishnah (Yoma 3:8), *YHVH* is simply rendered as *hashem,* "the name." At least by then (c. 200CE), the real pronunciation is lost to us, forever unclear and impermissible to all generations, forever hidden. So when we come upon this word, this name for God, this powerful metaphor, we become complicit in keeping its meaning hidden by mispronouncing the word, rendering it at times *hashem* and at times *Adonai,* which simply means "Lord."

The root of the word *YHVH* probably comes from the root *heh yod heh,* meaning "to be." If God is a verb—like the name of God in Exodus 3:14, "I will be what I will be"—then the word *YHVH* is in the third-person future-tense masculine—"He will be." But if *YHVH* is a noun, then the ending of the word *(kamatz-heh)* renders it feminine—something like "She is being-ness." And as we all know, by now, this "She is being-ness" is now hidden in plain sight under the utterance of the very masculine *Adonai,* or "Lord."

The Mixed Metaphor

And now the mixed metaphor. On the holiest moment of the year, while we are exhausted, vulnerable, and imploring, we say *avinu malkeinu,* "our father, our king"—a contradiction in terms, in imagery, and even in theology. Is God our father, or is God our king? The metaphor of father evokes the intimacy, love, and proximity of someone who hugs us, tells us bedtime stories, and protects us from the monsters of the dark. The king, by contrast, is distant, remote, and untouchable, ruling from a mountaintop castle and protected by a moat and guards who forbid our very approach. The king imposes debts, wages war, and hoards his wealth.

But it's a metaphor, a linguistic trick to enrich our understanding. The Hebrew word for "king" is *melekh,* from *kaf lamed mem,* the three middle letters of the alphabet—as if to say that God is the center of all we do, all we are, and all that is. The middle three letters are like the marrow of expression, just as God is the central power of the universe. And yet those letters become the word "king" only in reverse order, as if to teach us that when all is said and done, we, like Moses, still see only the "back" of God. Our words are mere shadows of reality.

"Our father, our king," taken together, proclaims two realities barely separated by a comma, as if we say: God is the king, but also the breath of life, the wind, the spirit, the father of all. But not really.

We ourselves live a mixed metaphor: life is a tangled, varied experience of delight and despair, of love and alienation. Our hearts expand to infinite capacities, holding great sadness at the pain of the human condition but also bearing witness to life's profound beauty and joy. Our concepts of God necessarily mirror life's complexity. We can hardly hope to articulate what we can barely fathom, so we exchange precision for poetry: the poetry of the ineffable. In the end, "our father, our king" is hardly separate imagery at all! Rather, it becomes song, melody, and, ultimately, silence. We do our best with words, and then we crawl into the silence of amazement, uniting speech with contemplation, and say, "May the words of my mouth and the meditations of my heart be acceptable." And after all, God is like a rock, *tzuri,* foundation and flint, stability and spark, unknown and so very known.[1]

PART V

How Prayer Book Editors Deal with Naming God

A British Father and a British King?

Rabbi Paul Freedman

Rabbi Paul Freedman is senior rabbi of Radlett Reform Synagogue, one of the largest and fastest-growing synagogues in the United Kingdom. He was final editor of *Haggadateinu*, the first British Reform Movement Haggadah and is coeditor of the next *machzor*. He is married to Vanessa, and they are proud parents of Katie and Joshua.

Perhaps it's not fashionable. Perhaps it's just not very British. For whatever reason, it's clear enough: we have trouble talking about God.

Admittedly, one person may announce that he believes in God, and another that she doesn't or can't. Someone else blames God for all that is wrong in her life, while another says he seeks comfort in God all the time. But conversation about what we actually mean by "God" is less common. The truth is, discussing God is hard work, and at the heart of it lies a paradox. On the one hand, we want God to be truly "other," transcendent, unfathomable, in which case human language may be wholly inadequate. On the other hand, if we do want to talk about God, then human language and our own experience are the only tools we have.

We could, of course, resort to mystical silence. If words cannot describe God properly, then we simply won't try. Certainly, abandoning all language would make the forthcoming British Reform *machzor* a slimmer volume! A more satisfactory approach is recourse to metaphor, simile, and symbol. We accept the impossibility of talking literally about God, but still we use human language to allude rather than to describe.

There is a danger in this approach. Even we who claim not to be fundamentalists are guilty of slipping into literal-mindedness, of forgetting that our metaphors are metaphors. Regularized liturgical repetition may make our God-language seem too holy not to be "true" in the absolute sense of describing God as God actually is, but calling God our father, our king, judge, guardian, shepherd, or rock is metaphoric nonetheless. Such words may be helpful in hinting at God or some aspect of God, but none of them can ever be sufficient. Indeed, any single one is, of necessity, insufficient. And if we become too attached to any particular metaphor there is the danger of taking it too literally, and (as theologian Neil Gillman reminds us)

> theological literal-mindedness is idolatrous, not because it claims to describe the transcendent God in human and natural terms—what other terms can we use?—but, rather, because it insists that these

descriptions are literally accurate and true.... The assumption that God's nature can be conveyed in a literal way by our natural language is as idolatrous as building a golden calf.[1]

If anything, we lack enough diversity in the liturgical images we customarily use because metaphoric diversity counters this tendency toward literal-mindedness. Look hard enough through the Bible and Rabbinic tradition, and you find feminine metaphors for God, for example, but they are relatively few and far between; their rarity gives the impression that God is somehow more truly masculine than feminine.

Of course, despite our anthropomorphisms, God is neither, but we cling to the masculine imagery as if it were more accurate rather than just more usual or comfortable. Similarly, we must be honest about whether our reaction to using feminine imagery is due to its being (in)accurate or just (un)comfortable. Liturgical usage is a particularly interesting lens through which to view the way in which we name God. We would hope to have prayer books that are edited with consideration for both theology and comfort, but what happens when too much concern for comfort prevents theological daring or when theological boldness makes us feel uncomfortable? The current trend in the liturgy of British Reform—as with other progressive movements—has been to balance these considerations by "degendering" the traditional masculine God. As we are reminded in the introduction to the British Liberal prayer book, "The truth is: literally, God is neither male nor female; metaphorically, God is both."[2] Accordingly, and were this the only consideration, we should not be *excluding* masculine language but rather *including* feminine language as well.

This inclusive approach of using more, not less, metaphorical language is beautifully illustrated by the *Chasidei Ashkenaz,* the German Pietist movement that arose in the twelfth and thirteenth centuries, particularly in a genre of theological poetry that its representatives initiated. One especially fine example is a *piyyut* that has been included in various positions in the liturgy, including the night of Yom Kippur, since at least the sixteenth century: *Shir Hakavod,* commonly known by its opening words, *Anim Z'mirot.*[3]

Of the poem's thirty-one verses, the bulk form a central section in alphabetical order, one for each letter of the alphabet, though intriguingly with an extra verse for the letter *resh*. When editors of progressive liturgies include a selection of verses rather than the complete poem, the acrostic pattern is inevitably lost, but it is the introductory and closing verses outside the acrostic that are most usually retained; these describe the poet's longing for God, but also the limitations of language in satisfying that longing. The poet characterizes language about God as imaginative, allusive, indirect, and metaphorical, while significantly reminding us of the important theological point that God is "one in all the imagery."

What then follows, however, in the unabridged *piyyut*, is the central section of the poem: verse after verse of blatantly anthropomorphic imagery. Even Israel Abrahams's classic but Orthodox *Companion to the Authorised Daily Prayerbook* describes these verses as "possibly too direct for modern taste" and sometimes reaching "the verge of anthropomorphic licence."[4] Nevertheless, it is this central section of the *piyyut*, with its range of metaphors for God, that reinforces the theological point made in the opening. It is the very range and variety of the divine metaphors—including, sometimes, even their mutual incompatibility—that remind us that they are metaphors and cannot be taken too literally.

To restrict the range of metaphors we employ is to increase the risk of their being understood literally. This seems to be a concept that is central in *Shir Hakavod*, a message that is lost when its central verses are missing. There may be value in retaining the poem's (literally incompatible, but very masculine) descriptions of youthful black hair and aging gray, as well as its rare sequence of verbs associated with giving birth that provide a feminine image of God as well.

If we furthermore take into consideration that the metaphorical language with which we are most familiar comes to us from another age, then we find another problem. Metaphors work by using something that is familiar to hint at something that is not. But here is the problem: no one actually imagines God looking like a big boulder in the middle of a field, whereas we can and do picture God as a ruler or parent. And a rock is, perhaps, still a rock, with all that that particular metaphor suggests about God. But is a king still a king? Is a lord still a lord, or even a father still a father?

I've met a British lord or two. And I'm very fond of my father. As a British subject, I'm young enough never to have had a king; Queen Elizabeth II has been the reigning monarch all my life. But I know what a king is, the way I know what lords and fathers are. Still, when we name God as *Adonai* ("Lord"), *avinu* ("our father"), or *malkeinu* ("our king"), I don't actually find myself thinking of any of them. I more or less know instinctively that these names are metaphoric—and altogether different—when used for God.

What is not so immediately clear is what these metaphors really say about God. I'm aware, for example, that lords, fathers, and kings are not what they used to be, but that doesn't mean that the old ones were better, more authentic, metaphors for God. Moreover, as much as a medieval king differs from a modern-day king, both of those kings are different from a biblical king, let alone a modern, female monarch. Calling God "king" may hint at God, but which one of all these kings (or queens?) ought we to have in mind? What *do* we mean to say when we label God "king"? Clearly, we should not become overly satisfied with any single metaphor at the expense of all the others, or even of one single example of any single metaphor, at the expense of all the other examples that the metaphor may suggest. However it is that we choose to vocalize or translate God's personal name, *yod heh vav heh*, we should hear within it something of the indescribable One who simply is, was, and will be.

This all presents a particular challenge for progressive liturgists when approaching *Avinu Malkeinu*. The first British Reform *machzor*, that of the West London Synagogue in 1842, was edited by Reverend D. Marks, who had been appointed minister of that newly established synagogue. He had a unique degree of freedom in his pioneering liturgical work as he sought to eliminate prayers that he considered "deficient in devotional tendency" or "known to be the offspring of feelings produced by oppression, and are universally admitted to be foreign to the heart of every true Israelite of our day."[5]

His *Avinu Malkeinu* incorporates nineteen verses. From their order, it appears to be (as might be expected given the background of the synagogue) an abbreviated Sephardi selection. Marks omitted verses deemed unacceptably particularistic in describing Jews as being singled out as a unique people, especially for oppression or punishment, but also as God's chosen heritage (lines 5–8, 11). Marks also rejected lines that include the image of a book in which we might be written, along with any similar suggestions of a divine decree or record being composed on high regarding the destiny or fate of worshipers (lines 21, 20, 23, 17, 14). Only one such verse creeps in, without explicit reference to the book, however, asking God to "*remember* us for a good life" (line 19). Finally, a verse about "exalting the horn of thine anointed" is deemed too messianic (line 26).

This *Avinu Malkeinu* has remained almost unaltered through decades of subsequent editions of the *machzor*, even as later editions were edited by other rabbis and used by other "associated synagogues" that eventually became the Reform Synagogues of Great Britain. In part, that might reflect the quality of Marks's selection, but also there is a strong conserving tendency from one edition to the next, particularly with regard to familiar sung texts.

The title page of the 1842 *machzor* highlights the volume's inclusion of an English translation. Over time, the English of one verse, in particular, has undergone an interesting history. In general, *malkeinu* has been translated as "Our King" in all editions to date, but the first edition appeared very early in the reign of Queen Victoria, which gives a special resonance to the translation "Our Father and King! we have no other *Sovereign* but thee" (line 2). The fourth edition was published in 1909, just a few years after Edward VII succeeded to the throne, and there the translation was changed to the perhaps more usual "Our Father and King! we have no *King* but thee."

The eighth edition was published in 1985 following a new edition of the "Shabbat and Daily" siddur in 1977, a book that departed radically from almost a century and a half of its predecessors, not least in (controversially!) introducing "modern idiom," with "You" replacing "Thee" and "Thou." The 1985 edition of the *machzor* follows this development, with the verse above now translated as "Our Father, our King, we have no king but You." The fact that the reigning monarch (for already three decades, by then) was Queen Elizabeth II did not prompt a return to the use of the word "sovereign."

It was also in this edition that the verses differed from the selection made by Marks in 1842. Of the original nineteen verses, five were dropped (lines 13, 18, 24, 30, 40) and replaced with three others (lines 5, 21, 20) that are found in Sephardi versions, along with two (lines 35, 36) that are more usually Ashkenazi. In particular, in a couple of the "new" verses, God again is described as "writing" (or at *N'ilah*, "sealing") us in a book, an image that Marks had excised. Choirs were apparently able to adapt their music for a different nineteen-verse *Avinu Malkeinu*. A final twentieth verse (line 44) was also appended, as it could be sung to a different, popular tune.

Following the 1977 siddur, a generation arose that knew not the God of "Thee and Thou," but for them, a new edition in 2008 involved a different change of language, one that was sensitive to gender, including the way in which we name God. Accordingly, "the Lord" became "the Eternal"; *Av Harachamim* is "Source of mercy," not "Father of mercy"; and *melekh* is more consistently "Sovereign," not "King." A corresponding new British Reform *machzor* is now being developed with a style of translation that will generally follow the model already laid down by the 2008 siddur. How will God be named in *Avinu Malkeinu?*

In 2014 a draft of the Erev Rosh Hashanah service was published with three alternative versions. First, the 1985 version is included, but with a new translation where *avinu malkeinu* is generally transliterated rather than translated. *Melekh* again becomes "sovereign." The second version also transliterates (that is, does not translate) *avinu malkeinu* but provides a different and shorter collection of verses, for musical reasons: it is intended to correspond to the musical setting of *Avinu Malkeinu* by Max Janowski.

The third version is a novel composition of eleven verses that can be sung to the same melody as the nineteen-verse version. Each verse contains two different names for God, one for each letter of the alphabet. The alphabetic acrostic suggests the important theological idea (in the spirit of the *Chasidei Ashkenaz*) that God might be named in innumerably more ways were it not for the constraint of the number of letters in the alphabet. (Similarly, for example, in the alphabetic confession *Ashamnu, bagadnu* suggests that our sins are more numerous than those listed.) The twenty-two names given for God (beginning with *avinu* and *malkeinu*, which *are* here translated as "Our Father, our King") center on a verse that names God using feminine grammar: *Sh'khinateinu, tikvateinu, chadshi aleinu shanah tovah,* "God who dwells among us, our Everpresent Hope, renew this year for us as a good year." Some who have experienced this new rendition of *Avinu Malkeinu* have commented that they miss the "traditional" version—from just 1985! Others have remarked on how moving it is to sing these "new" words to the "old" tune.

The Marks version of *Avinu Malkeinu* remained in use throughout the reigns of six consecutive British monarchs, a symptom of what might be called "musical conservatism." Around a quarter of the verses were substituted with different verses to create the 1985 edition—which remains in use today. When we name God, we create powerful metaphors or images of God that depend on historical and cultural context, but we should still not underestimate the importance of being able to sing those names.

Avinu Malkeinu and the New Reform Machzor (Mishkan HaNefesh)

Rabbi Edwin Goldberg, DHL

Rabbi Edwin Goldberg, DHL, serves as coordinator of the Central Conference of American Rabbis (CCAR) editorial committee on the forthcoming CCAR *machzor*. He has a doctorate in Hebrew letters from Hebrew Union College – Jewish Institute of Religion and is the senior rabbi at Temple Sholom of Chicago. He is author of *Saying No and Letting Go: Jewish Wisdom on Making Room for What Matters Most* (Jewish Lights). He contributed to *We Have Sinned: Sin and Confession in Judaism—Ashamnu and Al Chet*, *May God Remember: Memory and Memorializing in Judaism—Yizkor*, and *All the World: Universalism, Particularism and the High Holy Days* (all Jewish Lights).

Many years ago, during the Yom Kippur morning service, a certain rabbi was interrupted (albeit politely) by the oldest member of the synagogue. He asked if he could ascend the bimah and ask the rabbi a question. How could the rabbi say no? Here was the question: "On the High Holy Days how many *avinu malkeinu* s are there?" This was, in fact, a trick question. The old man was not asking for the traditional number of forty-four verses. The rabbi thought about the numerous repetitions of this recitation and blurted out something like, "One hundred." The gentleman, showing an amused grin, barked out, "No, Rabbi. In Judaism there is always just one *avinu malkeinu*." Of course, theologically he was correct: we believe in one God.

This tale highlights a challenge that my team of editors faced as we labored to create a new High Holy Day *machzor* for North American Reform Jews.[1] The task has taken five wonderful years, and the book is just now nearing completion. Issues regarding *Avinu Malkeinu* revolved around a set of interconnected questions:

- Are some verses no longer necessary or actually objectionable?
- Do some speak to our human condition more than others?
- And, can we afford to offer a text that does not synch with the widely used and justifiably beloved version composed by Max Janowski (and famously sung by Barbra Streisand)?

As is commonly known, a reference to *Avinu Malkeinu* first appears in the Talmud (Ta'anit 25b), purporting to go back to well-known authorities in the second century CE. From the beginning, it was understood to be an appeal for God's mercy.

Rabbi Eliezer once stood before the ark [during a drought] and recited the twenty-four benedictions for fast days, but his prayer was not answered. Rabbi Akiva stood there after him and proclaimed, "*Avinu malkeinu*, our father, our king, we have no king other than You; our father, our king, have mercy upon us," and rain fell.

Avinu ("our father") represents God's compassion. *Malkeinu* ("our king") signifies God's stern, judgmental face. Taken together, *avinu malkeinu* asks that God's judgment be tempered by God's mercy.

The theme of moving God from judgment to mercy is widespread throughout the Days of Awe but is also, by extension, a theme applied to us, as well as to God. Just as we seek God's compassion, so should we show compassion to one another—and to ourselves. So far so good. But many of us find objectionable the core idea that a drought is brought on by God as punishment for moral failings and the concomitant notion that punishment persists until we successfully petition God to bring it to an end.

Most of us—including myself—believe that people are responsible for their actions and that righteous people are aware of that responsibility. Being human, we will never meet the highest of divine expectations, but we do our best and believe that God understands. We do not believe that God harbors grudges against us such that droughts (or sickness, suffering, and plagues in general) are a sign of God's displeasure. Indeed, good people often suffer while bad people do not.

Our editorial committee was anxious to continue the centrality of *Avinu Malkeinu* in our *machzor* but to present alternative theological choices within it—a regular concern that we applied to other prayers as well.

We also wanted to make sure that worshipers not see the many repetitions of *Avinu Malkeinu* as redundant. To be sure, some Jews find its regularized recitation positive: a familiar signpost throughout the long set of services or a trance-inducing experience (in a good way).[2] Nevertheless, the sensibility of many of our people dictated a more nuanced, selective approach. But how to choose?[3]

Furthermore, there was the issue of music to consider. The traditional melody to the refrain would work no matter what, but the Reform community, over time, has developed a fondness for the Janowski melody that requires the wording of some verses, not just that one-line refrain. Knowing that so many people like to sing (or listen to) the Janowski version, we made sure to include the requisite lyrics. But the Janowski melody does not exhaust the entire set of verses that we might include, so we needed to determine a fuller statement of the prayer that we would feature—perhaps differently, however, for each service. The feeling tone changes through the various days and services, after all.

Ideally, the *Avinu Malkeinu* at, say, the beginning of Rosh Hashanah would be replaced by another one for the end of Yom Kippur.

Our prior *machzor*, *Gates of Repentance*, already illustrates this subtle difference in timing when it changes the translation for the traditional refrain for the last *Avinu Malkeinu*, during the concluding service of *N'ilah*. Normally, the prayer requests God's compassion *although* we have little merit. By *N'ilah*, however, the tone of the entire service shifts positively; standing before the open ark, we are expected to feel greater confidence in our ability to start over again. In keeping with this more heady expectation, the *N'ilah* version of the text was changed to read, "Have compassion upon us *even when* we have little merit." Sending us back into the world, it seemed logical and helpful that the prayer buoy us up by the sense that there will be times in the year ahead when we will actually have a fair amount of merit.

In keeping with this sort of calculus, our committee varied the rendition of *Avinu Malkeinu* to fit the mood of the particular services containing it. At the end of this essay I will offer some of the "creative" examples that we came up with. (They are still being piloted; it is too soon to say exactly which ones we will finally decide to use.) I turn first, however, to the normative *Avinu Malkeinu*, the one that would appear in most of the services, when creativity was not called for.

I have already alluded to the theological and musical considerations that went into deciding which verses to include. In addition, we knew we had to come up with a standard translation, and in that regard, the words *avinu malkeinu* themselves presented a challenge. We solved it by deciding (again, as in *Gates of Repentance*) not to translate them at all.[4] "Our father, our king" is too limiting in our age.

There remained of course the rest of the declaration, the wording in each line that follows the address of God as *avinu malkeinu*. After meeting with a number of experts in the art of translating Hebrew into English, we created for ourselves a spectrum from "literal" to "faithful." Literal is as close to a direct translation as is possible. Faithful refers to capturing the spirit of the Hebrew as best as possible.[5]

At times literal translations are absurdly wrong. The American poet Paul Zimmer, for instance, had a book translated into Japanese. The original dedication read, "To Sue, with Love." The Japanese, "To Press a Lawsuit with Love." The *machzor* editors know we cannot be perfect in our rendering. As Robert Frost observed, "Poetry is that which is lost in translation." Nevertheless we have attempted to offer the best that language can afford. In that regard, certain words stood out as especially problematic.

In general, the work of creating a new Reform *machzor* challenged us to find a different word for what generally goes by "sin." The word "sin," however, carries a great deal of cultural baggage in our country. Often it is considered in the Christian context of living in "a state of sin." Judaism does not understand sin in this way. Exactly what we do mean by it is not altogether certain, since so many metaphors have been offered through the centuries, and unlike Christianity, Judaism has fewer theological systems that try to fix the meaning of the term with all due certainty.[6] We took as our starting point the widely held assumption that for Jews, sin is a matter of missing the moral mark. It is not a state of being; it is a matter of doing something wrong.

With that in mind, we tried various translations, the usual "We have sinned before You," but also "We have missed the mark," and "We have transgressed." None of these seemed adequate. We finally came up with the following "breakthrough" wording that offered a new but faithful way of providing the concept of sin for moderns (it is being piloted even as I write this): "*Avinu Malkeinu*, we come before You in our brokenness."

Why such an approach? "Brokenness" captures our need for healing and repentance without using metaphors all too often associated with images of hell and damnation. It's not that there are no consequences for our acts; and "brokenness" means more than a need of healing—we must take responsibility for our choices. "Brokenness" does not get us off the hook. But it does offer a way of dealing with our shortcomings without putting us on the defensive or allowing us to slide into a non-Jewish view of sin.

Of course, *Avinu Malkeinu* is a litany: a series of lines that begin the same and end differently. The juxtaposition of several lines, one after the other, allowed us the opportunity to build on our central message ("we come before You in our brokenness") and provide it with context. For our pilot version we came up with the following:

> *Avinu Malkeinu,* Almighty and Merciful—
> We come before You in our brokenness.
> *Avinu Malkeinu,* Almighty and Merciful—
> You alone are our Sovereign.
> *Avinu Malkeinu,* Almighty and Merciful—
> Act toward us as befits Your Name.
> *Avinu Malkeinu,* Almighty and Merciful—
> Arouse within us new vitality to make this a good year.
> *Avinu Malkeinu,* Almighty and Merciful—
> Bring healing and wholeness to the ill among us.
> *Avinu Malkeinu,* Almighty and Merciful—
> Allay the harshness of the decree against us.
> *Avinu Malkeinu,* Almighty and Merciful—
> Remember our goodness and call it to mind.

> *Avinu Malkeinu*, Almighty and Merciful—
> Act for Your sake and save us.
> *Avinu Malkeinu*, Almighty and Merciful—
> Answer us with grace, for our deeds are wanting.
> Save us through acts of justice and love.

Note that we use "brokenness" in the first line, but then build upon it to provide a larger perspective on what we mean by the term. We also decided, after all (at least, in this version—we will get to others later), to translate *Avinu Malkeinu*, albeit in a non-genderized way ("Almighty and Merciful"). Just as "sin" is seen as a Christian word, I was concerned that "grace" (one line from the bottom) might also be seen that way. Our piloting did not confirm my fears.

I am in favor of retaining "brokenness" in the final version of the *machzor*. To be human is necessarily to be broken at times, and these Days of Awe come, in part, to remind us that awareness of our brokenness is often a requirement for healing. As Hemingway once wrote, "The world breaks everyone, and afterward, some are strong at the broken places." Some have claimed that the word is too passive, but I disagree. It is *moral* brokenness that leads us to wrongdoing in the first place, so that confronting our brokenness does not imply that we are absolving ourselves of our wrongdoings and failures. We are acknowledging our errors and our profound need for God's help as we seek to correct our ways.

I have now surveyed the three major issues that the committee faced with regard to *Avinu Malkeinu*:

1. How to translate the words *avinu malkeinu* themselves
2. Which of the traditional verses to reject and which to include
3. How to translate the verses we included

But as I said above, we were anxious also to provide theological diversity, and toward that end, committee member Rabbi Janet Marder came up with one particular "creative" version that deserves highlighting. It appears alongside the more "faithful" translation:

> *Avinu Malkeinu* ... We stand in awe; we draw close in love.
>
> *Avinu Malkeinu* ... The Power that passes through us and pervades all things.
>
> *Avinu Malkeinu* ... The Divine that is present within and among us.
>
> *Avinu Malkeinu* ... We speak this sacred truth aloud.
>
> *Avinu Malkeinu* ... We stand as one, accountable for our sins.
>
> *Avinu Malkeinu* ... We yearn for true compassion—for our children most of all.

Avinu Malkeinu ... May we resist the ravages of illness, fear, and despair.
Avinu Malkeinu ... Let us summon courage to withstand our enemies.
Avinu Malkeinu ... Let the goodness of this gift of life be engraved upon our hearts.
Avinu Malkeinu ... May we taste anew the sweetness of each day.
Avinu Malkeinu ... Let us wake up to the blessings already in our grasp.
Avinu Malkeinu ... However small our deeds, let us see their significance, their power to heal. May our lives be lessons in justice, rich in compassion, safety, and love.

This version is imminent in its theology and non-dualistic in its cosmology—that is, it does not consider God "out there" but rather a part of ourselves and the world. Although many people still resonate to the traditional view of a transcendent God who is wholly "other," we felt it important to offer this alternative approach to acknowledge a theology that has a revered (if rarely acknowledged) place in our liturgical images of the divine.[7]

In addition, we came up with the following remarkably innovatory alternatives.

Avinu Malkeinu: A Prayer of Protest (Rosh Hashanah and Yom Kippur Evenings) [an excerpt]

Avinu Malkeinu—
Hear our voice:
Some of us have cancer.
Some have lost strength of body; some have lost memory and speech.
Some of us are in pain.
Some can't find work.
Some of us bear the marks of human cruelty—inside, where the scars don't show.
Some live with depression; some battle addiction; many feel alone.
Some have known shattered marriages, trust betrayed, hopes destroyed.
Some of us have lost the ones we love, far too soon.
And some have lost a child.
All of us have seen suffering in our midst.
All of us know the ravages of war—for which there are no words.

The purpose of this innovation is to reflect our need not merely to appease, but also to wrestle with God. Many of us enter the Days of Awe with resentments, not just regrets. If we take the parental metaphor of *avinu* seriously, *Avinu Malkeinu* becomes an opportunity to address God as we would a real parent, expressing our disappointments and dismay, not just our thanksgiving and praise.

Avinu Malkeinu: An Opportunity for Reflection (Rosh Hashanah Morning)

Avinu Malkeinu ... We stand in awe; we draw close in love.
Avinu Malkeinu ... The Power that passes through us and pervades all things.
Avinu Malkeinu ... The Divine that is present within and among us.
Avinu Malkeinu ... We speak this sacred truth aloud.
Avinu Malkeinu ... We stand as one, accountable for our sins.
Avinu Malkeinu ... We yearn for true compassion—for our children most of all.
Avinu Malkeinu ... May we resist the ravages of illness, fear, and despair.

Here is an innovation that invites the worshiper to do more than just *recite* a litany of words—whether ancient or contemporary. Instead, we offer the opportunity to reflect on the meaning behind the words. The prayer-book text is presented as a jumping-off point for meditation beyond the literal meaning of the prayer itself. This approach allows the worshiper to slow down the speed of prayer and to "sit," instead, with the spiritual calling of what *Avinu Malkeinu* may mean at a deeper level.

Avinu Malkeinu: **A Call to Action (N'ilah)**

Soul-Sustainer, Source of Our Life
Ezrat Nafsheinu, M'kor Chayeinu,
our Soul-Sustainer, Source of Our Life—
we stand as one before the One.
Each solitary soul, each fragment of the whole:
a congregation of fears, dreams, and hopes;
regret and joy, questions unanswered:
Where is justice?
When will there be peace?
Who can mend our shattered hearts?
Some are starving. Some are dying alone.
Many are suffering, in need of our love.
How far can our hands reach?
Ezrat Nafsheinu, M'kor Chayeinu,
our Soul-Sustainer, Source of Our Life—
the gates of hope are ours to open.
Still the wind of Creation blows,
sweeping over the darkness,
building cosmos out of chaos;
evolving order and complexity;
shining light into the shadows;
wrestling beauty out of brokenness and failure.
Still the wind of Creation blows:
the world is still becoming,

and we are still emerging.
Ezrat Nafsheinu, M'kor Chayeinu,
let healing come—
let it come through deeds of *tz'dakah* and *chesed;*
let it come through us—our hands, our love.

The purpose of this innovation, provided specifically for *N'ilah,* is to prepare the worshiper for leaving the synagogue and beginning a new year of hope and betterment. We don't merely call to God for compassion. We also remind ourselves of our responsibility to be compassionate. And we do so, also, with an alternative strategy of naming. Having enlisted God earlier as the more traditional divine parent and ruler, we now turn to God as our spiritual helper *(ezrat nafsheinu)* and the source of life itself *(m'kor chayeinu).* We depart the synagogue convinced that we are intended for life strengthened from within with God as our spiritual guide.

In sum, our new *machzor* treats *Avinu Malkeinu* as a spiritual opportunity to find balance between consequence and compassion. *Avinu Malkeinu* reflects our responsibilities as well as our fondest hopes. We address God, and God addresses us. We summon God, and God summons us. There is only one God but also only one of each of us: made in God's image, each of us is also *echad v'yachid*, singly made and singular in nature. *Avinu Malkeinu* speaks to God but also to ourselves. There are many ways to sing it, and there are many ways to hear it. Our hope is that through the plurality of experiences, the parallel plurality of messages will come through.

What Is God's Name?

Rabbi David A. Teutsch, PhD

Rabbi David A. Teutsch, PhD, is the Wiener Professor of Contemporary Jewish Civilization and director of the Center for Jewish Ethics at the Reconstructionist Rabbinical College, where he served as president for nearly a decade. He was editor in chief of the seven-volume *Kol Haneshamah* prayer book series. His book *A Guide to Jewish Practice: Everyday Living* won the National Jewish Book Award for Contemporary Jewish Life and Practice. He is also author of *Spiritual Community: The Power to Restore Hope, Commitment and Joy* (Jewish Lights) and several other books. He contributed to *Who by Fire, Who by Water—Un'taneh Tokef*, *All These Vows—Kol Nidre*, *We Have Sinned: Sin and Confession in Judaism—Ashamnu and Al Chet*, *May God Remember: Memory and Memorializing in Judaism—Yizkor*, and *All the World: Universalism, Particularism and the High Holy Days* (all Jewish Lights).

Jewish tradition contains countless different names of God because God surpasses our understanding. The various names (like healer of the sick, bringer of rain, shield of Abraham, and so on) cannot actually encompass the divine, but they can at least describe separate aspects of it.

The multiplicity of names suggests the many aspects of divinity that we encounter, even though they say nothing about God's actual essence. Above all, perhaps, we experience God as the ultimate source of holiness—hence, the name Blessed Holy One *(Hakadosh Barukh Hu)*. But God cannot be grasped except in relationship to ourselves. We humans are not capable of experiencing *anything* (including God) except that way.

That reality is nowhere more obvious than in the Yom Kippur *piyyut Ki Hinei Kachomer* ("Like clay in the hand of the potter"), which describes God through similes that define the relation between God and human beings: potter/clay, carver/stone, blacksmith/ax, sailor/wheel, glazier/glass, draper/cloth, metalsmith/silver. These descriptions of God say nothing about God's essential "self"—which is unknowable—so much as they reflect our understanding of the divine presence as it is revealed in our lives.

Even those of us who do not think God intervenes personally to make individual decisions about us know, in our more lucid moments, how much we depend on factors we cannot control: our DNA, how our parents raised us, where we were born, war and peace, economics, weather conditions, the people with whom we go to school or work, and so on. Of course our conduct too affects what happens to us, but our creatureliness limits the possibilities open to us. Our very survival requires air, food, water, sleep, clothing, and shelter (all of which can be beyond our control), and no matter how competently we take care of ourselves, we still decline in old age—if we even manage to get that far.

The God imagery in *Ki Hinei Kachomer* vividly brings these limits home, but even as it does so, it asks that we think of ourselves on a different plane altogether—not just needy and dependent on accidents of birth (though we are that!) but also mortals who have received the gift of having consciousness of our relationship to "something more," the "something" we call God. We are invited to spend the day of Yom Kippur in contemplation of that higher reality, finding redemption through our covenant with God and our membership in the Jewish people, both of which uplift us, helping us to overcome the almost equally powerful reality of our weakness and transgressions.

Seeing God as potter, carver, blacksmith, sailor, glazier, and metalsmith is a way of understanding our relationship with God, which of course has many more perspectives to it than just those. These images are part of our effort to find our way into a relationship that is rarely easy and continuous; they exemplify our awareness of our dependence on something greater than ourselves and open the way to seeking that presence.

Vivid metaphors are particularly important during the *Yamim Nora'im*, when many of the people who are in the pews are out of practice at praying. The metaphors push us to face how profoundly limited is our control over our own lives. Each paired image of *Ki Hinei Kachomer* (e.g., potter/clay, carver/stone) chips away at our exterior defensive shells with the reality of who we are—a reality that we easily ignore on a day-to-day basis, when routine fills our lives and we become so easily distracted by an array of obligations and electronic devices. Recognizing our vulnerability is an important step toward being fully human; prayer awakens us to that reality, and the imagery of *Ki Hinei Kachomer* is an important step toward accomplishing that awakening.

In an earlier volume in this series,[1] we looked at *Ki Anu Amekha,* a poem that precedes the confessional *Ashamnu.* It too presents us with the sort of vivid imagery that we find in *Ki Hinei Kachomer.* Each of its lines obeys a common pattern setting up the relationship between Israel and God, beginning, "We are your people, and you are our God." The paired images then continue: your children/our parent, your servants/our master, your community/our lot, your possession/our destiny, your flock/our shepherd, your vineyard/our vintner, your work/our creator, your bride/our lover, your prize/our God, your people/our king, and so on. Instead of focusing only on our smallness, fragility, and finitude, these metaphors emphasize the capacity of our relationship with God to provide redemption.

Jewish tradition's metaphors for God thus say more about us than they do about God. This point is driven home in the beloved hymn *Shir Hakavod* ("Song of Glory," also known by its opening words, *Anim Z'mirot*), attributed to Judah the Chasid (1150–1217) of Regensburg.[2] In traditional synagogues, young boys often sing it as part of the conclusion to Shabbat *Musaf*. It comments powerfully on the metaphorical descriptions of God in Jewish tradition:

> I tell your glory, yet never have seen you; imagine you, find names for you, yet never have known you.
> By hand of those who prophesied and throngs who worshipped you, you gave imagination to the glory beyond view.
> God's greatness now unfolding, your might beyond all needs, they found the names for telling of the power of your deeds.
> Denoting you with likenesses, though less than you by far, they simply have equated what you've done with who you are.[3]

Worshipers need metaphors; they are our bridge to God, but they do not portray the divine self. The best way to judge these metaphors is to consider them functionally. Do they open us to aspects of the divine that are helpful? Do they move us in a way that spiritually elevates us? Do they inspire us to do *mitzvot* and live virtuously? These are the questions that should shape our theologies.

When I was growing up, the name for God used most often in both the prayer book and the Bible was "the Lord." As I grew older and started to think about theology more seriously, that name seemed problematic for a steadily increasing number of reasons: God is not a male. "Lord" is a term we have inherited from medieval hierarchies, which do not speak to my contemporary American experience. "Lord" suggests a God who perceives individuals and who acts personally in history—not my understanding of the divine.

The English word "Lord," moreover, has nothing to do with the word it purports to translate, the Hebrew four-letter name of God *YHVH* (the tetragrammaton), which is a form of the verb "to be" that is not supposed to be pronounced except by the high priest on Yom Kippur in the Jerusalem Temple. "The Lord" is just a translation of the Hebrew *Adonai*, which tradition substitutes for this unpronounced four-letter name—a translation chosen by the classical King James Version composed from 1604 to 1611 for Christian churchgoers, who knew what a British lord was and who thought of God as something higher but similar. More modern Bibles have followed suit, not just Christian ones, but the Jewish JPS (Jewish Publication Society) versions of 1917 and 1985 as well. Some contemporary prayer books have substituted

Adonai or *Adonay*—anglicized spellings of the traditional Hebrew word that allow the less knowledgeable to avoid facing the problem with "Lord" but do not solve the fundamental difficulty. In my college days, I noticed that some German Jewish prayer books prefer "the Eternal," a better translation than "the Lord," because "Eternal" addresses the tetragrammaton's connection to the Hebrew verb "to be." In college I started silently substituting "the Eternal" when siddur English was read aloud, which solved several theological difficulties for me.

When I first immersed myself in the study of philosophy and theology, I thought that everything we think about God needs to be systematically linked. As I moved through middle age and became less rigid, I increasingly came to see that our emotional and spiritual states determine the way we see God much more than do our intellectualizations. "Eternal One" continues to appeal to me intellectually, but in prayer, which depends on imagery, poetry, and metaphor, I experienced the repetition of any single name for God (including that one) as limiting and disruptive.

When I later chaired the committee that developed *Kol Haneshamah,* the Reconstructionist prayer-book series, we agreed that our translator, the poet Joel Rosenberg, should translate the four-letter name of God according to context rather than with a single name like "Lord" or "the Eternal." We set these names apart by putting them in HALF-CAPS in the way that many Bibles print "LORD." All these names taken together provide a kaleidoscope of imagery that is evocative rather than descriptive. They are meant to be encountered as poetry rather than as philosophical or political essays. The panoply of names that resulted (Faithful One, Fount of Life, The Creator, Dear One, and Compassionate One, to list but a few) helps us consider the many-sidedness of our relationship with God and the many ways that we can remain true to the Rabbinic ideal of *imitatio Dei,* our responsibility to imitate God.

Of course, none of these names means the same as the tetragrammaton, but collectively they provide a multiplicity of images, much the way that *Shir Hakavod* does.

We suffer from the misconception that the Hebrew word *Adonai* is actually a proper name, like Isaiah or Abraham Lincoln; and the Torah itself suggests that if you know the name, you have the key to the being. (See Genesis 32:25–31, for example, where Jacob wrestles with an angel, demanding its name, and where Jacob's name changes to Israel because he has "wrestled with God.") But God is not like people; with God, no single name will do. The decision by our prayer-book committee to adopt so many names for God was intended to move us beyond a magical focus on any single name.

When we see prayer as a means to awaken us spiritually and emotionally, and for Jews as a way to connect us to the Jewish people and its history and future, we cease to examine the words of prayer to ensure that they are all logically coherent with one another. We encounter the prayer book not as philosophy but in search of unitive experience and moral renewal. No imagery in the prayer book is as important in achieving that overall spiritual end as its God-language.

The stakes are especially high on the *Yamim Nora'im*, when the challenge of using prayer books to support worship is greatest. High Holy Day services are long, and they emphasize imagining God as *melekh* ("king"). The maleness of "king" can be surmounted in English by using a more neutral word like "sovereign"—an approach that can be employed in translating the formula for blessings as well. But the very notion of "king" (whether renamed "sovereign" or not) has less resonance today than it did in premodern times. Constitutional monarchs nowadays (as in England and Scandinavia) enjoy great affection but lack the power that the prayer book invokes when describing God as king.

In particular, it is the hierarchical relationship suggested by "king" that triggers American objections, partly because of the emphasis in American culture on the individual, autonomy, and personal choice. But the image of God as sovereign is helpful precisely for that reason. Our cultural presumptions to the contrary, we are not the fully autonomous beings we imagine. We are subject to moral demands, cultural norms, the constraints of relationships, and the vagaries of life itself. The image of God as sovereign reminds us that we are accountable nonetheless—as the Hebrew National hot dog commercial of my youth put it, "We are responsible to a higher authority."

It is this higher authority that is suggested by *avinu malkeinu*, literally, "our father, our king." I have already dealt with "God as king." What about "God as father"?

While "king" conjures up transcendent *power*, "father" suggests *care*. In our time, however, there are several reasons to be wary about the father metaphor. Some of us have grown up with two mothers at home or with one mother and no father. Then too, some fathers were abusive or largely absent. In addition, the rigid stereotypes of parental roles are increasingly giving way to more egalitarian moms and dads, and we do not wish to support sexist role differentiation.

Kol Haneshamah addresses these issues by translating *avinu malkeinu* as "our creator, our sovereign." But for people who remain painfully aware of the sexism inherent in the original Hebrew, it also provides a Hebrew alternative, *m'koreinu eloheinu*, for which the English is "our source, our God." Critics of these solutions have pointed out that the juiciness of "father" is missing from the alternatives. I believe that is a fair criticism, symbolic of the dangers that come from altering poetry, but I consider the trade-off justified in this case. We make up for it, at least in part, by the vivid imagery of the multiple words for God that appear elsewhere throughout the prayer book.

Even in *Avinu Malkeinu*, however, other images abound. God's "writ[ing] us in the book of life" conjures up a particularly vivid picture, even for those of us who believe that it is we, not God, who do the writing of our fate. Overall, *Avinu Malkeinu* expresses our hopes for the future along with the awareness that the fulfillment of those hopes is partly beyond our control. The placement of *Avinu Malkeinu* after the confessional prayers on Yom Kippur reminds us that the purpose in wiping the slate clean of our past transgressions is to lead a better life in the year to come. The motivation to change is rooted in that hope, so the imagery that accompanies it should be aimed at reinforcing hope.

At its best, the prayer book uses imagery that leads us to accept basic realities about ourselves that we might otherwise choose to ignore, lest they engender fear and doubt. In *Ki Hinei Kachomer*, we struggle with our frailty and dependence on forces beyond ourselves. In *Ki Anu Amekha*, we recognize how the many aspects of the relationship we have with God can give us strength and guidance. The imagery of *Shir Hakavod* celebrates the divine in our lives, even while cautioning that our experience of God yields no knowledge of God's true nature. *Avinu Malkeinu* brings us into touch with the redemptive power of hope and a vision of a better world ahead. All the images of the siddur and *machzor* combined remind us that no matter how vivid the pictures we paint with our words, the silent encounter with the divine goes beyond our capacity to articulate or to frame in rational thought. Prayer is meant to be a salvific moment of encounter that lifts us above our rational limitations.

Changing God's Names

THE LITURGY OF LIBERAL JUDAISM IN GREAT BRITAIN

Rabbi Andrew Goldstein, PhD and Rabbi Charles H. Middleburgh, PhD

Rabbi Andrew Goldstein, PhD, is the president of Liberal Judaism, UK, the rabbinic advisor to the European Union for Progressive Judaism, and coeditor of *Machzor Ruach Chadashah*. He contributed to *Who by Fire, Who by Water—Un'taneh Tokef*, *All These Vows—Kol Nidre*, *We Have Sinned: Sin and Confession in Judaism—Ashamnu and Al Chet*, *May God Remember: Memory and Memorializing in Judaism—Yizkor*, and *All the World: Universalism, Particularism and the High Holy Days* (all Jewish Lights).

Rabbi Charles H. Middleburgh, PhD, is the dean of Leo Baeck College in London, where he has taught since 1984. He is coeditor with Rabbi Andrew Goldstein, PhD, of the Liberal Judaism *Machzor Ruach Chadashah* and the anthologies *High and Holy Days: A Book of Jewish Wisdom* and *A Jewish Book of Comfort*. He contributed to *Who by Fire, Who by Water—Un'taneh Tokef*, *All These Vows—Kol Nidre*, *We Have Sinned: Sin and Confession in Judaism—Ashamnu and Al Chet*, *May*

God Remember: Memory and Memorializing in Judaism—Yizkor, and *All the World: Universalism, Particularism and the High Holy Days* (all Jewish Lights).

    The fundamental Jewish belief is that there is one God who is ineffable and whose personal name is unpronounceable. Yet God is known in Hebrew by many names and titles, reflecting the profundity of ways to connect to God in human experience. Some names, like *hamakom* (literally, "the place"), are impersonal; others, like *ribbon kol ha'olamim* ("master of all worlds"), emphasize God's greatness, while others still, like *harachaman* ("the merciful One"), reflect God's mercy. Alternative names arose as well because of the desire to treat God's actual name, as given in the biblical tetragrammaton, as too sacred to be mentioned. These substitutes (like those we mention above) increased in early post-biblical times, and nowadays, under the influence of traditional Judaism, God is simply referred to as *hashem,* "the name," which is to say, "no name at all." It is as if the sanctity of the tetragrammaton extends also to every other name of God we might use in its place.

    No wonder, then, as we began our mission to edit a new *machzor,* we discovered that our hardest task was to deal with two of the best-known names of God coined during the Second Temple period, *avinu malkeinu*—names that occur particularly prominently because they form the first two words, and title, of a favorite prayer. An even harder problem had preceded us but was solved in the siddur that we inherited (*Siddur Lev Chadash,* on which we had worked closely alongside its editors, Rabbis John D. Rayner and Chaim Stern, *z"l*): how to translate into English the tetragrammaton itself, the four Hebrew letters that are said to be God's actual name.

Tradition says that only the high priest in Temple days or mystics like the Baal Shem Tov ("master of the good name") knew how to pronounce the letters correctly. In its place, it became commonplace to say *Adonai*—literally, "my lords," or, as it is usually rendered, "the Lord." The principal challenge in *Siddur Lev Chadash* had been how to translate *Adonai* in a style that was linguistically satisfactory and genuinely spiritual. Others had struggled with the problem but (we believed) taken the easy way out by just transliterating and saying "Adonai"; others had resorted to *hashem*. Rayner and Stern had opted for "Eternal One" or "Eternal," and we followed the liturgical precedents set by our teachers as we developed our own *Machzor Ruach Chadashah.*

With that decision behind us, we turned to the challenge of rendering the two Hebrew words *avinu malkeinu*. A literal translation, "our father, our king" was clearly incompatible with a non-gender-specific *machzor*.

What, we asked ourselves, is *avinu malkeinu* from a congregant's perspective rather than a liturgist's? Surely it is a mantra, just the rote repetition of *avinu malkeinu,* "our father, our king"—easy to remember and tripping off the tongue, and disproportionately precious as a result.

We deliberated the obvious (and easiest) option of transliterating the words rather than translating them but rejected this possibility. It felt like a soft option, and we were far from convinced that it would satisfy those who wanted to reinterpret this classic phrase in a way that gave it resonance. We discussed replacing *Avinu Malkeinu* altogether with petitionary prayers of similar structure found in other *machzorim,* such as the Sephardic *Eloheinu Shebashamayim*[1] ("Our God in Heaven") or the medieval litany *Rachamana D'anei* ("Compassionate One"). But we concluded ultimately that the line-by-line list of requests, each line beginning *avinu malkeinu,* was so popular with worshipers, so comforting in its imagery, and so embedded in the High Holy Day consciousness that we could neither leave it out nor replace it with a completely different text.

We knew as well that the usages and translations in *Siddur Lev Chadash* were now accepted and familiar: *av* as "divine parent" and *melekh* as "sovereign" occurred regularly, but that was in prayers where the two words, if not utterly incidental, were at least less high profile than with *avinu malkeinu,* where they stand out by virtue of juxtaposition (they appear together), repetition (line after line after line, several times throughout the High Holy Day period), and familiarity over the years (even casual worshipers recognize this prayer). We tried a range of options: "Our parent"? Too politically correct. "Our father and mother"? Too confusing. "Our divine parent?" A bit of a mouthful.

In the end we decided to translate *avinu* as "our creator"—not a literal rendering, but in view of the fact that human fathers are co-creators of life and God is called the creator of all life we felt this worked. We had to admit that "creator" was not a word that implies the warmth, closeness, and comfort that "father" or "mother" conveys, but we were reminded by several colleagues that these terms do not universally evoke love in those whose childhood has been unnaturally hard.

Malkeinu, "our king," presents the opposite image to the close and comforting *avinu,* "our father," in that it evokes a distant figure with ultimate authority over us and our lives, an image wholly appropriate to the theme of the Days of Awe and its liturgy, even though most congregants no longer conceive of God in this way. Rosh Hashanah is said to be based on the ancient Mesopotamian coronation festival, and in any event, all origins aside, our liturgy makes much of the word *melekh,* "king," as do the Rabbis who assembled the liturgy in the first place and then commented on it through the generations.

So central is this image that Rabbinic literature consistently compares God to earthly kings or uses the image of the earthly king *(melekh basar vadam)* to discuss lessons on how human beings should behave. This insistence on royal imagery is curious because the literature in question was composed in eras when actual Jewish kings were a historical memory and when many Jews lived in lands where the king was a tyrant and not particularly kind to their community.

In any event, the image of God as "king" runs deep in Jewish tradition, and we did not want to jettison it. Fortunately, there were easy synonyms for the masculine "king" and the translation of the Hebrew *melekh* had already been tackled in *Siddur Lev Chadash,* where the word comes up in most standard blessings: "God" there is regularly *melekh ha'olam* (literally, "king of the universe"). Instead of "king," "ruler" had been tried but found rather banal, and so "sovereign" became the chosen translation. It was non-gender-specific, it had a certain majesty about it, and for British Jews in a country whose head of state is our Sovereign Lady Queen Elizabeth II, it worked very well.

Having chosen our formula, "Our Creator and Sovereign...," there was the lesser problem of how many verses of *Avinu Malkeinu* to include. *Seder Rav Amram* (our first extant Jewish prayer book, from roughly 860CE) has 25 lines, the various Eastern *minhagim* have 29–31, and

Ashkenazi Rites vary between 38 and 44 (though the prize goes to that of Salonika, with 53). A total of 44 lines makes some sense, as it completes a double Hebrew acrostic (the Hebrew alphabet has 22 letters in it), but curiously none of the rites used an acrostic form for *Avinu Malkeinu*—unlike the other High Holy Day doxology of *Al Chet*, which uses the alphabet to set a limit to the number of sins that might easily be enumerated.

Reviewing the progressive liturgies, we discovered that the American *Union Prayer Book* of 1894 had 9 verses, while a later edition of 1923 had 11, and it was this version that the founding rabbi of Liberal Judaism in Britain, Dr. Israel Mattuck, chose for his *Liberal Jewish Prayer Book*, the movement's first High Holy Day prayer book of 1923. Its replacement in 1973 *(Gates of Repentance,* edited by Rayner and Stern) increased the number to 12. A similar variety of numbers could be seen in contemporary non-Orthodox *machzorim*. How many should we choose?

The British Reform Movement's current *Forms of Prayer* has 20 lines, the Israeli *Kavanat Halev* has 28, and the Reconstructionist *Kol Haneshamah,* 19. There seemed to be no obvious rationale behind these various choices; presumably, editors customarily chose whatever lines they found the most appealing or relevant. This was certainly our *modus operandi* in ending up with 13 verses, with the unintentional added bonus that the number mirrors the thirteen attributes of God (*Adonai, Adonai, el rachum...*) liturgically associated with *Avinu Malkeinu* in the High Holy Day services.

Having settled this key part of the service, we then felt that we should follow the example set by the Israeli Progressive *machzor, Kavanat Halev,* and add an extra litany, similar thematically to *Avinu Malkeinu,* but with imagery that was explicitly feminine, to offset the association most people have (regardless of what translation we use) of *avinu* with "father" and *malkeinu* with "king." We generally inserted this new litany as a supplement to *Avinu Malkeinu,* but on Yom Kippur afternoon, it replaces it altogether. And unlike *Avinu Malkeinu,* which consists of a list of requests from us to God, the feminine substitution provides seven verses that urge us to reconsider our own nature and failings. For example: "*Shechinah Mekor Chayyenu*—Divine Presence, Source of our lives, teach us to use the gentle answer that turns away wrath."

Liturgists learn from and are inspired by the work of their predecessors and contemporaries. We included (for example) in our meditations Ruth Brin's groundbreaking poem of 1959:

> When men were children, they thought of God as a father;
> When men were slaves, they thought of God as a master;
> When men were subjects, they thought of God as a king;

But I am a woman...."[2]

Perhaps the most inventive addition and counterbalance to *Avinu Malkeinu* is in the Conservative *Mahzor Lev Shalem* (2010). It has a series of alternatives to *avinu* and *malkeinu* that follow the same linguistic pattern (a name for God with the first-person plural Hebrew suffix-*einu*) and successfully provide a whole new range of imagery for God: *Boreinu*—our Creator, *Go'aleinu*—our Redeemer, *Vatikeinu*—Ancient One, *Shomreinu*—our Guardian, *Tomcheinu*—our Benefactor.[3]

Machzor Ruach Chadashah was published in 2003, seven years ahead of the Rabbinic Assembly's text, so we missed out on an added incentive for such a radical alternative. But maybe next time.

PART VI
Masculine Imagery; Feminist Critique

So Near and Oh So Far

Rabbi Laura Geller

Rabbi Laura Geller, senior rabbi of Temple Emanuel of Beverly Hills, was one of the first women to be selected to lead a major metropolitan synagogue. She was twice named one of *Newsweek's* 50 Most Influential Rabbis in America and was featured in the PBS documentary *Jewish Americans*. She is the author of many articles in books and journals and was on the editorial board of *The Torah: A Women's Commentary*. She is a fellow of the Corporation of Brown University, from where she graduated in 1971. Ordained by Hebrew Union College – Jewish Institute of Religion in 1976, she was the third woman in the Reform Movement to become a rabbi. She contributed to *All the World: Universalism, Particularism and the High Holy Days* (Jewish Lights).

The very first change I made in the High Holy Day liturgy when I became the senior rabbi of Temple Emanuel in Beverly Hills was in *Avinu Malkeinu*.

My childhood in a classical Reform synagogue with magnificent cathedral ceilings left me with very clear memories of *Avinu Malkeinu* as both terrifying and comforting. It was terrifying, because even as a child I understood its message of fragility and impermanence; I was sure that God the king was somewhere up in those stained-glass windows remembering that I had sinned against Him. But it was also comforting because I was standing next to my parents, and God the father was holding my hand. There was both judgment and unconditional love. There was God far away and God very near.

The refrain from *Avinu Malkeinu* was the one melody the whole congregation sang together in Hebrew: *Avinu malkeinu, choneinu va'aneinu ki ein banu ma'asim; aseih imanu tz'dakah vachesed, aseih imanu tz'dakah vachesed v'hoshi'einu* ("Our father, our king, be gracious to us and answer us, for we have no merit; act justly and lovingly with us and save us"; line 44). Although I was probably too young to fully understand, I could tell by the tears of some of the congregants that something important was going on. The underlying message, "Even though we are not worthy, be good to us," came through in the music.

At the very same time, I knew, of course, that God was not my "real" father, but since I intuited that there was something in the way my father loved me that taught me something about God, then I suspected I could learn something about God from the way my mother loved me as well. (And I thought, also, that maybe I was supposed to learn something about how to love God by how I loved both of my parents.) But I was left wondering, since nobody ever talked about any of this back then.

So the very first change I made in Temple Emanuel's liturgy was to substitute the Hebrew phrase *avinu malkeinu* for the English "our father, our king," an option that appeared in the first edition of *Gates of Repentance,* the Reform *machzor* that most congregants still use.[1]

At Temple Emanuel, we chant together, "*Avinu malkeinu,* hear our prayer; *avinu malkeinu,* keep far from us pestilence, war, and famine," and so on, through the prayer; until the final refrain that we sing together in Hebrew—a small change, perhaps, but, especially for those who still have (or still remember) the words "our father, our king" in their prayer books, the substitution reminds us that how we speak toward God is important.

Dr. Rabbi Rachel Adler taught me that God wants the truth, a lesson she finds in the Talmudic story that asks how it is possible that Jeremiah and David abolished God-language established by Moses. Rabbi Eliezer explains, "Since they know the Holy One is truthful, they would not lie to God."[2]

But it is hard to speak the truth about God in the language of a tradition that pictures God so differently from the truths I know. The God of Jewish liturgy is a transcendent "other" who judges, rewards, punishes, and forgives. The God to whom I want to speak is the self of the universe, of which my self is a part. The truth I aspire to is that everything is connected and that

I, therefore, am called to respond to others with compassion.

The images in our prayer books actually get in my way.

Over the years, in my own private prayer life, I have experimented with different names of God. Most powerful has been the name Moses hears at the burning bush: *ehyeh asher ehyeh*, "I will be what I will be" or "I am what I will be" or "I will be what I am"—from which we seem to get the four-letter name of God, *YHVH*, which might be interpreted as the present tense of the verb "to be." So another name for God is simply "Is"; or, maybe, "Is-ness." I am moved by what I learned from Rabbi Arthur Waskow: that the name *YHVH* is unpronounceable not because we are *forbidden* to pronounce it, but because trying to pronounce these aspirated consonants without any vowels is simply to breathe.

Paying attention to my breathing as a way of connecting to God has become the core of my spiritual practice. The Rabbinic tradition that one should say a hundred blessings daily is a reminder that I should pause multiple times each day to appreciate the fact that each and every breath links me to the divinity that connects me to everything. *Kol han'shamah t'hallel yah*, "Every breath praises *yah*." So, again, learning from Rabbi Waskow, I translate the blessing formula before a *mitzvah*: "Holy One of Blessing, whose presence fills creation, who makes us holy through connections and connects us to each other and to You through [fill in the blanks]."

While this "works" for me in private prayer and meditation, it is problematic when I pray in community, especially when it is a community that comes together for the High Holy Days but not very often otherwise. The High Holy Days are the most formal of our services and one where worshipers are most resistant to taking risks. Even Reform Jews become very "conservative" when it comes to changing High Holy Day liturgy.

But we are in a very different place from where we were almost forty years ago when I became a rabbi. The early feminist critique of the mid-1970s argued that exclusive male language for God reinforces patriarchal domination, a groundbreaking view that led two Brown University students, Naomi Janowitz and Margaret Wenig, in 1979, to create a feminist English-language *siddur*—the first one, actually—that referred to God using only female imagery and pronouns.

Later feminist thinkers like Judith Plaskow, Marcia Falk, and Rachel Adler refined the conversation, asking other questions: about transcendence and immanence, prayer as metaphor, and the challenges of altering the Hebrew and presenting innovative English interpretations of prayers. New and recovered names for God began appearing—first in independently produced prayers books from synagogues and *minyanim,* and then in movement prayer books like the Reconstructionist *Kol Haneshamah* (1989). Some of these siddurim employed feminine imagery from traditional Hebrew sources, like *Shekhinah* and even *av harachamim,* reinterpreted not as the literal "father of mercy" but "source of motherly love," from the root *rechem* ("womb"). Others chose gender-neutral terms like *hamakom* ("the place"), *tzur yisrael* ("rock of Israel"), *m'kor hab'rakhah* ("source of blessing"), or *m'kor hachayim* ("source of life"). All of these names add to my vocabulary in speaking toward God.

The most radical innovation has been the work of Marcia Falk, a poet and liturgist, who offered an altogether new take on the daily, Shabbat, and Rosh Chodesh liturgy (1996) and more recently (2014) on the High Holy Day liturgy as well. Her reworking of the traditional blessing formula from *Barukh atah Adonai* ("Blessed are You, Adonai") to *N'varekh et m'kor hachayim* ("Let us bless the source of life") radically changes the dynamic of prayer. The traditional formula suggests that prayer is a case of reaching out to a God who is *atah* ("You")—totally "other" from ourselves; God is a separately existing source of blessing that we merely acknowledge, in the hope of being the grateful recipients of whatever God chooses to give us. Falk's alternative version casts ourselves as initiators of blessing and finds God as immanent, within and among us, rather than as transcendent, beyond us. Her imagery also offers an alternative way to look at the problematic images of kingship and judgment.

A new Reform *machzor* will soon be published. In so many ways it reflects the changes that have transformed Jewish prayer from the days when I believed that God was in those far-off stained-glass synagogue windows. On one side of the page is the Hebrew, the full transliteration, and an English translation that speaks of a God who transcends gender, who is both mother and father, our very source of life. On the facing page are poetry and texts that open whole windows onto alternative ways to image God.

The children of my congregation who will grow up with this new prayer book will never have memories of God as father and king. Instead, they will know that although God is one, we must speak of God in many ways; and that even when God seems very far away, the true love of both their fathers and their mothers teaches them something about the way God loves them and is so very near.

Our Rock, Our Hard Place

Catherine Madsen

Catherine Madsen is the author of *The Bones Reassemble: Reconstituting Liturgical Speech; In Medias Res: Liturgy for the Estranged;* and a novel, *A Portable Egypt.* She is librettist for Robert Stern's oratorio "Shofar" (on the CD *Awakenings,* Navona Records NV5878) and bibliographer at the Yiddish Book Center. She contributed to *Who by Fire, Who by Water*—Un'taneh Tokef, *All These Vows*—Kol Nidre, *We Have Sinned: Sin and Confession in Judaism*—Ashamnu and Al Chet, *May God Remember: Memory and Memorializing in Judaism*—Yizkor, and *All the World: Universalism, Particularism and the High Holy Days* (all Jewish Lights).

On the High Holy Days we name in metaphor what we are forbidden to name—or incapable of naming—outright. No metaphor for God can satisfy all of the people all of the time; its subject is too elusive and too complex. A metaphor is a form of audacity, a glimpse into an ultimate privacy. The Rabbis, who seldom openly admired audacity, hedged the Torah's anthropomorphisms with the disclaimer *kiv'yakhol,* "so to speak," lest anyone suppose God really had a physical mighty hand and outstretched arm. In Yiddish the expression evolved into *kavyokhl,* and can be used as noun, in place of God's name like *hashem:* you can say "hot kavyokhl gezogt" for "God said." Thus a word meant to signal "this is a metaphor" acquires almost an edge of irony—as if God himself were a figure of speech.

The pleading metaphors of the traditional *Avinu Malkeinu* take God as utterly real, and trust that our prayers can move him. The prayer is an effort to comprehend the relation between our deeds and their consequences, to make moral sense of our lives. But if our lives could actually make moral sense we wouldn't need liturgical efforts. Even while pleading we know that cause and effect isn't a rational process, that the wicked may prosper and the good may suffer, that meaning can be wiped from our lives slowly or all at once. We know prayer isn't a quid-pro-quo proposition or even a wager: it's a cry into a realm altogether hidden from us, and disappears in its distances. Behind the pleading metaphors, the knowledge remains that we don't really know how mercy and forgiveness and deliverance work, that if God hears prayer he has no obligation to answer it, that religion has no reproducible results.

In the late 1980s or early '90s, several revisions of *Avinu Malkeinu* began circulating, aimed at gender-balancing the traditional language and reworking the metaphors for current sensibilities. Did they take God as utterly real?

It was hard to be sure. Invariably they used positive, benign metaphors; invariably, even in addressing serious matters, they avoided strong emotions like anguish and doubt. Their audacity was political and theological, not existential; they were trying to fix something, not to comprehend something. This was around the time of my conversion, a years-long effort that had filled me with anguish and doubt; I believed in, and had written, new liturgical language, but starting from a lonelier and more uncertain place. I could accept the traditional *Avinu Malkeinu* as a distilled shot of the moral longing of ages, but I could not accept the new versions as anything but a tepid brew of nice thoughts. If my life was going to make moral sense it would not be through substitutes like these.

It's a slippery slope, revising a prayer: one audacity calls forth another. Present your own metaphors, all fresh-sprung and still damp from the intellectual womb, and you authorize—or provoke—all sorts of upstart metaphors besides your own, some of them from people who do not share your aims. I was not sure whether God was utterly real, but I knew liturgy was. I tinkered for a few months and produced my own version, more or less as a protest:

> Our father, our king, we resent fathers and kings.
> Our mother, our teacher, we resist mothers and teachers.

Our eclipse, our no-one, renew for us a good year.
Our figment, our construct, hear us, pity us, and spare us.
Our guess, our denial, seal us in the book of pardon.
Our hope, our dismay, speed our liberation.
Our doubt, our division, temper us to your need.
Avinu malkeinu, for your sake if not for ours.
Our limit, our secret, remember us till we live.
Our rock, our redeemer, give us endurance in pain.
Our place, our midst, root us in the cracks of your being.
Our breath, our life, evade all our theologies.
Our midwife, our surgeon, bring out of us what is in us.
Our infant, our patient, demand from us till we provide.
Our lover, our consoler, lie down beside us in loneliness.
Our enemy, our catastrophe, goad us to act justly.
Our mugger, our rapist, shatter our lives with your claims.

Our maker, our destroyer, build us again
from the ground up, carefully.

Whatever this may be worth as liturgy—certainly it differs violently from both the original prayer and the updated versions—it does attempt to think about God from the full range of our ambivalence. If, as *(l'havdil)* George Herbert suggests, prayer is "the souls bloud," it may be coursing joyfully through the soul's arteries or leaping from a wound; it may be pulsing tranquilly or swarming with deadly infection. We need language for all these chances. Not more acceptable metaphors but more accurate metaphors; not metaphors without danger but metaphors without evasion. (I don't apologize, by the way, for "rapist": it was suggested by Jeremiah 20:7, translated by no less an authority than A.J. Heschel as "O Lord, Thou hast seduced me, and I am seduced; Thou hast raped me and I am overcome." It isn't meant to be tolerable.) Metaphor that is carefully vetted for painful associations and sharp edges will never prepare us for—or heal us of—real life.

Public prayer generally shuns ambivalence. The Psalms sometimes come close with their sharp juxtapositions of agony and praise, but the material surrounding them in the liturgy seems designed to muffle our private ambivalences and wrap us in a collective sense of trust. For the contemporary sensibility, the metaphor "father" self-evidently undercuts that trust. How can we pray trustingly to a God who may be bad-tempered, commit sudden violence, have inexplicable moral lapses, or disappear altogether—whose love may seem, or be, entirely conditional? The possibility of female God-language was raised to solve that problem. But are we really less ambivalent about mothers? Ask any woman who has one. Unconditional love can be a burden; it can also be profoundly conditional without ever admitting it, always threatening to withdraw itself if you cross some invisible emotional line. The intimate, immanent, gender-balanced God may not renounce power and domination at all, she may just approach it differently: "You're wearing *that*? You should eat a healthier breakfast. Don't say I didn't warn you. You never call." Still the superego, still the moral arbiter, still never entirely on our side. Can any parental metaphor suggest a God we don't have to be wary of?

About kings we're not really ambivalent; give us any stilted and multisyllabic euphemism to avoid the discredited K-word, "sovereign" having been exhumed as the current favorite. But consider what kingship is to people who live with it. There's the king of Denmark, the king of Belgium, "the Royals" of Britain; not all kings are George III or Henry VIII. As a citizen (or a subject), you recognize your rulers and know them, perhaps not up close but not at an uncrossable distance. You think of them with a certain proprietary affection; they are human-scaled, with personalities attached. "Théoden King, Théoden King! Farewell! As a father you were to me, for a little while," says Merry in *The Lord of the Rings,* and he means a good father. Of course the king's personality may be dangerous, or dangerously detached—he may be exacting, ill-tempered, or bellicose, he may simply have too much power. Yet King David, whose reign decidedly had its low points and who was not a good father, nevertheless holds a place in the Jewish heart. The picture is complicated; there is something in the office itself, for all its anachronism in the global corporate culture, that invites a kind of tenderness along with the awe and caution. And longing: we want someone with power and resources to think of our well-being. We may even want (whisper it!) someone to rule us: someone to govern our scattered energies for a high purpose, someone to belong to. Can we get that from a faceless government initiative, however well-designed and benevolent, or from the perilous euphoria of following a charismatic leader? *Hamelekh*—the exacting, ill-tempered, bellicose God of the Torah, to whom the Jews have been trustingly praying for centuries—is a king we can argue with; perhaps he offers the best of both the anarchic and the monarchical worlds. Perhaps we don't have to trust him full-time.

Given the historical uses of God as a bludgeon in the hands of religious officials, colonial powers, angry parents, and other threatening authorities, we are not entirely wrong to mistrust metaphors of power and domination. We even mistrust metaphors of consolation and hope, when they seem intended to pacify us. But just as we cannot survive without consolation and hope, we cannot eliminate power and domination from our experience. We are "dominated" every day of our lives by circumstances and people beyond our control, from people above us like our employers and our political leaders and our enemies, to people who depend on us like our customers and our students and our children. To omit power relations from our definition of God—even a liberating God who wields, *kiv'yakhol,* a mighty hand and an outstretched arm—is mere wishful thinking. Even to omit power and domination from our definition of ourselves is psychologically and spiritually crippling. For years I had an aversion to power relations so extreme that I shied away from private music lessons until humbled by my own incompetence, avoided jobs where I would have to supervise anyone, found the thought of raising children a horror, could not imagine my way to a profession that would help me achieve my heart's desire. The atmosphere of the '60s counterculture offered a woozy rationale for this abdication, as a renunciation of privilege and an embrace of nonviolence, but it only worked until you wanted to do something definite. Which metaphors can help us to determination and self-discipline and purpose—in spite of, maybe even with the help of, ambivalence?

Rock. I like geology: the solid residues of liquid fire, the fossil record of ages of ages, the bones of the earth. Lava, obsidian, tuff, shale, slate, sandstone, granite; agate, peridot, jade, garnet, carnelian; olivine, graphite, marble, serpentine, soapstone. Tectonic plates; faults, earthquakes, volcanoes, glaciers, geysers; caves, moraines, pingos, sinkholes, cirques. Rocks don't care about us; they have no gender; prayer does not move them. To use the word "rock" of God is to suggest more than firmness, density, permanence; it invokes that vast and indifferent realm where the inanimate is in charge, where theological debates are mere puffs of vapor, where our physical and moral ineptitudes are not forgiven or cured but are not very big. Why do we have metaphors for God at all? Because we come up against the hard surfaces of the world; because we are clay in the hands of the potter, who thickens or thins it at will. Maybe we are insects trapped in the clay, our sins fleeting as the lives of mayflies, ubiquitous and messy and then suddenly gone. If, *kavyokhl* forbid, we take the whole ecosystem with us, the rocks will remain and grow another.

What will become of God when we're no longer here to devise metaphors for him? If there are no ears to hear—O Israel—will he still make a sound? God was and is and is to be, says *Adon*

Olam; do the rocks know that in their structure? And is God *Adon Olam,* who may be impervious to our implorings, or *Avinu Malkeinu,* who may respond to them? We are not equipped to tell. All we can do is grant the simultaneous validity of contradictory metaphors, and send our prayers beyond them into the distance.

What's in a Word?

OR, HOW WE READ AND HEAR OUR PRAYERS

Ruth Messinger

Ruth Messinger is the president of American Jewish World Service (AJWS). She contributed to *Who by Fire, Who by Water—Un'taneh Tokef, All These Vows—Kol Nidre, We Have Sinned: Sin and Confession in Judaism—Ashamnu and Al Chet,* and *All the World: Universalism, Particularism and the High Holy Days* (all Jewish Lights).

This is very much a personal essay. Both of this volume's prayers *(Avinu Malkeinu* and *Ki Hinei Kachomer)* resonated strongly for me throughout my child- and young adulthood, because of the imagery evoked by their English translation—and because my perspective on that imagery has changed over time. I am one of the large and growing number of Jews who attend High Holy Day worship but know almost no Hebrew—so must either mouth the ancient words that we remember from years past or read the English and let our minds take us where that leads. Those who prepare our prayer books or conduct worship from them should, I think, attend to personal reflections like this one.

Avinu Malkeinu is the best example for me because I can recall how I read it, heard it, and understood it at various points in my life. Originally it was very reassuring in the way, perhaps, that its authors intended it to be. There I was, a young woman, being promised an all-powerful God who was father and sovereign; who was master over his and my whole universe; who, if He received enough prayers, would tend to the problems of the world at least as they affected me; who would use his astonishing power in the world to protect me. It felt reassuring, and it made the regular recitations and repetitions of the prayer seem somehow worth it. Already then (and still today) I was most moved by the Yom Kippur switch from "inscribe us" to "seal us," especially at *N'ilah*, when it became especially urgent to pray that much harder because it was all really being decided then and there, and heartfelt prayer was the way to bargain for another year of life and good fortune.

And then there were the many years of adulthood, not entirely lost even now, where I bristled at the overwhelming masculine imagery of the religion, of the prayers in general, and of this prayer in particular. How dare they, whoever "they" were, insist on imagery with the clear and patent message that whoever I might be praying to was definitely a man. Women, it followed, could "be" and "do" but only up to a point. Only men—fathers, kings, and a father/king God who looked like them—could actually change the world, protect individuals, and create a better future for us all.

If I wanted to be part of a better world; if I wanted to have a God who would forgive, pardon, care, and act for good; if I wanted to be sure that I would be among those treated favorably; if I wanted, especially, to be sure I was sealed for the year, then I needed in my prayers to invite a male—not just any male but an all-powerful one—to do these things for me and for my people. It grated, and it took me time to get beyond it. I have done that, partly by making occasional suggestions in informal settings, when the name of God is invoked, that "She" will take care of it; it may seem silly to some, but I see the practice in all its seriousness: I was attempting to construct an alternative mental image without which I would be unable to engage in the regular recitations of the prayer.

It is perhaps [hah!] a sign of some maturity that I am largely beyond this second stage and much more focused now on the things we are asking God to do—whoever God is or is not—and, most importantly, on recognizing that as I understand Judaism, the real question is what I am doing as God's partner to rid the world of oppressors, to create health for more people, to make myself someone who can hope to be renewed. I am, in other words, able, largely, to get beyond the gender issue but also beyond the notion that we are praying only because every aspect of our being and our fate is determined somewhere outside of ourselves. I am focused on what I consider the essence of *Avinu Malkeinu*: an attempt to lay out all we want for a more perfect world to come about, including another immediate year of a good life for all. Its very repetition encourages us to use our prayer time to muse on these desires and ask some force in the world *and ourselves* to make them come true.

And yet, and yet, the other prayer, *Ki Hinei Kachomer,* has always resonated differently. One might not imagine this to be the case. After all, it has the same element of divine powerfulness. Shaped by God the way an inert element is hammered into being by an artist, we are as nothing; we don't count, really, since God makes us as He or She would have us be.

But this is an example of the power of different words to create different and somehow more engaging images. The notion of God as a craftsperson, as someone taking time and care to mold us, choosing to keep us in his or her hands so that we emerge better for the experience, evoked a different and more positive image within me. I was moved by the sense of being held, of being worthy of careful attention from the divine. I appreciated the way different specific attributes of this divine person were identified, because I could resonate to the possibilities of God—and of me—being at different times gracious, stern, healing, and forgiving. I liked the insistence with which we were charging God to do the best possible job upon us, rather than summarily toss us aside and leave us as unworthy.

And I know that I gravitated differently to this particular prayer because the first few times I heard it in English—in a synagogue near Boston that I attended on the High Holy Days when I was in college—it was read by a cantor in a deep voice, with a British accent, and in a cadence slow enough to allow the images to form, as he more or less instructed God to listen and respond. I resonated to the notion that I might be nothing more than clay or cloth without a body or soul, were it not for God who was crafting these materials into something more profound that would be "me."

To this day, I am struck by the power of words, melody, and presentation to engage us, to bring us to a place where we are open to thinking about who the divine is and who we ourselves are in relationship to that presence. Even as I write this essay, I am reminded of how much we need to hold different images of ourselves and of God, and how the right images can help us emerge from prayer empowered to act in such a way as to be worthy of whatever the divine craftsperson intended us to be.

Rescuing the Father-God from Delray Beach

Rabbi Jeffrey K. Salkin, DMin

Rabbi Jeffrey K. Salkin, DMin, is a noted author whose work has appeared in many publications, including the *Wall Street Journal, Reader's Digest,* and the *Forward*. He is editor of *The Modern Men's Torah Commentary: New Insights from Jewish Men on the 54 Weekly Torah Portions* and *Text Messages: A Torah Commentary for Teens;* and author of *Being God's Partner: How to Find the Hidden Link Between Spirituality and Your Work,* the bestseller *Putting God on the Guest List: How to Reclaim the Spiritual Meaning of Your Child's Bar or Bat Mitzvah,* and *Righteous Gentiles in the Hebrew Bible: Ancient Role Models for Sacred Relationships* (all Jewish Lights), among other books. He contributed to *We Have Sinned: Sin and Confession in Judaism—Ashamnu and Al Chet* and *All the World: Universalism, Particularism and the High Holy Days* (both Jewish Lights).

One of my longtime congregants approached me during the Yom Kippur breakfast. After telling me that he enjoyed the services for the Days of Awe, he went on to say that he had just one small question.

"Why is it that we don't translate *avinu malkeinu* as 'our father, our king' like it says in the prayer book? What's so wrong with calling God 'father' or 'king'?"

The overtly male metaphors for God seem constraining, I explained to him, as well as somewhat outmoded.

To which he replied, "My dad died twenty years ago, and I still miss him. Something to think about." He returned to the rugelach.

So I thought about it: maybe the "father-God" is not as bad as we once thought.

I know, I know: God is beyond our power to imagine. The Shabbat hymn *Anim Z'mirot* admits that God is beyond all allegories and pictures but bombards the worshiper with a cloud of God-metaphor anyway.

Let us assume that many people want some kind of prayerful relationship with God. We need a metaphor for that relationship, and when we go through the catalog of possibilities, the parental relationship stands out as the Holy of Holies—which is probably why the Fifth Commandment, to honor your parents, is the Ten Commandments' "swing vote" that links the God-centered utterances to the human-centered ones.

Rabbi Richard Levy once asked, "How would you like your mother to be? How would you like your father to be?" His answer gives one pause: "Your parents have the potential to be that way, but God is that way now. The kind of parent-love you want ... it's there in God."[1]

That being said, there is no such thing as a "generic" parent. When your daughter stubs her toe, she does not run into the house yelling, "Parent! Parent!" We have reclaimed the *Shekhinah*, thus redeeming the maternal presence of God. So, if we can have *Shekhinah*, what's wrong with *abba*?

But what kind of *abba* can God be?

I suggest that if we look into our own parenting, we will discover the answer. Our toddler takes her first steps. She stumbles. Of course, we want to catch her. But not always, and not forever. So, too, God watches humanity mature and exercises increasing self-restraint from intervening.

To paraphrase Oscar Wilde: when we are young we idealize our parents; when we are adolescents we judge them; when we are older we understand them. In ancient times, when we were young, we Jews idealized the God who intervened in history to keep us from falling. In our Jewish adolescence (from the destruction of the Temple in 70CE to the Shoah), we judged the God who no longer reached out to save us from falls. Now that we are older, perhaps we "understand" God better as a God who (like our human parents) is not all-powerful and who needs us as much as we need God.

So what kind of "father" is this God of our more mature understanding?

God Is a Nurturing Father

The Jews are, like Moses, an adopted people:
> He found him in a desert region, in an empty howling waste.... Like an eagle who rouses his nestlings, gliding down to his young, so did He spread his wings and take him.... He fed him honey from the crag, and oil from the flinty rock." (Deuteronomy 32:10–13)

Or, consider this midrash:

> When did the Holy One Blessed be He make the population of Israelites grow so dramatically in Egypt? Exactly how did this happen?
>
> When Pharaoh decreed, "Every male child shall be thrown into the Nile," what did the Israelite women do? When a woman sensed the onset of labor, she went into the field to have the child. Once the child was born, the mother would look to heaven and say, "I have done my part, just as You told me, 'Be fruitful and multiply.' Now You do *your* part!"
>
> And what did the Egyptians do? When the Egyptians saw the Israelite women going into the fields to have their children, they sat opposite them at a distance. When the women finished delivering their children and returned to the city, the Egyptians took stones and went to kill the babies. The

babies would be swallowed up in the field, and then reappear at a distance, and again be swallowed up, and again reappear at a distance. The Egyptians finally wearied of this and left.

And how did the babies survive out in the fields?

Some say that the angels took care of the Israelite children. But others disagree. Rabbi Chiyya the Great said: God Himself washed and clothed the children. He fed them and cleansed them. And the babies continued to grow in the field like the plants. They would sneak back into their houses by mixing in with the flocks of sheep....

But how did they know to go to their own parents?

The Holy One Blessed be He went with them and showed each one his parents' house, saying, "Call your father by this name, and your mother by that one." The child would ask the mother, "Don't you remember bearing me in a certain field on a certain day five months ago?" The mother would respond, "Who raised you?" And the child would answer, "A certain young man, with nice curly hair—there is no one like him—but he is standing right outside the door."

They would look for him, but could not find him.

But when they arrived at the Red Sea, they saw Him.

The children pointed Him out to their mothers, saying, "This is my God. This is the One who raised me in the fields."[2]

God Is a Father with Emotions and Vulnerabilities

God is like Shakespeare's King Lear—the "original" *avinu malkeinu,* the simultaneous father-king, who watches his three daughters (Judaism, Christianity, and Islam?) fight, who would divide his kingdom for them, and who ultimately and tragically winds up alone.[3] God is Lear with a hitch—God does not wind up alone. But this does not stop us from sorrowing with God and feeling a sense of what Heschel would call divine empathy, especially for the God who suffers along with his people as they go into exile.

Again, the midrash is decisive.

"In that instant, the angel Metatron came, bowed low, and spoke up before the Holy One: 'Master of the universe, let me weep, not You.' God replied, 'If you don't let Me weep, I will go someplace where you cannot go and weep there.'"[4]

God Is a Nonauthoritarian Father

In the oft-quoted "oven of Akhnai" passage in the Talmud, the Sages argue with a *bat kol,* a voice from God, over an arcane question of law, and the Sages are proved right. "What did the Holy One do in that moment?" The Talmud asks. "God laughed with joy, saying, 'My sons have defeated Me, my sons have defeated Me.'"[5] It is like the parent who loves being beaten in chess or in football by his child—or who loves it when her child comes back with a witty retort.

There is far more to the religious imagination than we know. When we access the full imagery of that imagination, we become better, richer, and deeper. Henry Slonimsky once wrote, "God is primarily and preeminently a great heart, caring most for what seems to be important and sacred to us, namely, our loves and aspirations and sufferings."

I long for the day when there is a truly gender-neutral way of talking about—and to—that great heart, without having to trip over our tongues in doing so. But until that day comes, I wind up thinking about what I would lose if God the father were to suddenly move to a retirement home in some cosmic Delray Beach and not return my calls.

I Do Not Know Your Name

Rabbi Sandy Eisenberg Sasso, DMin

Rabbi Sandy Eisenberg Sasso, DMin, is rabbi emerita of Congregation Beth-El Zedeck in Indianapolis, where she has served for thirty-six years, and director of the Religion, Spirituality, and Arts Initiative at Butler University in partnership with Christian Theological Seminary. She is the author of award-winning children's books, including *God's Paintbrush, In God's Name,* and *Shema in the Mezuzah: Listening to Each Other,* winner of the National Jewish Book Award (both Jewish Lights); *Creation's First Light,* a finalist for the National Jewish Book Award; and *Anne Frank and the Remembering Tree.* She is also author of *Midrash: Reading the Bible with Question Marks* and coauthor of *Jewish Stories of Love and Marriage: Folktales, Legends, and Letters.* She contributed to *Who by Fire, Who by Water—Un'taneh Tokef, All These Vows—Kol Nidre, May God Remember: Memory and Memorializing in Judaism—Yizkor,* and *All the World: Universalism, Particularism and the High Holy Days* (all Jewish Lights).

God said to Moses, "I will send you to Pharaoh that you may bring my people out of Egypt." ... And Moses said to God, "I do not know your name. When I come to the children of Israel, and say to them, 'The God of your fathers has sent me to you,' and they shall say to me, 'What is his name?' what shall I say to them?" And God answered, "*Ehyeh asher ehyeh*—I am that I am, I will be what I will be.... This is my name forever." (Exodus 3:10–15)

What? Just one name forever? There are seventy-two names for God in Jewish tradition! Still, during the High Holy Days we say over and over again, *avinu malkeinu,* "our father, our king."

That is how my ancestors knew You: they called You *avinu malkeinu,* but I do not know your name! What are You to me; what can I call God?

In Psalm 29:4 we read, "The voice of Adonai is in strength." The Rabbis suggest that the voice of God is in the strength and capacity of each individual—the youth, the elderly, and the children. The divine voice sounds differently depending on your age and experiences. Therefore the Holy One said, "Do not be misled because you hear many voices. Know that I am one and the same: I am Adonai your God."[1]

When the people of Israel journeyed in the desert, their sustenance consisted of manna. According to the Rabbis, the taste of the manna depended on the needs of those who consumed it. For the infants manna tasted like mother's milk, for the young it tasted like rich bread, and for the old it had the taste of a wafer made with honey.[2]

What was true of manna is also true of God's voice, word, and name.

When Moses came to the bush that burned but was not consumed, the Rabbis suggest the voice that he heard telling him to go to Egypt to free his people was that of his father. God spoke in a way that Moses could understand: a parent's loving voice that calls a child to his responsibility.

The High Holy Days is a time once again to listen to that voice. What does it sound like as it echoes in our own souls? Is it the voice of father, mother, healer, redeemer? What do we require for the coming year—comforter, peacemaker, friend, a still small voice?

What would it mean to invite people to find the name for God that speaks to them, the voice they need to hear, that comes from their own experience?

One woman told me what God had become for her. "I want to name God 'an old warm bathrobe.'" I had heard many names for God, but never that one. One year later the same woman came to see me. "I want to thank you," she said.

"For what?" I wondered.

She responded, "For the opportunity to name God. My mother died this past year, and I took her old warm bathrobe and wrapped it around me, and I felt the presence of God."

I do not know your name, but I think You must wrap around us like an old warm bathrobe.

A young intelligence officer had recently returned home from a tour of duty in Iraq. He didn't talk much about the war. He was tired and glad to be home. He called me: "Do you remember when we were in class years ago and you asked us what our name for God was? I did not know then, but I know now. I want to call God, 'my trampoline.' It is what allows me to bounce back after falling down."

I do not know your name, but I think You must feel like a young man flying.

I asked children at one Yom Kippur family service what was their favorite name for God. A five-year-old boy, one of a set of triplets, stood up in the large sanctuary and said, "I want to call God, 'healer.'" His mother was dying of breast cancer. On Yom Kippur some twenty years later, I told my congregation how that story had changed me, taught me something about prayer and faith I had not known.

After services, that boy, now a young man studying astrophysics in college, came to greet me. I asked, "Did you recognize yourself in my sermon?" He said, "Yes, that little boy who called God 'healer,' that was me." I said, "I will never forget that name or that moment." He looked at me and said, "Neither will I."

I do not know your name, but I think You must sound like that little boy praying.

Looking at a picture book with his father at bedtime, my six-year-old grandson asked, "Dad, where is God?"

"Where do you think God is?" my son replied.

"I think, maybe, maybe there She is," he answered, pointing to a picture in one of his books.

"That's God?" my son asked, surprised.

"I think, maybe," my grandson replied.

"And what do you think God's name is?" my son inquired.

Sitting on my son's lap, he said, "I think God's name is 'between.'"

I do not know Your name but I think You must be somewhere between a son and his dad.

For generations it has mostly been adult males who have given us our names for God. When leaders were kings and fathers, the primary authorities, *avinu malkeinu* spoke to the heart of the worshiping community. But as long as the ultimate was known only through masculine metaphors, something was missing; our understanding of the sacred was impoverished. If men *and* women are created in the image of God, then we must all see ourselves reflected in that image.

Abraham's God was *magen Avraham,* "the shield of Abraham," the one who protected him on his way to a new land. Isaac's God was called *pachad Yitzchak,* "the awe of Isaac," a name that reflected the fear he knew bound to the altar as his father held a knife above his throat. Jacob's God was *avir Ya'akov*, "the power of Jacob." God was the Mighty One who protected Jacob on his journey from his brother's wrath and back home again.

We know of one biblical woman's name for God. Hagar calls God *el ro'i*, "the One who sees me." Alone with Ishmael in the desert, God helps her see the well that is before her so that she might quench her son's thirst.

There are ways in which our journeys, our fears, and our hopes help us to name God as our ancestors did. But there are also ways in which our paths, our difficulties, and our visions move us to speak new names for God. We are reminded that God is called *ehyeh asher ehyeh*, "I will be what I will be; I will become what I will become." Every time a new year beckons, we search the darkest places to discover a small light, what the divine has become for us.

We include those names that men, women, and children have spoken from the depths of their souls: father, king, warm bathrobe, trampoline, healer, between, mother, friend. No name is better than another; all the names for God are good. They are all partial reflections of the One who has many names and none.

And God said, "Do not be confused if you hear many voices, know that I am one and the same. I will be what I will be. I will become what I will become. This is my name forever."[3]

PART VII
What's in a Name?

Abracadabra

THE MAGIC OF NAMING

Rabbi Bradley Shavit Artson, DHL

Rabbi Bradley Shavit Artson, DHL, holds the Abner and Roslyn Goldstine Dean's Chair of the Ziegler School of Rabbinic Studies and is vice president of American Jewish University in Los Angeles. He is a member of the philosophy department, supervises the Miller Introduction to Judaism Program, and mentors Camp Ramah in California. He is also dean of Zacharias Frankel College in Potsdam, Germany, ordaining rabbis for the European Union. A regular columnist for the *Huffington Post*, he is author of many articles and books, including *God of Becoming and Relationship: The Dynamic Nature of Process Theology* and *Passing Life's Tests: Spiritual Reflections on the Trial of Abraham, the Binding of Isaac* (both Jewish Lights). He contributed to *All the World: Universalism, Particularism and the High Holy Days* (Jewish Lights).

Avinu malkeinu, we sing out, assigning these titles to God as if they were names, as if they define and label the divine.

Who are we to name God? What's in a name? Or, more precisely, what's involved in the act of naming? In biblically based religions, the stakes to that question are pretty high, since humanity's relationship to animals and men's relationship to women are expressed in a story about what it means to bestow a name:

> Adonai God said, "It is not good for man to be alone; I will make a fitting helper for him." And Adonai God formed out of the earth all the wild beasts and all the birds of the sky, and brought them to the man to see what he would call them; and whatever the man called each living creature, that would be its name. And the man gave names to all the cattle and to the birds of the sky and to all the wild beasts; but for Adam no fitting helper was found. (Genesis 2:18–20)

God authorizes Adam, the man, to name each creature. What does that permission entail? What does it mean in terms of how humanity is to relate to the animal world? The Torah places this process of naming the beasts in the context of finding an appropriate helper for the man. If we can explicate what is implied in the act of naming, we might understand how Adam is to relate not only to the animals but to the woman as well. Does this biblical story endorse the superiority that many men impose on women and that much of humankind presumes over nature? Or is there another way to read this story?

Most commentators—medieval and modern—construe this biblical naming as an assertion of power. Thus, Rabbi Joseph Herman Hertz explains that "in giving names to earth's creatures, he [man] would establish his dominion over them." In his magisterial study of animals in Jewish tradition, Rabbi Elijah Judah Schochet remarks:

> To bestow a name upon an entity ... denotes a mastery of the nature of that entity. God, as the Lord of the universe, bestows names upon the structures of the universe and the dimensions of time, while man, designated by God to be the lord of the animals, is here granted similar power to bestow names upon his own animal subjects.[1]

So how do we summon the temerity to dare to name God? And on the holiest days of the year?

Viewing naming as an assertion of power can certainly find support in the Bible and in Rabbinic writings. But such a construal also threatens an environmentally sensitive understanding of the proper place of humanity within creation and impedes establishing a non-hierarchical relationship between men and women. If the only way we can understand Adam's bestowal of names is in terms of *his* power over the objects named (animals and woman), then it is our flawed reading that aligns the Torah with the doubly repugnant equation: man is to woman as humanity is to nature. For the goodness of creation, for the divine image reflected in all men and women, for the traditional Jewish claim (shared by many other wisdom traditions) that God is loving and just, we would do well to seek out another way to understand what naming is all about.

Rather than reading naming as an assertion of dominance and supremacy, I would propose recognizing the gift of a name as an expression of empathy, an act that demonstrates understanding and respect by the one doing the naming for the one being named. Naming is a way to articulate awareness of another. When parents comb through a book of babies' names to select the perfect name, their meticulous attention is not a bid for control; it is an invitation to share a new intimate relationship through the child and for the child to become better known through an identifying name. To name, then, is to initiate a relationship, to strengthen the bonds of recognition and of love. Thus, Jewish tradition bids new parents to bestow the name of a relative, linking the infant and the older namesake.

Naming makes the invisible visible. We do not fully acquire a quality until we name it, because only by giving a value concrete linguistic form do we make it possible to attend to its implications and to make ourselves familiar with its ways. It is only by naming a value that we can begin to feel it.

This understanding of what it means to name is hardly new. In a wonderful midrash, we are told that humanity's wisdom exceeds that of the angels precisely through our insight to name properly:

> God assembled all the domestic animals, all wild beasts and fowl, and made them pass before the angels. God asked, "What are the names of these creatures?" But the angels did not know. When God created the first human, however, God assembled all domestic animals, all wild beasts and fowl, and made them pass before Adam. God asked, "What are the names of these creatures?" Adam replied, "This one—the name 'ox' fits. And this one—the name 'horse' fits. And this one—'camel.' And this one—'eagle.'"[2]

Adam is unique in creation by virtue of his ability to know an animal's true nature and then to be able to name it appropriately—a demonstration of deep empathy and wisdom, and evidence also, perhaps, of being made in God's image. By bestowing a name on each creature, Adam simultaneously articulates that creature's special virtues and elevates it as it uniquely is into human consciousness.

Seeing naming simply as a form of mastery and a demonstration of sovereignty denigrates Torah. But even when filtered through terms of power and sovereignty, naming need not reflect an assertion of domination, for power, even sovereign power, need not be dominating. Indeed, at least one ancient Rabbinic author comes to the same conclusion:

> God asked Adam, "And you, what is your name?" Adam replied, "Adam." God asked, "Why?" Adam replied, "Because I was fashioned out of the earth [adamah]." God asked, "And I, what is my name?" "Adonai." God asked, "Why?" "Because You are the sovereign [adon] over all your works."[3]

Surely Adam is not asserting *domination* over God—even though he names God! In this instance, at least, to name something cannot imply control. What it does suggest is that the one giving the name truly *understands* the one receiving it. Adam names God because, made in the divine image, Adam loves God and intuits God's essence. That is why nicknames are a sign of special friendship and why lovers share secret names with their *beshert*—their destined one.

Adam's naming of his *eizer k'negdo,* his equal helper, reflects a similar comprehension and warmth. Indeed, the Torah itself explains the naming in terms of oneness: "Hence a man leaves his father and mother and clings to his wife, so that they become one flesh" (Genesis 2:24). To name is to relate, since naming always reveals the connection between namer and named. The man names the woman in such a way as to indicate that they are one. He even says, first, "She is bone of my bones, flesh of my flesh," and only then, "she will be called woman"

(Genesis 2:23). So, too, is humanity and the rest of creation one, at least to some extent—all creatures are gifted with life, after all. Naming discloses at least an aspiration for some degree of connection. Names reveal who we are but also what we hope to become, and they do so in terms of relationship between namer and named.

So naming is not an assertion of power. It is an invitation to connect, an expression of relationship, a discovery of common ground. But relationship is more than recognized commonality; it honors the distinctiveness of those whom we name as being creatures in their own right, not just carbon copies of ourselves. We grow in a relationship precisely because we learn to love and to internalize traits that are not our own. We expand mere self-centeredness to include the desires and needs of someone else. Relationship is the name we give to the connection forged between two different creatures. Naming, then, is a celebration of difference.

We are distinguished by our names, but our essence also exceeds what our names reveal. Perhaps that ineffability, too, is an expression of our having been made in God's image. God cannot be fully described by a name either: "You have no known name, for You pervade all names; You are the fullness of them all."[4]

God's essence cannot be spoken; it can only be experienced. God's reality remains beyond articulation. So too with God's creatures: we cannot be reduced to our titles, our achievements, or our names. Naming is an act of allusion: we point, through naming, to the individual, knowing all the while that each of us embodies an irreducible and ineffable reality. The name serves as a sign, representing—but not embodying—its bearer. We are always more than our names.

In naming, then, we voice our connection with another, we recognize distinction and uniqueness, and we allude to what remains beyond naming. To name is not a grasping for power; to name is to intuit and to love. Even God.

My Name Is Vulnerability

Rabbi Tony Bayfield, CBE, DD

Rabbi Tony Bayfield, CBE, DD (Cantuar), is professor of Jewish theology and thought at Leo Baeck College in London. He is also president of the Movement for Reform Judaism in the United Kingdom. He contributed to *Who by Fire, Who by Water—Un'taneh Tokef*, *All These Vows—Kol Nidre*, *We Have Sinned: Sin and Confession in Judaism—Ashamnu and Al Chet*, and *All the World: Universalism, Particularism and the High Holy Days* (all Jewish Lights).

Passages from the Torah are always ripe with meaning—with *meanings*, actually, since they always have more than one. This multiplicity of understandings is especially important in considering Exodus 3:13–14, where Moses seeks to know God's name.

For years, I have had an enduring attachment to one particular understanding of this passage—the realization that even though Moses says it is the *Israelites* on whose behalf he is asking, it is really he himself who wants to know. Names are about ownership and control. "If I can name God," thinks Moses, "I can command God's presence and demonstrate God's power." But God responds, "I'm not that kind of God.

I'm not a genie in a bottle. I don't have a name like Amun or Baal. I am who I am."

I still find that reading helpful, but my recent discovery of Abraham Joshua Heschel's extensive study *Heavenly Torah*[1] has taught me that there is a far greater complexity to the subject of naming—or not naming—God. I've never been a great Heschel fan—admiring his ethics and use of language but agreeing with Arthur A. Cohen that he tends to pursue theology through rhetoric that, however elegant, avoids the really pressing questions.[2] That isn't true of *Heavenly Torah,* a three-volume exploration of Rabbinic Judaism, published posthumously.

Heschel explores the different theological stances of two of the founding giants of Rabbinic Judaism, Rabbi Ishmael and Rabbi Akiva. What is so significant about both of them is that they stood in the shadow of the second *churban* (destruction of the Second Temple), just as we stand in the shadow of what Ignaz Maybaum called the third, the Shoah.[3]

The Talmud tells us that, as a child, Ishmael ben Elisha was taken captive to Rome. Rabbi Joshua, on a visit to Rome, was told of a boy with beautiful eyes and face and curly hair who was being held in prison. Rabbi Joshua visited him, paid the ransom, and adopted him as his student.[4] Ishmael's victimization during the chaotic conditions of Roman occupation is deeply significant. The focus of his career, his very raison d'être, was reestablishing order in Jewish life.

Heschel shows incisively how, toward that end, Ishmael and later his school of interpretation understood God as wholly distant, an understanding that allowed Rabbinic leaders to legislate in the face of chaos rather than bemoan the absence of God. Ishmael is thus famous for formulating hermeneutic rules by which halakhic exegesis can develop. He concentrates on interpreting Torah through halakhic midrash. He thereby becomes a towering and decisive figure in the Rabbinic enterprise of developing the portable way of life that had become so necessary following the Temple's destruction and the growth thereafter of Jewish communities worldwide. In this post-*churban* project of restoring order to Jewish life, creative obedience to the Torah text is, in itself, a gritting of the teeth, an unflinching response to disaster.

But Heschel goes further:

> The Rabbis in the generation we are considering experienced things that others have not seen: the sacking of Jerusalem, the humiliation of the House of Israel, and the profanation of the Holy Name in the sight of the whole world. Stormy eras filled with human agony also harbor troubling thoughts; even the pillars of heaven shudder. And a nation that has been belittled by the nations of the world is likely to verge on belittling the great presumptions: that God is merciful and compassionate and that God is the great and the powerful. If there is mercy,

there surely is no power; and if there is power, there surely is no mercy! For could one maintain that the Holy and Blessed One empathizes well but does not carry through?

Now in the school of Rabbi Ishmael they expounded "Who is like You, God, among the mighty [ba-elim]" (Exodus 15:11)—"Who is like You, God, among the mute [ba'ilemim], who is like You in how you see the humiliation of Your children and remain silent?"[5]

Nowhere more than in that interpretation of God as wholly silent in the face of disaster is the gritting of teeth and unflinching gaze apparent. Why must God be thought of here as mute, silent? Because it's better to accept divine silence than to compromise divine omnipotence. Ishmael names God as great, mighty, omnipotent. "I am who I am" is not just an indication of not being open to human ownership and control. It has become the affirmation of God as wholly/holy transcendent. God is, for Ishmael, unnamable.

Not so Akiva! Akiva names God as *Shekhinah*, an actual divine presence—profoundly immanent rather than exclusively transcendent. God responds to the catastrophe of the second *churban* by going with Israel into exile:

> Wherever Israel was exiled, the *Shekhinah* accompanied them. They were exiled to Egypt, and the *Shekhinah* accompanied them.... They were exiled to Babylonia, and the *Shekhinah* accompanied

> them.... They were exiled to Eilam, and the *Shekhinah* accompanied them.... They were exiled to Edom, and the *Shekhinah* accompanied them.... And in the future, when they will return from exile, the *Shekhinah* will, as it were, accompany them as well.[6]

Israel has been exiled from its Temple, from its land. The divine presence goes into exile with it. Israel has been humiliated and weeps. So too the divine presence:

> When the Holy and Blessed One revealed himself to Moses at the thorn bush, he said to him, "Do you now sense that I dwell in sorrow just as my people Israel dwells in sorrow? Know that in speaking to you here in the midst of the thorns, I participate in their suffering."[7]

Israel suffers and God does not—cannot?—intervene to prevent that suffering. More than that. There is a connection between worldly and heavenly afflictions. As Heschel says, "The Holy and Blessed One is a partner in the suffering of his creatures; He is involved in the lot of His people, wounded by their sufferings and redeemed by their liberation."[8]

Jeremiah says, "Because my people is shattered I am shattered; I am dejected, seized by desolation" (8:21). Rabbinic tradition understood those words as applying to God rather than the prophet himself:

It is analogous to a young prince who attempted to lift a heavy rock. As he lifted it, it fell and crushed him. When the king heard that his son had been crushed, he began to cry, "I've been crushed." The palace guard, uncomprehending, said to him, "Your son has been crushed. Why do you say *you* have been crushed?" Such was the reaction of the Holy and Blessed One, as it were: because my people are shattered, I am shattered; I am dejected, seized by desolation.[9]

If we apply the two views of Ishmael and Akiva to *Avinu Malkeinu,* we see that Ishmael emphasizes one and Akiva the other. For Ishmael, God is *malkeinu,* so distant as to be like a far-off ruler—omnipotent, to be sure, but silently above and beyond the fray of human suffering. By contrast, Akiva focuses us on *avinu.* We are the children of our parent. To be a parent, as we know all too well, is to be vulnerable. As our children grow in independence, we become less and less able to protect them. They are wounded by life and we feel the pain. It hurts us as it hurts them. We feel their suffering more acutely than we feel any other suffering. Akiva spells out the overwhelming conclusion. God is *avinu;* God is passible; God's name is vulnerability.

In the shadow of the third *churban* (the Shoah), Jewish theology has had overwhelming difficulties. Some "theologians" have gone so far as to deny to God any metaphysical meaning at all—thus abandoning the task of doing theology altogether. Others have radically reinterpreted the concept of God—naming God, for instance, as "holy nothingness."[10] But to the extent that theology has survived at all, it has tended to follow Ishmael, seeing God as wholly/holy transcendent. God has turned God's face away.[11] God has withdrawn to a distant, other place, and we are left to carry on with Jewish life in silent Job-like noncomprehension. If God has a name, it is "inscrutability."

In the Western theological/philosophical tradition, the term "theodicy"—maintaining God's omnipotence and goodness on the one hand, and the reality of evil on the other—is attributed to German philosopher Gottfried Wilhelm Leibniz (1646–1716). Akiva's understanding runs radically counter to this theodicy. He also challenges Ishmael's transcendent and omnipotent God by naming God as immanence, present-presence, empathy, vulnerability. For me personally, that response, forged in the grim shadow of the second *churban,* is the only road I can follow in response to the third.

We Are But Dust

Dr. Erica Brown

Dr. Erica Brown is a writer and an educator. She is a faculty member of the Wexner Foundation, an Avi Chai Fellow, and the recipient of the Covenant Award. She is author of *Inspired Jewish Leadership: Practical Approaches to Building Strong Communities*, a National Jewish Book Award finalist; *Spiritual Boredom: Rediscovering the Wonder of Judaism*; and *Confronting Scandal: How Jews Can Respond When Jews Do Bad Things* (all Jewish Lights); and coauthor of *The Case for Jewish Peoplehood: Can We Be One?* (Jewish Lights), *Return, In the Narrow Places, Leadership in the Wilderness,* and *Happier Endings*. She contributed to *Who by Fire, Who by Water—Un'taneh Tokef, All These Vows—Kol Nidre, We Have Sinned: Sin and Confession in Judaism—Ashamnu and Al Chet,* and *All the World: Universalism, Particularism and the High Holy Days* (all Jewish Lights). Her articles have appeared on the *Newsweek/Washington Post* website "On Faith."

Every year on our Days of Awe and the days in between, we open the ark multiple times to pour out our collective requests that God—our parent, our "authority figure"—remember us for good, treat us with abundant mercies, and erase our wrongdoings.

All of this makes good seasonal sense. It is hard to start off the year without a slate wiped clean of transgression and readied—as a clean slate is—for new scribbles of possibility and redemption. But there is one line of *Avinu Malkeinu* that trips me up each year. It used to make no sense to me: "Our father, our king, remember that we are but dust" (line 33).

Do I need to remind God that I am dirt, nothing, a mere divine afterthought? In those darkest, most vulnerable moments of Yom Kippur, I want and maybe need to believe that God thinks more of me than I think of myself. We are infinitely small before our king. We are unworthy. We bow in humility. I understand. But dust? If I am but dust when I approach God, then I have no substance, no form, no shape worthy of praying and supplicating.

There are ample proof texts from our Hebrew Bible to support the use of "dust" as a metaphor of humility. In Genesis, God condemns the snake to be a lowly creature: "Upon your belly shall you go, and *dust* shall you eat all the days of your life" (3:14). When Abraham prays to God, he invokes his diminished status in the face of God, his covenantal partner: "Here I venture to speak to my lord, I who am but *dust* and ashes" (18:27).

Dust in the Bible also reminds us of our mortality (which need not imply lowliness). It is used in rituals of mourning, for instance. We hear that "Joshua rent his clothes, and fell to the earth upon his face before the ark of Adonai until the evening, he and the elders of Israel, and put *dust* upon their heads" (Joshua 7:6). In Job, the same context of mourning appears somewhat differently. Here dust is hurled into the air—perhaps as a further sign of righteous anger. As Job's friends encounter Job while he is suffering from disease and mourning his lost family, "they rent every one his mantle, and sprinkled *dust* upon their heads toward heaven" (Job 2:12).

I am but dust, yet on the Days of Awe does that mean I am simply lowly? Instead I may use the imagery of dust as a way to signal my mortality. I will return to the earth one day, yet I can feel anger or injustice about the premature or painful death of others or express my own existential angst that all human life must end in death.

Dust also has a positive meaning in *Tanakh*, symbolic of a numeric future for the Israelites beyond count. "And I will make your seed as the dust of the earth: so that if a man can number the dust of the earth, then shall your seed also be numbered" (Genesis 13:16). We may be subtly reminding God at the start of the year of this commitment: "God, do not forget the promise of dust. Continue to let this small people grow and become more numerous and influential so that we have strength in numbers." This would be a compelling prayer for a people marked by history for persecution yet able to regenerate and replenish its numbers with an alacrity that could only be regarded as divine intervention.

And yet, asking God on the Days of Awe to remember that we are dust must have a meaning more profound than a simple wish for expansion. I return, therefore, to dust as a sign of being human. That is how we find dust used for the very first time in our sacred texts—as an ingredient in our very composition. "The Lord God formed the man from the *dust* of the ground and breathed into his nostrils the breath of life, and the man became a living being" (Genesis 2:7). With this polar opposite of ingredients did God design us—the dust of the earth and God's own breath. We embody not only the simplest, most earthy material but also the stuff of transcendence. We house these potentially conflicting forces within us, aspiring to be worthy of our godliness while also acknowledging our earthly origins and nature. God reminds Adam of his "earthiness" when meting out punishment to him as the first mortal—with "dust" as the master metaphor: "By the sweat of your face you shall eat bread, till you return to the ground, for out of it you were taken; for you are *dust*, and to *dust* you shall return" (Genesis 3:19). Much later, in Ecclesiastes—that biblical book of melancholia and of wisdom—we are told once again of our fate: "The *dust* returns to the earth as it was, and the spirit returns to God who gave it" (12:7).

Elsewhere too, Scripture details the recipe of human creation, telling us that dust is essential to our very composition. One verse, in particular, inches closer to the language of *Avinu Malkeinu*: "As a father shows compassion to his children, so Adonai shows compassion to those who fear him. For He knows our frame; He remembers that we are dust" (Psalm 103:13–14). God is a loving father who has compassion upon us because He made us. When we mention dust, it is as if we say to God, "This is what *You* made me of. Remember that whoever I am is directly a consequence of how You formed me. I am part of You. Remember me. Have mercy on me. Grant me grace. Grant me peace."

Two other passages, one in Psalms and the other in Job, detail the delight we take in our physicality, an attitude that reflects well on its creator.

> For You formed my inward parts; You knitted me together in my mother's womb. I praise You, for I am fearfully and wonderfully made. Wonderful are your works; my soul knows it very well. My frame was not hidden from You, when I was being made in secret, intricately woven in the depths of the earth. Your eyes saw my unformed substance; in your book were written, every one of them, the days that

were formed for me, when as yet there was none of them. (Psalm 139:13–16)

God made each of us—so worthy of mention that God even made note of us in a book. The Psalms passage, however, omits reference to dust. A parallel conversation by Job, however, does add dust to the mixture, thereby agreeing with Psalms, albeit in a more somber and macabre way:

> Your hands fashioned and made me, and now You have destroyed me altogether. Remember that You have made me like clay; and will You return me to the *dust?* Did You not pour me out like milk and curdle me like cheese? You clothed me with skin and flesh, and knit me together with bones and sinews. You have granted me life and steadfast love, and your care has preserved my spirit. (Job 10:8–12)

Job wishes to remind God that God is essentially a creator, not a destroyer. If God created us in love, God must continue to love us; rather than cause us suffering, God must raise us up so that our dust is overshadowed by God's breath.

"Our father, our king, remember that we are but dust."

So yes, we are dust, but not just lowly dust. We are the holy dust of humanity, dust mixed with the very breath of God; dust that God chose for us, in love. To say we are dust is not, therefore, to say that we are unworthy. It is to remind God of the love that God poured into that dust when we were formed and to pray that God, our creator, continue to love us still. We are the descendants of that magnificent creature, the first human being. Dust was the raw material that God gathered up from the ground and imbued with life. God, we implore You, we beg You, not to forget that it is You who made us. Please sustain us and let us live so that with our lives (dust that we are), we may honor our creator.

Two Pockets

Rabbi Joshua M. Davidson

Rabbi Joshua M. Davidson is the senior rabbi of Congregation Emanu-El of the City of New York. Prior to his appointment in 2013, he served for eleven years as the senior rabbi of Temple Beth El of Northern Westchester and for five years as assistant and associate rabbi at New York City's Central Synagogue.

Rabbi Simcha Bunam taught we should carry with us two statements: one from Genesis, *V'anochi afar va'eifer*, "I am but dust and ashes" (Genesis 18:27); and the other from Mishnah Sanhedrin, *Bishvili nivra ha'olam*, "For my sake the world was created."[1] One goes in our left pocket to impress upon us our smallness; the other in our right pocket to remind us of our greatness.

This tension "between vulnerability and action,"[2] as Rabbi Milton Steinberg called it, confronts us throughout the High Holy Days.

"I Am But Dust and Ashes"

One *Kol Nidre* Eve a rabbi decides to model repentance for his congregation. Humbly he approaches the ark. Beseeching the Almighty for forgiveness, he beats his breast, proclaiming,

"Before You, God, I am nothing. I am nothing." The cantor sees him and joins in. "I am nothing. I am nothing," she cries. The temple president, sensing that he too must get in on the act, now comes up. "I am nothing. I am nothing," he sobs. In the silence that follows, the rabbi turns to the cantor and whispers, "Look who thinks he's nothing."

For ten days a year, the *Yamim Noraim* challenge us to adopt a posture that says, "Before You, God, we are nothing." We recite the words *Avinu malkeinu, z'khor ki afar anachnu*, "Our father, our king, remember that we are but dust" (line 33). But as that joke suggests, saying the words is one thing; meaning them is quite another.

Yet unless we allow the reality of our insignificance before God to penetrate on some level, then the spiritual rebirth that should come with the Days of Awe won't come for us. So we must consider the words "I am but dust and ashes." What do they mean?

First, that each of us is terribly small—as we read, "a particle of dust floating on the wind."[3] Relative to God we are inconsequential.

Second, our power over our lives is limited. "Who shall be tranquil and who shall be troubled"[4] remains beyond our control.

Third, each of us is mortal ... dust.

Kol Nidre confronts us with our mortality. With its scrolls removed, the ark is but an empty box, an *aron*, a casket. The *kittel*, the traditional garment worn by men on Yom Kippur, is white like a funeral shroud. *Kol Nidre* brings us face to face with the end. Each of us will die. None can escape.

Not even Moses, who was furious with God for his fate that he would not enter the Promised Land despite forty trying years of leadership. According to the Midrash, Moses resists. He draws a small circle around himself, stands defiantly inside it, and threatens, "Master of the universe, I will not budge from here until You void your decree."[5]

No circle can protect him. His death may be terribly unfair, but life is not fair. We don't need the slip of paper or the story of Moses to teach us what we've already learned from the pain of our own misfortune or the illness and loss of loved ones.

However, the note and the Midrash do teach us something: While there will be places we will not go, goals we will not reach, questions we will never answer, these do not represent our failures or signal God's disfavor. They are simply the limits of our lives. We do not live forever. Those we love do not live forever. Bad things do happen to good people. This is the way of the world. We do not understand it, and we cannot control it. Moses himself had to exit the circle of life, and so must we.

This is Yom Kippur's message to us ... but only part of Yom Kippur's message. There is more. "Everyone has two pockets," Simcha Bunam taught, "to use as the occasion demands":

one if we become haughty and forget our place in God's universe, and another if we despair and lose our way.

"For My Sake the World Was Created"

So now the other slip: "For my sake the world was created." How different an outlook this is! It does not deny the inevitability or the unfairness of death. Rather, it affirms the potential of life! If the High Holy Days remind us of the limits, they also teach us that we have the power to live lives of extraordinary meaning.

The message is conveyed most beautifully in the *piyyut Ki Hinei Kachomer:* "Like a wheel in the hand of a sailor, at will, holding it, and at will, letting it go, so are we in your hand, God who is good and forgiving" (line 4). The moment will come when God's hand will close on the wheel, but until that moment arrives, we are the navigators of our life's journey.

And we are not inconsequential. We are taught that "man stamps many coins with one die and they are all alike; but the Holy One stamps all humanity with the mold of the first human being and every one of us is different! Therefore each of us is duty-bound to say, 'For my sake the world was created.'"[6]

Each of us is precious. Each of us brings a gift to this world that no one else can, without which God's creation would be incomplete. And our uniqueness bears witness to God's greatness. The historian Harry Elmer Barnes argued, "Astronomically speaking, man is almost totally insignificant," to which the theologian George Albert Coe rejoined, "Astronomically speaking, man is an astronomer."[7] "For my sake the world was created" teaches us to look at ourselves and the joys of our lives, great and small, as gifts to be treasured, nurtured, and explored.

And "For my sake the world was created" teaches us that we are not powerless. When Abraham utters the words, "I am but dust and ashes," he is in the midst of arguing with God to save Sodom and Gomorrah for the sake of the righteous. He defies God: "Shall not the judge of all the earth deal justly?" (Genesis 18:25).

"How can dust become the one whose thought is more than dust?"[8] We can make our lives stand for something. We can rail with Abraham against the world's injustice. We become more than dust when we fight for our ideals and aspirations and remind ourselves of their enduring value and give our lives transcendent meaning. Indeed the High Holy Days summon us to repair the broken places of this world. That is why so many of us wrestle with the global challenges of poverty and hunger and homelessness.

And the High Holy Days beckon us to repair the fractured relationships in our own lives, to bridge whatever divides us from those we yearn to be near again, be they spouses, siblings, parents, children, colleagues, or friends. If we insist on waiting for them to reach out to us, we risk getting snared in the trap of smug self-righteousness. And the chance for healing may be lost forever.

Each of us will die; the decree cannot be averted. But *Un'taneh Tokef* promises, *Ut'shuvah, ut'filah, utz'dakah ma'avirin et ro'a hag'zeirah*, "And repentance, prayer, and charity help the hardship of the decree pass." And now we understand what that means. We cannot prevent death. But we can make certain that when death does come, we will not look back with regret—because we have reached out to repair relationships, because we have attempted to right some wrong, because we have linked our lives to enduring values and by doing so given our lives lasting worth.

During *N'ilah* we read, "In woman and man, children of dust and offspring of heaven, You have blended two worlds: perishable earth and immortal soul; finite matter, locked into time and space, and infinite spirit, which endures through all eternity."[9]

Each of us will die. But the meaning of our lives need not die. According to the Midrash, Moses was desperate to live. So on the day of his death he busied himself writing the Torah, the scroll of God's teachings he had come to embody for his people. The Torah—the text of Moses's life, a life linked to divine purpose—would be his immortality! So can the message of our lives live forever.[10]

That is why Bachya taught, Our "days are scrolls. Write upon them what you wish to be remembered."[11] Write upon them acts of kindness and fairness toward your fellow human beings, expressions of love toward those most precious to you. The High Holy Days impel us to consider the texts of our lives, the stories we will leave behind. And they assure us that if the values of Torah infuse them with gentleness and justice, then our lives too will have transcendent meaning.

Keep One Slip in Each Pocket: You'll Know When You Need Them

"I am but dust and ashes."
"For my sake the world was created."

Keep one slip in each pocket. You'll know when you need them.

Rabbi Simcha Bunam, who gave us those two slips, taught that we are always moving back and forth through two doors.[12] During *N'ilah,* at the close of the High Holy Days, we return to those doors, to the ark, the *aron,* and blast the shofar one final time. That sound has been compared to the wail of a woman in labor and to a newborn's cry. If we are willing to consider the truths in our pockets, then *N'ilah* can be our rebirth into a new year of reconciliation and repair, humility and wonder.

Re-imaging God

Rabbi Lawrence A. Englander, CM, DHL, DD

Rabbi Lawrence A. Englander, CM, DHL, DD, has been rabbi of Solel Congregation of Mississauga, Ontario, since its inception in 1973. He is author of *The Mystical Study of Ruth;* former editor of the *CCAR Journal;* and a contributor to *We Have Sinned: Sin and Confession in Judaism—Ashamnu and Al Chet*, *May God Remember: Memory and Memorializing in Judaism—Yizkor*, and *All the World: Universalism, Particularism and the High Holy Days* (all Jewish Lights).

In a nightclub act, the comedian Mel Brooks plays a two-thousand-year-old man who is asked by the interviewer, Carl Reiner, how religion first developed. "It was like this," the aged patriarch replies. "When I was a kid, there was a guy in the neighboring tribe who was twice as big and as strong as anyone else—his name was Phil. Everybody was afraid of Phil when he came into our camp, because if he was in a bad mood he would beat people up as he went along. We used to pray, 'Please don't be mad at us, Phil. Please don't step on us or break our arms. Be nice to us, O great and powerful Phil!'

"One day, it started raining really hard. As Phil came over the hill, a bolt of lightning flashed down from the sky and knocked him dead in his tracks." Brooks concludes, "It was then we knew: there was someone bigger than Phil!"

Using the comedic technique of exaggeration *ad absurdum,* Brooks depicts the divine as mysterious, powerful, and fearful. Before we dismiss this image as silly and childish, must we not admit that we find a similar description of God in the High Holy Day *machzor?* The God of our liturgy is judge and jury of our deeds—and sole determiner of our fate.[1] *Avinu Malkeinu* adds the related images of father and king—likewise, all-powerful beings in the culture of late antiquity that the Rabbis inhabited—whom we beseech to be kind and forgiving, even though we are undeserving of such favor. Aren't these prayers reminiscent of Mel Brooks's entreaties to Phil? More importantly, how can we, in our own time, relate to a God who is depicted this way?

Before we dismiss these prayers entirely, I suggest that there is more than one way to interpret them—and I suspect the Rabbis who authored these entreaties were aware of this, too. Names and images of God can be best understood if we relate to them as *metaphors*.

Metaphors explain unfamiliar phenomena through familiar imagery. A computer, for example, becomes understandable when we think of it as having "files" and "documents"—even though (as we are well aware) there is no actual paper lurking behind the screen. These metaphors help us comprehend how binary electrical impulses organize data into words and pictures.

Metaphors of things we understand help us relate to objects we do not.

In addition, metaphoric imagery can be interpreted in more ways than one. In "The Highwayman," for example, poet Alfred Noyes describes the moon as "a ghostly galleon tossed upon cloudy seas." We might imagine the movement of clouds giving the impression that the moon is sailing over them; alternatively, its pale light in an overcast sky might give the moon a macabre appearance.

The pioneering feminist, poet, and liturgist Marcia Falk explains how metaphor is especially important for *metaphorical theology*.

> The way to avoid verbal idolatry is to keep reminding ourselves that *all* theological naming is really a naming-toward; all honest talk about divinity has an "as if" embedded in it. And when we recognize the naming of divinity for what it is—the act of *metaphor-making*—we approach it with a new freedom.... The empowering quality of metaphor exists only as long as we remember that it *is* a metaphor we are speaking, not literal truth and not fiction. When a metaphor is treated as literal truth, it becomes a lie.[2]

I stated above that metaphors play two roles: they allow us to relate to what is otherwise difficult to know, and they open the possibility of multiple interpretations. Metaphorical theology allows us to apply both functions to the difficult terms we encounter in prayer. Images such as "father/parent" and "king/sovereign" help us *relate to* a God who is too complex to be captured in ordinary prosaic language, and furthermore they can be interpreted in different ways.

Take *Avinu Malkeinu* for example.

First, *avinu*.

A parent can be at times stern and demanding, at other times loving and forgiving. But one constant aspect of parenthood is that our parents give us life. God, as the source of *all* life in the universe, can therefore be perceived as our divine parent.

By calling God "parent," we metaphorically stretch our imagination to appreciate God not as the all-powerful head of a family, but as the guiding presence in nature. In calling God *avinu*, we affirm nature's ordered pattern that makes the world more *cosmos* than *chaos*. Affirming this order evokes our wonderment at "the miracles that are with us every day" (as expressed, for example, in the daily thanksgiving prayer in the *Amidah*).[3] It is this sense of wonder that enables us, at the birth of a child, to encounter God as *oseh ma'aseih v'reishit* ("renewer of creation"). It is this sense that moves a botanist, peering into the complexities of a rare flower, to perceive beyond the microscope the *m'kor hachayim* ("source of life"). It is this sense that inspires a person at prayer to feel the nearness of

Shekhinah (God's indwelling presence). By relating to God as *avinu*, we apprehend that we, too, were brought into being as an integral part of the divine pattern. There is, indeed, "someone bigger than Phil."

Next, *malkeinu*.

When this prayer was composed, kings were potentates who ruled vast territories and whose word was final. Today, we are more accustomed (especially in those countries ruled by the British monarch) to a constitutional sovereign who is responsible for the welfare of the people. Theological metaphor might, therefore, recast God as sovereign to be more like our senior partner in the covenant that began with Abraham and Sarah, was ratified on Mount Sinai, and is renewed even now by every individual who chooses to live a Jewish life.

If *avinu* suggests the God of nature, *malkeinu* denotes the God of history, the God we acknowledge at every Passover seder as the *go'eil* ("liberator") of Israel and, by extension, of all the world's inhabitants. This is the God we call *notein hatorah* ("giver of Torah") every Shavuot, as we pledge our commitment to the covenant. And yes, this is also the God who acts as *shofet* ("judge") on the High Holy Days, urging us to bear witness to our deeds and to become our better selves. By relating to God as *malkeinu*, we affirm that there is not just order, but also purpose in the world,[4] a messianic dream toward which we must work together. This is a

God whom the worshipers of Phil could never even dream of.

Metaphorical theology thus enables us to retain traditional names of God by translating them into terms that apply to our own life experience. When it comes to God, after all, there is no single truth: the more metaphors, the stronger our relationship with the Holy One. And *Avinu Malkeinu* is just the beginning of the High Holy Day list. Another well-known prayer for the occasion, *Ki Anu Amekha* ("For We Are Your People"), imagines God as parent, but also master, shepherd, and lover, to name just a few.[5]

But isn't there a problem in proliferating so many images of God? Are there no boundaries to metaphor making? How can we know which of them are "true" and which are false or misguided? The response to these questions rests in yet another metaphor. Imagine a huge precious gem dangling from the ceiling in the middle of a room. From one end of the room, I see a spherical-shaped gem illumined by sunlight coming through a window to my upper left, causing the square-shaped facets to sparkle with a yellow hue. But from the opposite end of the room, you see an irregular-shaped gem illumined from the upper right, with hexagonal facets that radiate a pink color. Which one of us is "right"? We solve this dilemma by walking around the entire circumference of the gem and seeing its appearance change, depending on our perspective.

Each appearance is "true," yet a much fuller appreciation comes by sharing our multiple perspectives. The same is true of our relationship with God. When we call God by many names, when we learn from others the names and relationships that they cherish, we also serve to enrich our own.

"Would You Still Love Me If...?"

Rabbi Shoshana Boyd Gelfand

Rabbi Shoshana Boyd Gelfand received her rabbinic ordination in 1993 at The Jewish Theological Seminary in New York. She has served as chief executive of the British Movement for Reform Judaism and prior to that was vice president of the Wexner Heritage Foundation in New York. Currently she is director of JHub, an operating program of the London-based Pears Foundation. She contributed to *All These Vows—Kol Nidre*, *We Have Sinned: Sin and Confession in Judaism—Ashamnu and Al Chet*, *May God Remember: Memory and Memorializing in Judaism—Yizkor*, and *All the World: Universalism, Particularism and the High Holy Days* (all Jewish Lights).

My children often ask to play the game "Would you still love me if...?" Each time we play (usually as a ploy to delay bedtime!) they try to imagine something they could do that would make me stop loving them. Of course, the main point of the game is that they never come up with anything that could diminish my fundamental love for them. But an added benefit is that the examples they choose remind them why we need rules and that even if they never forfeit my love, breaking rules does have consequences.

At some point, when my children are parents themselves, I'll share with them the technical language for what the game teaches. Psychologists call it conditional versus unconditional love. Good parenting requires balancing the two: children enjoy the security of knowing that they are inherently lovable regardless of their actions (unconditional love). But they learn also that their actions matter in that they inevitably evoke reward and punishment (conditional love). That's just the way the world works.

This psychological principle of balancing conditional and unconditional love applies to theology as well. At the heart of Jewish belief is our fundamental faithfulness with God (covenant). This relationship exists unconditionally; it cannot be broken. But we also have rules, which establish expectations for behavior *(mitzvot)*. And when we break these rules (sin), God calls us to task and expects us to change *(t'shuvah)*. So covenant is at the heart of God's unconditional love for us, while *mitzvot* form the basis of God's conditional love, for which we are rewarded or punished depending on how we fulfill God's *mitzvot*.

T'shuvah is possible only because of the unconditional love that underlies our covenantal relationship with God—like the bond between parent and child. It is our unconditional covenant that gives us the audacity to request God's mercy—and feel confidence in advance that we might get it. But were God to exhibit the attribute of mercy alone, we would be like spoiled children, where rules have no consequences. The attribute of mercy is thus balanced by the attribute of justice, which holds us accountable, even though the whole point of the Yom Kippur "game" is for God to pardon us in return for our *t'shuvah*. We know in advance that is how the day will end.

The constant tension of these two attributes is expressed in the well-known midrash in *Genesis Rabbah* (12:15):

> God is like a king, who had some empty glasses. He said, "If I pour hot water into them, they will burst; if I pour cold water into them, they will contract and crack." What did the king do? He poured a mixture of hot and cold water into them, and they remained unbroken. So too, the Holy One of Blessing said, "If I create the world with the attribute of mercy alone, its sins will be too many; if with justice alone, how could the world endure? So I will create it with justice and with mercy, that it may endure!"

Whether in parental psychology or Jewish theology, this tension between conditional (justice) love and unconditional (mercy) love is a "polarity"—a set of interdependent opposites that exist in ongoing constructive tension with one another. As with any polarity, neither can exist without the other, and choosing one pole at the expense of the other is simply not an option, as they are interdependent.

Our world is awash in polarities: inhale/exhale, activity/rest, process/product, stability/change, and so forth. As Dr. Barry Johnson, a leading expert in organizational behavior has taught,[1] polarities require a response of *both/and*. You can never "resolve" a true polarity by choosing one side over the other, because when one side "wins," both sides inevitably "lose" and you end up back where you started. (If you don't believe this, try choosing just inhaling over exhaling or vice versa!)

Conditional (justice) love and unconditional (mercy) love are just one of many polarities within Judaism. Our tradition embraces numerous polar tensions that are inherently irresolvable:

- *Halakhah* (law) and *aggadah* (lore)
- *Keva* (fixed prayer) and *kavanah* (spontaneous prayer)
- *Din* (justice) and *rachamim* (mercy)
- *Torah sheb'al peh* (oral law) and *Torah shebikhtav* (written law)
- Commentary and codification
- *Adonai* (God's name implying mercy) and *elohim* (God's name implying justice)

- *Mitzvot bein adam l'chaveiro* (relationships among people) and *mitzvot bein adam lamakom* (relationship with God)

Judaism is chock-full of polarities. The very nature of Talmudic discourse assumes that differing opinions will lead to truth—not through compromise but through allowing those opinions to remain in dialectical tension with one another.

Perhaps the most succinct and powerful expression of the Jewish love of polarities comes from the very first recitation of *Avinu Malkeinu:*

> It is related of Rabbi Eliezer that he once stepped before the ark [to lead the congregation in prayer] and recited the twenty-four benedictions [of the *Amidah* for fast days called on account of drought], and his prayer was not answered. Rabbi Akiva stepped before the ark after him and exclaimed, "Our father, our king, we have no king other than You! Our father, our king, for your sake have compassion on us!" And rain fell. (Talmud, Ta'anit 25b)

Why did God answer Rabbi Akiva, not Rabbi Eliezer? Perhaps it was because Akiva framed his plea in terms of conditional/unconditional polarity. Later generations expanded *Avinu Malkeinu* into an entire litany of lines and made it a core element of the High Holy Day service. But the polarity is already there in Rabbi Akiva's original version:

Our father, our king, we have no king other than You!

Our father, our king, for your sake have compassion on us!

The first line emphasizes the attribute of justice (God's uncompromising sovereignty), while the second line emphasizes compassion (God's parental mercy)—the very same polarity as in the game "Will you still love me if...?" Unconditional love lies at the heart of compassion. Conditional love is the essence of justice. In two short lines, Rabbi Akiva identifies the dialectic of unconditional/conditional love as the parallel polarity of mercy/justice.

Not only do the first two lines embody this tension; the first two words do the same! The juxtaposed image of God as parent (*avinu*) and sovereign (*malkeinu*) creates a repeated chorus that forms a rhythmic reminder of unconditional and conditional love—the two polar opposites that are God.

SOVEREIGN	PARENT
Awesome	Intimate
Transcendent	Immanent
Just	Compassionate

This dualistic typology constitutes the ultimate polarity of conditional and unconditional love, which all human beings seek.

Figure 1 below outlines both the positives (upper quadrants) and the negatives (lower quadrants) of these two kinds of love:

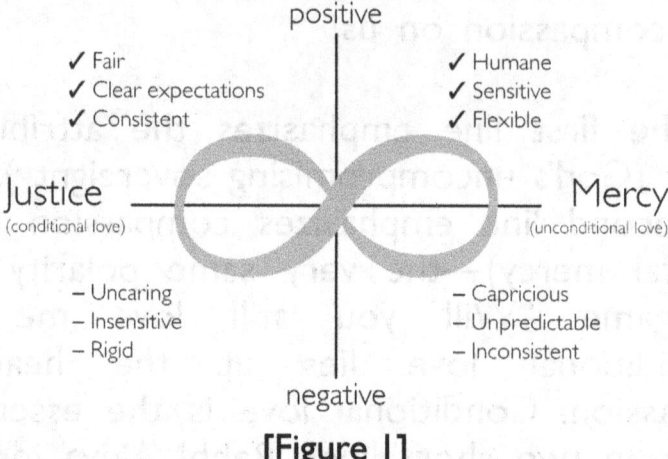

[Figure 1]

If we had only the unconditional love (mercy) of a parent, the world would be capricious and unpredictable. But with only the conditional love (justice) of a sovereign, it would be uncaring and insensitive. As the aforementioned midrash in *Genesis Rabbah* expresses so beautifully, it is only through the juxtaposition of conditional and unconditional love that the world endures.

Even in Rabbi Akiva's initial prayer, unconnected to the High Holy Days in its original context, *Avinu Malkeinu* is a powerful expression of the justice/mercy polarity. But the fact that it has been enhanced and incorporated into the liturgy of the *Yamim Nora'im* only enhances its resonance, because of the Rabbinic interpretation of those days as a time of *t'shuvah*, the act of "returning."

T'shuvah is usually interpreted as a spiritual returning to our own true selves, returning from having "missed the mark" and gone off course through sin. We usually understand *t'shuvah*, therefore, as the opportunity to correct our course and realign ourselves in terms of the direction in which our lives are heading.

But the study of polarities provides a more subtle understanding of *t'shuvah*. Instead of simply correcting the direction of our path, *t'shuvah* is about assessing where we sit within a particular polarity dynamic at any given moment and trying to adjust our position so as to manage that polarity better. Are we overemphasizing "mercy" at the expense of "justice"? Or vice versa? How are we managing the tension between the parental mercy of unconditional love and the monarchic judgment of conditional love—and not just regarding God, but in *all* our relationships: our parents, siblings, and children; our friends, neighbors, and colleagues; that is, everyone.

Avinu Malkeinu asks God to love us both conditionally and unconditionally but invites us to do the same relative to others. In that sense, *t'shuvah* is not only a straight line leading away from sin and toward God. It is also an invitation to manage yet another polarity: our relationship with God but also with each other.

It is an opportunity to say both to God and to our loved ones, "Would you still love me if…?"

Celebrating a Conflicted Relationship with God

Rabbi Asher Lopatin

Rabbi Asher Lopatin is the president of Yeshivat Chovevei Torah Rabbinical School, an Orthodox rabbinical school that teaches an inclusive, open, and inquisitive Torah. He is the former rabbi of Anshe Sholom B'nai Israel Congregation, a modern Orthodox synagogue in Chicago, and is a founding rabbi of the multidenominational Chicago Jewish Day School. He contributed to *Who by Fire, Who by Water—Un'taneh Tokef* and *All the World: Universalism, Particularism and the High Holy Days* (both Jewish Lights).

It is one of the most haunting and beautiful tunes of the High Holy Days. It is the tune we all sing together, our eyes lifted from the words on the *machzor* page, and then half-closed, half looking up to heaven, to take in the power of the moment. *Avinu Malkeinu, choneinu va'aneinu ki ein banu ma'asim* ("Our father, our king, be gracious to us and answer us, for we have no merit").

Some congregations sing it twice. Some slower or faster, some softer or louder, but inevitably, although it ends on a low note, it constitutes an emotional crescendo to the service.

Even though there is no Jewish legal obligation to say *Avinu Malkeinu*—not the first line, not the last line; not any of the lines—it feels as obligatory as the *Amidah* or the *Sh'ma*. The service would not be complete without it.

Except ... on Shabbat.

On Shabbat, halakhah prohibits *Avinu Malkeinu*. The general reason given is that it is too petitionary to be appropriate for Shabbat. On Shabbat, we are to experience the world as perfect, with nothing lacking, nothing still uncreated, nothing yet to work on. So *Avinu Malkeinu* needs to step aside, despite its grandeur, beauty, and power.

It is consistent for *Avinu Malkeinu* to take second fiddle to Shabbat, because when Rosh Hashanah falls on Shabbat, Shabbat completely dominates it. Halakhah cancels even the blowing of the shofar then (if we cancel the shofar, we can certainly cancel *Avinu Malkeinu*).

Yet things are not that simple, because Yom Kippur, in many ways, takes precedence over Shabbat. Normally, we are supposed to eat even an extra "third meal" on Shabbat *(s'udah sh'lishit)*,[1] but on Yom Kippur we fast. We dress up for Shabbat, but on Yom Kippur we wear plain, non-leather shoes. Yom Kippur is filled with crying and sadness, with requests for God's forgiveness and for blessings in the New Year.

Almost none of this penitential liturgy is suppressed on Shabbat.

Yet, on Yom Kippur, *Avinu Malkeinu* is halakhically banned—smuggled in only at the end of *N'ilah*, when it is hardly Shabbat anymore (the sun has set a long time ago). We cling to the end of Yom Kippur—and our chance, finally, to sing *Avinu Malkeinu*—and ask humbly for everything we could not mention during all of the long day just over.

Why is this? Why do we allow every other Yom Kippur consideration to override Shabbat but not *Avinu Malkeinu*? Even the few parts of the service that are changed when Yom Kippur occurs on Shabbat are more than compensated for—for example, we drop the thirteen attributes that we would normally sing when we take out the Torah, but we then say them multiple times over in other parts of the service throughout the day. Not so *Avinu Malkeinu*: it must wait until Shabbat is over; only then do we say it with gusto, with passion, with all the love that we might have for a precious child or sibling who has disappeared for so long and finally returns. Why is *Avinu Malkeinu* so absolutely antithetical to Shabbat that we eliminate it even from a Yom Kippur that falls on Saturday?

Perhaps the reason is deeper than just the usual notion that it seems too petitionary for Shabbat.

Perhaps the reason is found in its very name, which starts every single one of its lines. The phrase *avinu malkeinu* reflects the need for the Jew, the human being, to break the one and only God almighty into two different attributes. *Avinu*, our father, our mother, the God we love, the God to whom we look for help; and *malkeinu*, our king and ruler, but the God we cannot figure out, who makes us angry, who acts in ways that distance us, the God with whom we cannot even usefully fight or disagree.

We know God is one. We know the same God that permits all the horrors in this world is the same God who makes blessing and goodness possible. Yet in *Avinu Malkeinu*, God is split. We look to *avinu* for our salvation, but recognize *malkeinu* in the deaths of innocents—*yonkei shadayim shelo chatu*, "our young ones and babies who have not sinned." One God alone, mind you! Not a bad God and a good God, but a single God we love but also fear and fail to relate to.

Not only is God split; so too are we. We are nobodies to ask something from God *(ki ein banu ma'asim,* "we have no merit"); but at the same time we are the ones entrusted with sanctifying God's name, the ones sacrificing to pursue lives that make God a presence in this world. We are the lowest of the low who begin by confessing, "We have sinned before You," and end by admitting, "We have no merit." But in between we demand from God a huge list of things that we need and, by implication, we have every right to demand. And "demand" is exactly the right word—we do not just petition or request, we demand due justice and kindness from a God of justice and kindness. From *avinu*, we get it; from *malkeinu*, we may not.

Shabbat has none of this ambivalence. It is altogether beautiful, holy, the greatest gift any people has ever received. Shabbat is simple: God rested, we rest; God completed the world's creation, we live in a fully created world. Shabbat, said the Rabbis, is a "taste of the world to come." It is a simple sheltering cave, an abundant oasis, a "palace in time," as Abraham Joshua Heschel called it. Shabbat celebrates one God, one Jewish people, and one unified world of humanity, all of us God's creatures. On Shabbat, God's dreams for the world all come together in perfection—as symbolized so beautifully by the way we hold together the two split *challot* at the Shabbat meal and then eat them as one. On Shabbat, everything is simple; everything makes sense.

Avinu Malkeinu is the opposite: It is the prayer that tells us that God does not always feel like the parent God really is; where God's judgments, the king's edicts, do not always make sense—even for God's own goals in this world. It is the prayer that juxtaposes our defects and our lowliness with our power and purpose. *Avinu Malkeinu* reflects a broken world that is not easily put together—like separate *challot* that cannot be pressed together to make everything nice and neat. We love You, God, *avinu*—it says—but how can You, God, *malkeinu,* allow our children—any children—to be killed and tortured and used as pawns in senseless wars? Are You a God who wants the world to be sanctified or a God who is willing to let it be destroyed by evil? Should we submit to injustice or demand righteousness from You?

The ambiguity of *Avinu Malkeinu* is too much for Shabbat. Shabbat can handle fasting and even crying, pleading, and petitioning. But it cannot live with ambivalence about God and our own self-doubt as to what and who we really are. *Avinu Malkeinu* is reality; Shabbat is a dream, a vision, a hope. Our tradition loves Shabbat too much to challenge it—even on Yom Kippur—for if it were to fall, so too would everything we stand for. It cannot be threatened by *Avinu Malkeinu.*

Yet we love *Avinu Malkeinu* as well. Our people has survived not only because of our Shabbat vision, but because we respect reality too. On the High Holy Days, particularly, we admit how challenging the world is. We see God as *malkeinu,* not just *avinu,* avoiding the easy pitfall of lulling ourselves into a dream where God is sweet, the world is sweet, and we need never awaken to the fact that even the kind and loving God is answerable for a world that makes God look harsh and uncaring.

And who are we? Nobodies or everybodies? Weak and humble, but also proud and critical about a world that demands improvement. We not only live with these contradictions, we celebrate them, we sing them. Together, out loud, with tears and triumph in our eyes.

God, You are our loving parent but also a ruler over a harsh and bleak world. On Shabbat we put aside the great questions of our tradition and their critique of life's realities. But otherwise, the High Holy Days demand we face these fissures in life's smoothness. In the end, we need them both: the calming dream of Shabbat, and the searing reality of *Avinu Malkeinu*.

God the Cashier

A PARABLE OF THE DUBNER MAGGID'S

Rabbi Jack Riemer

Rabbi Jack Riemer, well-known author and speaker, has conducted many workshops and seminars to help people learn about the inspiring tradition of ethical wills and to prepare their own. As head of the National Rabbinic Network, a support system for rabbis across denominational lines, he gives sermon seminars to rabbis throughout the United States. He is editor of *The World of the High Holy Days* and *Wrestling with the Angel,* and coeditor of *Ethical Wills and How to Prepare Them: A Guide to Sharing Your Values from Generation to Generation* (Jewish Lights). He contributed to *May God Remember: Memory and Memorializing in Judaism—Yizkor* and *All the World: Universalism, Particularism and the High Holy Days* (both Jewish Lights).

Nowadays it is the custom to sing the last line of *Avinu Malkeinu* out loud. It has become one of the most beloved and familiar songs of the High Holy Days. Everyone knows the melody, and even those who cannot read much Hebrew love to join in this song.

But in Eastern Europe the custom was to sing all the rest of *Avinu Malkeinu* out loud and then to recite the last line in a whisper. The Dubner Maggid was once asked why, and he responded, as was his way, with a parable.

This is what he said:

Once there was a grocer who lived in a small village. Once a year he would go to the big city in order to order merchandise for the coming year. When he entered the warehouse each year, he was dazzled by the amount and the variety of the merchandise that was on display there. He got so carried away that he would go down the aisles, ordering everything that he saw. He would say, "Give me some of this" and "Give me some of that." And then, when he got to the cashier and totaled up his bill, he was embarrassed and would say in a whisper, "I am sorry, but I don't have enough money with which to pay for all these things that I have ordered. Could you please give them to me on credit, and if I have a good year, I will be able to pay for them all when I come back next year."

So it is with us, said the Dubner Maggid:

When we think of all the things we would like to have in the new year, we are carried away with desire. And so we call out: "*Avinu malkeinu*, give us health; *avinu malkeinu*, give us wealth...." But when we come to the last sentence and we realize how little merit we have, we say in a whisper: *Avinu Malkeinu, choneinu va'aneinu, ki ein banu ma'asim; aseih imanu tz'dakah vachesed v'hoshi'einu,* "Our father, our king, be gracious to us and give us all that we have asked for on credit, because we have no good deeds with which to pay for them. Give us another year of life and we will try our best to be better, and to justify your faith in us, and to pay You back for all that You give us on credit."

I like this parable because it speaks to my heart on the Days of Awe, for I am both: a sinner who needs grace and a penitent who hopes that he has earned some trust.

There are many, many different names for God in our tradition. We call God king, prosecutor, judge, jury, shepherd, friend, partner, and many other names as well. But in the last sentence of the *Avinu Malkeinu,* we call God our cashier, the One who keeps a record of all that we would like to have; whom we ask to give them to us on credit, even though we do not deserve them; and to whom we promise that we will try to do better next year.

Let me be clear. This name and all the other names of God that we recite in our liturgy are not meant to be taken literally. *Ein lo d'mut haguf v'eino guf,* "God has no body"[1]—so no name can contain or capture Him—including "Him." Anything that we say about God is an understatement. And yet we use names as figures of speech to describe God, because we have no way other than words with which to do so, and because each name for God describes and defines, however feebly, what we believe is at least one dimension of God's nature.

What then do we mean when we describe God as the cashier?

I think it is our way of saying that the things that we want from God ought really to be earned and that the only currency we have with which to pay for them is good deeds. But we know that in the end, our lives, and all the blessings that we receive within our lives, are favors that God gives us, not things that we have earned. Life itself, after all, is just a gift that we didn't earn. We are born and we will die without being asked, and in between, we hope for health and good fortune, even though we know that for reasons we cannot fathom, bad things happen even to good people.

But no one wants to live totally as the recipient of unearned and undeserved favors. And so we call upon God the cashier: we confess our knowledge that when He goes over our long list of requests, He will see that even though we have not earned them, we ask that God grant them to us anyway—on credit; and we promise that if God does so, we will try to earn our blessings with good deeds in the year to come.

It is a thin line we walk between knowing that our lives are a gift of divine grace and wishing that we could earn at least some of our blessings by our deeds. The former can lead to a sense of helplessness and passivity, in which everything we have and everything we are comes only from God's kindness. The latter can lead to a sense of pride, to a feeling that we deserve all the blessings that we have, that we have indeed actually earned them. The last line of the *Avinu Malkeinu,* at least as the Dubner explains it, is a prayer that strives to avoid both dangers. It keeps us from false pride by reminding us that we cannot ever rightfully claim to have earned the good things we receive in life. But it keeps us from helplessness, by reminding us that, for the blessings we receive, we owe God and that we should promise to pay for them in the only currency that counts in the divine economy—good deeds.

And so, let us not just sing the last words of this prayer, sweet and tuneful as they are. Even as we belt out their melody, let us whisper to ourselves the profoundly awesome message of the two great lessons that they teach: that we are the recipients of divine favor, many times over; and that we ought to try to pay God back for that favor, to whatever extent we can.

Piety and Protest

Rabbi Dennis C. Sasso, DMin

Rabbi Dennis C. Sasso, DMin, has been senior rabbi of Congregation Beth-El Zedeck in Indianapolis, Indiana, since 1977. He lectures worldwide on Caribbean and Central American Sephardic Jewry and teaches about Reconstructionism and on interfaith relations. Rabbi Sasso is a founder and past president of the Reconstructionist Rabbinical Association. He serves on the board of directors for the United Way of Central Indiana, the Greater Indianapolis Progress Committee, and the Lake Family Institute for Faith and Giving of the IUPUI Center on Philanthropy. He is affiliate professor of Jewish studies at Christian Theological Seminary (Disciples of Christ). He contributed to *All the World: Universalism, Particularism and the High Holy Days* (Jewish Lights).

The repetitive refrain of the High Holy Days litany, *Avinu Malkeinu* is as beloved as *Kol Nidre* itself. Like *Kol Nidre*, *Avinu Malkeinu* enjoys a position of privilege: if *Kol Nidre* opens Yom Kippur eve, *Avinu Malkeinu* virtually closes it—coming just before the customary concluding prayers, *Alenu* and *Kaddish*. The same is true of other services on the High Holy Days. By closing *N'ilah* too, *Avinu Malkeinu* provides a capstone to the entire High Holy Day experience, setting the stage for Yom Kippur's concluding proclamations of faith and the final *t'kiah g'dolah* shofar blast.

In all the lengthy Ashkenazi litany, no refrain is better known than the closing words, *Avinu malkeinu, choneinu va'aneinu ki ein banu ma'asim; aseih imanu, tz'dakah vachesed v'hoshi'einu*, "Our father, our king, be gracious to us and answer us, for we have no merit; act justly and lovingly with us and save us" (line 44). It is largely absent in both the Sephardi and the Yemenite traditions and is slightly modified in *Machzor Vitry* (eleventh to twelfth centuries), where it reads, *Avinu malkeinu, choneinu va'aneinu ki ein banu tz'dakah vachesed; aseih imanu l'ma'an shemekha v'hoshi'einu* ("Our father, our king, be gracious to us and answer us, for we have no justice or love; act with us for the sake of your name and save us" (line 44a).

Unique is the Yemenite version, which, among other things, ends *Avinu Malkeinu* with a repetition of the two key words *(avinu malkeinu)* but nothing after them. It is as if it intended yet another line of prayer but stopped short of providing it, thereby inviting worshipers (so to speak) to offer an ending of their own.

Similarly, the Yemenite version ends *N'ilah* with just a short litany, instead of the usual long one:

Avinu malkeinu, You are our father.

Avinu malkeinu, we have none other than You.
Avinu malkeinu, have mercy on us.
Avinu malkeinu, be gracious to us and answer us, for we have no merit; act justly and lovingly with us and save us.

Again, it is as if the Yemenite prayer book were saying, "Here is the basic idea of *Avinu Malkeinu*, but as for filling it out, you may create an entire *Avinu Malkeinu* of your own, before leaving Yom Kippur behind for another year."

Avinu Malkeinu is associated with Rabbi Akiva (second century CE). The Talmud (Ta'anit 25b) describes a time of drought when Rabbi Eliezer was unable to obtain divine favor, and Rabbi Akiva took his place, addressing God as *avinu malkeinu*, "our father, our king." The rains promptly descended. The narrative is quick to dismiss any notions of the greatness of one sage over another but notes that Rabbi Akiva was a more forgiving person *(ma'avir al midotav)* than his colleague, hence God's favorable response to his entreaty.

The theme of forgiveness explains the association of this prayer with the High Holy Days. In the course of time, it was expanded to reflect life as Jews knew it in different settings and circumstances of the Middle Ages. Hence the differences in wording and length among the various liturgical traditions. The Sephardi Rite typically includes 29 verses; the German, 38; the Polish, 44; and the Salonika Rite, 53. Rav Amram Gaon's prayer book (c. 860CE) lists 22 verses in alphabetical order. Neither Saadiah nor Maimonides includes *Avinu Malkeinu* altogether. The Yemenite liturgy provides 24 verses, or, for *N'ilah,* the affirmation cited above as a brief final entreaty.

What is this prayer's appeal? The commentaries highlight the obvious contrasting qualities of the addresses, *avinu* (our father/parent) and *malkeinu* (our king/sovereign/ruler): the first is a statement of intimacy and immediacy, symbolizing God's compassion; the second, a statement of divine authority and transcendence. But the prayer's origins suggest another important frame of reference.

Like many other early Rabbinic prayers, *Avinu Malkeinu* originated during the Roman period and needs to be understood in the context of Roman occupation and oppression. Rabbi Akiva himself is known for his support of the Bar Kokhba revolt (132–135CE).

In a variety of works (especially his *Religion and Empire*), Richard A. Horseley reveals the early Rabbis as mediators between Roman rule and the Judean struggle to maintain tradition in the face of assimilation. The Roman destruction of the Temple and capture of Jerusalem challenged the biblical and Rabbinic view of God as the supreme, benevolent, and just ruler of the world and savior of Israel. The synagogue and the academy provided settings for buttressing Jewish social, cultural, and religious loyalties.

Worth noting is the Roman belief that the birthday of the emperor marked the beginning of a new year—a new creation—even as Rosh Hashanah had come to symbolize God's creation of the world and annual re-enthronement as sovereign of the universe. In his earthly empire, the Roman caesar reigned supreme, imposing *pax romana,* "Roman order/peace," sometimes in benevolent, sometimes in ruthless ways. His titles attest to his powers: *pater*—father; *dominus noster*—our lord; *sebastos/augustus*—majestic, venerable; *auto-krator, imperator*—ruler; *basileus*—king; *soter*—savior.

The forms of divine address in Jewish prayer are a repudiation of Roman claims. It is the God of Israel who is our father, *avinu;* our ruler/king, *malkeinu;* and our compassionate, venerable, and just lord and savior.

While some of these divine terms can be found in earlier periods of Jewish literature, they acquire special resonance during Roman times. More than a language of piety, they constitute a terminology of protest and resistance. We find this also in early Christian circles. Christianity, however, became the religion of the empire and appropriated Roman imperial terminology for Jesus. Judaism remained a minority faith.

A significant number of the phrases in *Avinu Malkeinu* co-opt forms of addressing the emperor for the God of the covenant: the One who is forgiving; the source of new beginnings; the One who grants amnesty; the One who makes or blots out entries in the judicial record of our lives; the One who is just and compassionate, all-powerful, yet forbearing.

Avinu Malkeinu is spiced with insurrectionist, messianic references to the restoration of the Davidic dynasty—a hope we find also in other Jewish prayers of the period, such as the *Amidah, Birkat Hamazon,* the haftarah blessings, and so on. Hence, any effort to comprehend the theological nuances and implications of *Avinu Malkeinu* without understanding its context in the Roman period yields incomplete results.

The refrain *avinu malkeinu* ("our father, our king") resonated with our Judean ancestors in ways that we cannot fully appreciate today. More than a prayer, it was a protestation of fidelity to the God of Israel and a statement of protest against the "divine" Roman emperor. It was a statement of insubordination toward the empire and of subordination to the God of the covenant.

While the invitation to write this essay pointed us, for comparative purposes, to another *s'elichah* ("poem for pardon"; plural: *s'lichot*), *Ki Hinei Kachomer,* I find a more powerful parallel and counterpart in *Ki Anu Amekha* (covered in *Prayers of Awe, We Have Sinned: Sin and Confession in Judaism—Ashamnu and Al Chet,* pp.94–96):

¹Our God and our ancestors' God, forgive us, pardon us, absolve us.
²For we are your people, and You are our God.
³We are your children, and You are our parent.
⁴We are your servants, and You are our master.
⁵We are your community, and You are our lot.
⁶We are your possession, and You are our destiny.
⁷We are your flock, and You are our shepherd.
⁸We are your vineyard, and You are our vintner.
⁹We are your work, and You are our creator.
¹⁰We are your bride, and You are our lover.
¹¹We are your prize, and You are our God.
¹²We are your people, and You are our king.
¹³We are your declaration, and You are our declaration.
¹⁴We are arrogant, and You are forgiving.

¹⁵We are insolent, and You are patient.

¹⁶We are full of sin, and You are full of compassion.

¹⁷We are the ones whose days are like a passing shadow, and You are the One whose years are unending.

The vocabulary of this prayer goes beyond the paternal and monarchical roles of God in *Avinu Malkeinu*, and evokes a whole list of relational terms, inspired by Song of Songs: "I am my beloved's, and my beloved is mine" (2:16). *Ki Anu Amekha* completes the cycle of *s'elichot* that introduces the *Vidui*, or confessional, in the Yom Kippur services. In form, it presents an introductory line (line 1) followed by twelve expressions of human-divine intimacy, feelings of warmth and affection (lines 2–13). The final four lines alter the tone of the prayer by citing human defects (lines 14–17) and prepare us to recite *Ashamnu* (the short confessional).

In the first part of *Ki Anu Amekha*, we are God's people, children, servants, community, possession, flock, vineyard, work (of God's hands), bride, prize, people (again), and declaration (the ones God has spoken for, as it were). In turn, God is our parent, master, lot, destiny, shepherd, vintner, creator, lover, God, king, and declaration. Here we are presented with a cornucopia of divine-human relational vocabulary that suggests our modern efforts to find powerful, moving, and relevant names for God.

As the mood changes and we are ready to beseech God's forgiveness, we move from terms of endearment and confidence to terms of self-abnegation and denigration. We are arrogant, insolent, full of sin, a mere passing shadow. Yet God will hear our prayers, because God is forgiving, patient, full of compassion, and the One whose years are unending.

Ki Anu Amekha ends on a similar note to *Avinu Malkeinu*. God, who is a loving father (parent) and benevolent king (sovereign), will have compassion and answer us, even though we have no merit to plead our cause. We beg for justice *(tz'dakah)* tempered by mercy *(chesed)* and trust in God's saving powers and forgiving nature.

What the Roman emperor was to his subjects, the God of the universe is to Israel. The Jewish people contended with a brutal, worldly, and wicked empire but trusted a benevolent God whose ruling power transcended Rome's and would ultimately triumph. Many of us come to the synagogue, especially during the High Holy Days, seeking comfort in tradition's nostalgic repetition of ancient prayers and familiar melodies. *Avinu Malkeinu* reminds us that the purpose of prayer is not *just* to find refuge and solace, but to arouse us to protest moral and social injustice, to rally against complacencies and idolatries, to consider what we stand for and to whom we are accountable.

Avinu Malkeinu reminds us that prayer can be subversive, a negation of accepted norms and practices. The synagogue is the community where we measure ourselves and society in light of our faith and its ultimate values. Perhaps this is the intent of the last, unfinished version of *Avinu Malkeinu* in the Yemenite ritual—an invitation to add our voice, piety, and protest—in keeping with the spirit and tradition of our sacred heritage.[1]

The Most Difficult Name for God, "You"—Or, How Is Prayer Possible?

Rabbi Jonathan P. Slater, DMin

Rabbi Jonathan P. Slater, DMin, was ordained at The Jewish Theological Seminary of America and has a doctor of ministry degree from the Pacific School of Religion. He is the author of *Mindful Jewish Living: Compassionate Practice* and *A Partner in Holiness: Deepening Mindfulness, Practicing Compassion and Enriching Our Lives through the Wisdom of R. Levi Yitzhak of Berdichev's* Kedushat Levi. He is also codirector of programs at the Institute for Jewish Spirituality as well as an instructor in meditation at the JCC in Manhattan and other venues. He contributed to *Who by Fire, Who by Water—Un'taneh Tokef, All These Vows—Kol Nidre, We Have Sinned: Sin and Confession in Judaism—Ashamnu and Al Chet,* and *All the World: Universalism, Particularism and the High Holy Days* (all Jewish Lights).

When we pray, we open our mouths to say what we hope is true: that we are grateful for our lives; that we look forward to the future; that we are fearful of all that we know may harm us, and even more of that which will harm us but about which we do not yet know. We express our wonder at the incomprehensible universe; at the mystery of love—its acceptance, expectation, and tenderness; at the persistence of our people and our hope for its future; at our hopes for humankind in general. In prayer we locate ourselves in time and space, in history and community.

Yet, there is more to say: that we are imperfect beings who make mistakes; that we are terrified our mistakes will cause greater injury than we already know; that we are capable of causing harm to ourselves, to those we love, and to people we do not even know; that we, so often and without thought, participate in the destruction of our precious world, condemning future generations to suffer. It is painful to recognize these truths; excruciating to bring them to speech. If we hardly dare acknowledge them to ourselves, how much the less can we speak them aloud?

It is not only that we are unwilling to reveal our deepest truths to another. A close reading of the Talmud suggests that doing so may even be impossible. "Rava said: Every person is considered a relative to themselves, so no one can incriminate themselves" (Sanhedrin 9b). To be sure, Rava's adage refers to a court of law, where, in Jewish law as in American, we are not permitted to testify against ourselves, bearing witness to our own falsehood and moral failures.[1] But it is true in another sense as well.

The Hebrew *adam karov etzel atzmo*—which we could understand to mean "no one is closer to us than we ourselves"—implies that only we can know what is in our hearts, so only we can speak it. Yet even there we are liable to shade that truth, bend it, bury it, or parade it with pride. So surely, as soon as we speak it aloud, we inevitably "incriminate" ourselves, and for Rava that is impermissible. Acknowledging the truth to ourselves is difficult; presenting it before another is impossible.

What then are we to do? How can we pray altogether if we cannot even speak the truth aloud?

We read: "More devious is the heart. It is perverse—who can fathom it? I, Adonai, probe the heart, search the mind—to repay every man according to his ways, with the proper fruit of his deeds" (Jeremiah 17:9–10). The same heart that knows its faults and flaws feels pain and grief over them. Yet it cannot tell the truth to ease that pain, and so the truth persists. Though we remain unwilling and unable to speak the truth does not mean that it is gone.

What are we to do? Must we remain silent, unable to offer an honest word, to utter anything true? Are we left bereft of speech, alone in our inner turmoil, or solitary in our celebration of the good in life? Is there any way short of speech that can release us from the overwhelming gravity of our self-consciousness and let us hope for deliverance, redemption, salvation? In a word, "Can we still pray?"

The psalmist found himself in this position. Psalm 130 (deliberately introduced into the morning service from Rosh Hashanah to Yom Kippur) presents the struggle of a master poet who wishes to pray but settles for a cry: "From the depths I call You, Adonai.... Hear my cry; let your ears be attentive to the sound of my supplication" (vv. 1–2).

The psalmist speaks no specific confession here; unable to convert his heart's truth into words, he focuses all his pent-up pain and yearning for forgiveness into a wordless cry as if to say, simply, "Hear just the sound of my unspecified supplication." Calling out without words, he tells God what he knows to be true of his own condition: "When I keep account of my sins, noting and feeling them fully, I can hardly stand; I cannot move." This confession just of his condition brings him relief. It becomes his prayer, and he is redeemed.

In the profoundest way, the *Zohar* (3:70a) describes an inner dynamic to understand how the cry itself delivers us:

> Rabbi Abba said, "[*A song of ascents.*] *From the depths [I call You, Adonai]* (Psalm 130:1)—there is a hidden place above ... from which streams and springs issue in every direction. That deepest depth is called *Teshuvah,* and one who wishes to be purified of his sins must call to the blessed Holy

One through this, as is written: *From the depths I call You, Adonai.*"[2]

For the *Zohar*, "from the depths" does not denote the place where the worshiper is situated. Rather, it is where God lies hidden. Through our cry for healing, God emerges "from the depths." As Daniel Matt explains:

> *The depths* mentioned in this verse do not refer primarily to the depths of the human heart or the depths of despair, but rather to the cosmic depth, *Binah*.... She is known as *Teshuvah* (Return), since all emerges from Her and ultimately returns to Her.
>
> Human *teshuvah* should be focused on this deep realm. From this depth, one should seek to draw forth the divine stream: *From the depths* [in which You are] *I call You* [forth].[3]

For the *Zohar*, aspects of the divine character are represented by spiritual qualities, called *sefirot*. Of these, *Binah* ("Understanding") is the realm of divine comprehension where all potential exists in its original undifferentiated state—no difference yet between good and bad, before and after. *Binah* is the supernal mother, the womb of all existence, where everything still is possible, including change. That is why she is identified with *t'shuvah*: repentance, transformation, and wholeness.

As undifferentiated knowledge itself, *Binah* is the realm of divine energy that best comprehends our own inability to differentiate the depth of our sins in the full specificity of words. If we are unable to find language to access the fullness of what lies within us, we have the option of simply crying out for *Binah* and letting the divine emerge from the depths within us.

We need not remain mired in self-consciousness and pain. Instead, we cry out to the source of compassion and the seat of *t'shuvah*, opening ourselves to transformation. We beg that these qualities emerge from their deep sources to flow into us—and then out again in prayer. Perhaps they will cleanse our hearts, clear our minds—and *finally* (!) open our mouths to speak our truths. Reaching out may let us reach in.

When we prepare ourselves to honor our speech as a constant "reaching out," a plea that we say something true, even though we cannot find the words to do it, we learn to pray. Saying "You," getting out of ourselves by presenting ourselves before another, is the only way out. It is to recognize that we simply cannot do this alone—and that we are not alone.

Poet and Zen teacher Norman Fischer wrote:
> Making language is making prayer. Our utterances, whether silent or voiced, written or thought, distinct or vague, repeated or fleeting, are always essentially prayer, even though we seldom realize it. To speak, to intone, to form words with mouth and heart and spirit, is to reach out and reach

in. What we're always reaching out and into, even when we don't know that we are, is the boundless unknowable, the unnameable. In the end, prayer is not some specialized religious exercise; it is just what comes out of our mouths if we truly pay attention. Debased as it so often is, language at its core always springs forth from what is fundamental in the human heart.[4]

Reaching out to the source of love and transformation is to reach in to our own hearts, to say the truth. Paradoxically, presenting ourselves in truth before another frees us to acknowledge the truth in our hearts, to experience release from shame and pain, and to undertake *t'shuvah*. It is, ultimately, how we come to pray. Recognizing God as the other, as "You," may be the most difficult act of prayer, but without it we cannot speak.

Machzor and Malkhut

THE CHALLENGE OF NAMING A KING

Rabbi David Stern

Rabbi David Stern is senior rabbi of Temple Emanu-El in Dallas, Texas. He contributed to *Who by Fire, Who by Water—Un'taneh Tokef*, *All These Vows—Kol Nidre*, and *May God Remember: Memory and Memorializing in Judaism—Yizkor* (all Jewish Lights).

One day, the king summoned the jester into the royal court, determined to outwit him.

"Jester," he said, "I hear told that you can make a joke about any subject!"

"Yes, Your Highness," the jester replied, "It is true!"

Flushed with victory, the king answered, "I dare you then, to make a joke about me!"

The jester replied, "Ah, but Your Highness, the King is not a subject!"

I do not call any of my children by their given names. Our daughter Lili is Billy or Squib; our daughter Nina is Beans or Boo; our twenty-one-year-old son Jacob still lets me call him Goosie in public.

It's my own parental version of negative theology. No single name could possibly capture or contain the richness of feeling I have for them: the depth of love, the horizon of hope, the judgment and frustration and wonder and glee. So meet my wife's and my progeny: the Squib, the Bean, and the Goose.

If we can't even figure out what to call our own children—finite in body but reaching infinite depths in their parents' hearts—how in the world are we to figure out what to call God? Names delimit, and God is limitless. Naming gives power to the namer over the named—but to imply our power over the Holy One would be to un-God God. Some, like Marcia Falk, suggest that even to call God *atah* ("You") posits a separation between subject and object, a segmentation of being that contradicts the notion of God's oneness. But even if *atah* did not suggest such separation, a blunt and mere "You" does not seem to be the most intimate and tender form of address for the source of all life and hope. (Romance-language translations of Hebrew prayers commonly use the formal rather than the informal second-person singular pronoun for *atah*, opting for transcendence over immanence. I wonder: if Hebrew gave us the option of both formal and informal address for the divine *atah*, would we always make the same choice?)

It seems that the psalmist gives us a hushed and helpful path out of the thicket: *L'kha dumiyah t'hillah*—"To You, silence is praise" (Psalm 65:2).

We will simply remain mum on the issue of divine naming. We won't cheapen the Holy One—or our relationship to every breathtaking sunset—by slathering it with words. We'll just sit up straight, plant our feet on the floor, and breathe.

All of which is good, until you have to write a *machzor*. Until you want to create communal norms, and language and ritual. Until you have to wrestle with the inspiring and vexing nature of naming the unnameable. When even images that feel just right—like *Ein Sof*, or YHVH—endlessness and being—still consist of finite letters in finite words on a finite page.

But we keep at it because we recognize that our own leap toward the ineffable requires some tangible springboard, some kind of image that—if we are at our best—will not limit our sacred imaginations, but launch them. It's how the great poet Marianne Moore famously described the poet's task: the presentation of "imaginary gardens with real toads in them."[1] You can't get to abstraction via abstraction. The word "God" might not get me thinking about the transcendent, but the word "sunset" just might.

The word "sunset," and maybe even the word "king." That's right—as if this whole enterprise of naming weren't challenging enough, we're now going to stir the contradictory brew of verbal necessity and verbal inadequacy with a royal scepter. We're going to take our good twenty-first-century Jews—already struggling with the notion of God, or indifferent, or stuck in fairy-tale conceptions—already tending to be trapped within the confines of words on a page rather than using them as invitations to prayer or sacred imagination—and to that noble, struggling twenty-first-century Jew, we're going to give a bonus challenge: the notion of divine sovereignty.

If you think addressing God as "You" is problematic, try saying "You" to a God who dwells on a throne. Try triggering every modern ambivalence about authority: our zealousness about personal autonomy, our wariness of submission, our vigilance about the oppressive narrowness of gendered language. If our tradition had to go and name the unnameable, why did we have to pick a name that would end up being so complicated?

We're smart enough to know why the anthropomorphism of *melekh* ("king") might have been valuable, and might be still: in conventional interpretation, it signifies protection, providential care, the assertion of order over chaos, a world governed by good.

But there is an irony to our using a human king as metaphor for the divine. In fact, the modern Jew who wrestles with ambivalence about divine sovereignty echoes the concerns of the debate that ensued when Israel first demanded a human king (I Samuel 8). Seeing that wish as an implicit rejection of God, the prophet Samuel warned the people with an angry litany of potential abuses by mortal sovereigns. Ironically, some of his critique now taints our notions of divine rule as well: we worry that the divine *melekh* too might render us powerless or demand that we surrender too much.

How do we keep the king a subject of prayer? We have some options.

We could take an approach I call resigned or rejectionist: simply eliminate the term *melekh* and, with it, any sense of historical or theological continuity.

Alternatively, we can keep using it but give up on gaining meaning from it. It would be as if, centuries from now, God were to paraphrase Exodus 6:3 to say, *Ush'mi melekh lo nodati lahem*, "By my name 'king' I was not known to them." "Yes," God might explain, "the term *melekh* was in use, but those limited moderns were never able to grasp that dimension of my being." It might be humility rather than rote obedience that makes us keep a term in play—even knowing that it does not resonate universally with the sensibility of our own Jewish communities nowadays.

Then too, we could maintain the imagery out of a sense of romance or nostalgia. When Rabbi David Hartman, z"l, returned to his congregation in Montreal after visiting Jerusalem in the weeks following the Six-Day War, he walked into his synagogue on Tisha B'av to find his congregants sitting on the floor and mourning the destruction of Jerusalem. He stood before them and said, "The Jews in Jerusalem are presently jubilant!" He later compared his congregants' jarring chant of *Eichah* (Lamentations) to "the case of a parent who continues praying for a child to get well even after the child's recovery because [the parent] fell in love with the prayer."[2] How could we keep using a term that smacks of gender and power, that all but undermines what Rabbis Elyse Frishman and Peter Knobel have called a "theology of human adequacy," that seems to fly in the face of modern need and modern truth? Maybe we're just in love with the prayer.[3]

But maybe—just maybe—the term *melekh* still has something to teach us. So here are some things I believe. I believe *m'lo khol ha'aretz k'vodo*, "the wholeness of the earth is God's glory" (Isaiah 6:3)—that is, God is all-encompassing being: warp and woof and *din* ("judgment") and *rachamim* ("mercy") and sunset and baby's cry and the way you know your lover's fingerprints in the palm of your hand.

And I embrace (after a lot of struggle) even the hierarchy implied by *melekh*, because it teaches me humility. In the immortal words of Mel Brooks's 2000 Year Old Man, "There's something bigger than Phil." I am part of, and not greater than. And by learning and relearning humility, by practicing and re-practicing, I am able to connect anew to the all-encompassing presence that is *melekh* precisely because it is all-encompassing—sovereign in time and space.

It is for me a deeply sacred spiral when I can find the path: from wonder to humility to wonder again.

The challenge for a *machzor*, of course, is that we depend on it to provide springboards and portals of possibility for our spiritually diverse communities and for any one person's spiritually varied life. So one day I may enter the space of prayer as an overconfident sovereign self, in need of humbling. On another I might already be stricken with *kotzer ru'ach*, what Rashi to Exodus 6:9 calls "shortness of breath"—insecurity, really, about who I am and my right to stand before God; and then I need all the bolstering and nurturing I can find. There may be moments when I need a God who is *melekh*—when a sense of hierarchy or God's-greater-than is healing and anchoring to me. Or moments too when I am already feeling so diminished that assertions of divine power and my own smallness may be the last alienating and discouraging straw.

Here, the use of counter-texts in our prayer books serves a valuable purpose. Counter-texts—divergent translations, interpretations, or reflections that appear in juxtaposition with traditional translations on the page—can offer multiple approaches to the theme of a given prayer and thereby provide theological or philosophical diversity for the worshiper, while retaining the worshiper's relationship to the core themes of the service. Counter-texts help the *machzor* stay true to our varied communities and our variegated selves.

As a concluding reflection on the question of divine sovereignty and human meaning, I'd like to offer a question raised by a moving excerpt from the sixteenth-century kabbalist Moshe Cordovero's *Or Ne'erav*, and two potential responses from the High Holy Day liturgy.

From Cordovero:

> An impoverished person thinks that God is an old man with white hair, sitting on a wondrous throne of fire that glitters with countless sparks....
>
> But if you are enlightened, you know God's oneness; you know that the divine is devoid of bodily categories—these can never be applied to God. Then you wonder, astonished: Who am I? I am a mustard seed in the middle of the sphere of the moon, which itself is a mustard seed within the next sphere. So it is with that sphere and all it contains in relation to the next sphere. So it is with all the spheres—one inside the other—and all of them are a mustard seed within the further expanses. And all of these are a mustard seed within further expanses.
>
> Your awe is invigorated, the love in your soul expands.[4]

I believe that I am a mustard seed in the middle of the moon, which is itself but a mustard seed within the next sphere, and on and on. The challenge is to get from that awareness to

Cordovero's last sentence, about awe and love. How can I help myself—and help others—to see that being a mustard seed on the surface of the moon is in fact a source of awe and not diminution, of nobility and not dehumanizing distance?

One answer lies in the liturgical passage beginning *Hamelekh yosheiv al kisei ram v'nisa* ("King, seated on a high and exalted throne") from the *P'sukei D'zimrah* on Rosh Hashanah morning—the very place that the prayer service for the morning technically begins. (See *My People's Prayer Book,* vol.10, *Shabbat Morning: Shacharit and* Musaf, pp.42–43.) Traditionally, the cantor begins the regular Shabbat service with the words *Shokhein ad marom v'kadosh sh'mo* ("Abiding forever, his name is exalted and holy"), a reference to God's eternality. On the High Holy Days, however, the cantor starts a few words earlier, at "King, seated on a high and exalted throne, abiding forever." So we begin with a powerful declaration of God's eternal sovereignty: "King, seated on a high and exalted throne, abiding forever."

But the prayer then pivots on the first verse of Psalm 33, which proclaims the central human role in exalting the divine: "Acclaim Adonai, all you righteous, for it is fitting for the upright to offer praise." The prayer then continues:

> You will be lauded by the mouths of the upright;

> You will be praised by the words of the righteous;
> You will be exalted by the tongues of the faithful;
> You will be sanctified by the lungs of the holy creatures.

The prayer that begins with a God who is enthroned, distant, and even isolated on high thus moves into a powerful endorsement of human agency. God may be exalted and eternal, but human beings are potentially "upright," "righteous," and "faithful."

In fact, another reading of the final line suggests the necessity of the human prayer community in sanctifying the divine. The Hebrew for "You will be sanctified by the lungs of the holy creatures" is *uv'kerev k'doshim titkadash*. The translation given here ("by the lungs") follows from the fact that it is poetically in parallel to the three lines immediately above it, so must be translated similarly: God is variously "lauded, praised, exalted, and sanctified" by the "mouths, words, tongues, and lungs" of the "upright, righteous, faithful, and holy."

But *uv'kerev* can mean not only "by the lungs of," but "in the midst of"—suggesting that the righteous human community is necessary for God to be enthroned. It is only *uv'kerev k'doshim*—"in the midst of the holy ones," the worshipers who gather—that *titkadash*, "You are made holy."

God's greatness and our agency, God's holiness and human holiness, are therefore not mutually exclusive, but interdependent—there is plenty of *k'dushah* ("holiness") to go around.

An even more poetic affirmation appears in *Ein kitzbah lishnotekha* ("Your years are boundless"), the final passage of *Un'taneh Tokef* (see *Prayers of Awe, Who by Fire, Who by Water*—Un'taneh Tokef, p.47). The passage describes God's unbounded presence, and then *Un'taneh Tokef*, replete with its sometimes overwhelming juxtaposition of our mortality and God's eternity, ends with these three words: *ush'meinu karata vishmekha*—"You named us after You," or "You have linked our name with your own." We are small, but never untethered from the One whose presence fills the earth. We are a seed-speck upon the moon, but never insignificant. *Ush'meinu karata vishmekha*—somehow, our name echoes within the name of God—subject and sovereign, sovereign and subject—all in the call of a single breath.

"We Guess; We Clothe Thee, Unseen King"

Rabbi Margaret Moers Wenig, DD

Rabbi Margaret Moers Wenig, DD, teaches liturgy and homiletics at Hebrew Union College – Jewish Institute of Religion in New York and is rabbi emerita of Beth Am, The People's Temple. She contributed to *Who by Fire, Who by Water—Un'taneh Tokef, All These Vows—Kol Nidre, We Have Sinned: Sin and Confession in Judaism—Ashamnu and Al Chet, May God Remember: Memory and Memorializing in Judaism—Yizkor,* and *All the World: Universalism, Particularism and the High Holy Days* (all Jewish Lights).

> We guess; we clothe Thee, unseen King
> with attributes we deem are meet
> each in his own imagining
> sets up a shadow in Thy seat.[1]

God is ultimately unknowable: the Hidden One, ineffable, unmeasurable, and unfathomable. In the words of the quintessential High Holy Day prayer *Un'taneh Tokef*, "None can describe the chariots of your glory and none can explain the mystery of your name" *(ein sh'un l'mark'vot k'vodekha v'ein peirush l'eilom sh'mekha*").[2] Naming God? It's either a presumptuous endeavor or a marvelous feat of imagination.

"I tell your praise though I have not seen You," proclaims the medieval author of a famous liturgical poem *(Anim Z'mirot)*:

> I describe You though I have not known You
> Your prophets imagined You not as You really are
> They described You by your acts alone
> They multiplied metaphors for You...
> They saw You both in old age and in youth
> With your hair now gray, now black
> As a wise old judge, as a handsome young warrior...

We've inherited many imaginative metaphors for God, among them eagles' wings, a strong hand, an outstretched arm, shield, rock, shepherd, father, and king. But on Rosh Hashanah, the most favored by far is king, appearing in many different formulations: "the king" *(hamelekh)*, "the holy king" *(hamelekh hakadosh)*, "king over all the earth" *(melekh al kol ha'aretz)*, to name but a few.

A personal caveat is in order regarding the elegant substitutions for the gendered word "king." *Machzorim* like *Kol Haneshamah* prefer

"Eternal One," "Almighty One," "Majestic One," "Mighty One," "The One Alone," "Sovereign of all worlds," and the like. I deeply appreciate such alternatives; I have employed them myself.[3] But I wish also to retain the traditional gendered "God as king" as well as to create new gendered names and images for God. I do not object to imagining God as both immanent and transcendent—even as a "power over us." In fact, as empowered as I feel to have been created by God, in the image of God, I am also profoundly cognizant of my human limitations, and I prefer religious language that acknowledges them.

So what might those who call God "king" imagine God to be?

The first metaphoric reference to God as king appears in the Song of the Sea, sung when the Israelites escaped the hot pursuit of *melekh mitzrayim* ("the king of Egypt"). Surely, at that very moment in mythical time, singing *Adonai yimlokh l'olam va'ed* ("God will rule forever and ever"; Exodus 15:18) must have conveyed a conviction that there indeed *is* One more powerful than any mortal king, ruler, or sovereign.

But calling God "king" does not imply a *similarity* between God and a mortal ruler. Quite the contrary. Nothing makes that clearer, perhaps, than the prayer still recited by Jews in the United Kingdom for "Our Sovereign Lady Queen Elizabeth, Duke of Edinburgh, Charles,

Prince of Wales, and all the Royal Family," in which God is referred to, no fewer than three times, as "king, king of all the kings" *(melekh malkhei ham'lakhim)*[4] whose reign is a "reign for all time" *(malkhuto malkhut kol olamim)*.[5]

The reign of mortal kings *(melekh basar vadam*, as the Rabbis say, "a king of flesh and blood") comes and goes. Terms end, elections are lost; human kings are beheaded, presidents impeached; policies of one ruler are reversed by another; and for the brief time that an emperor, sultan, president, or prime minister is sovereign, he or she rules but one nation or empire on earth. The rule of *hamelekh* ("the king"), by contrast, is *chai v'kayam* ("undying"), not for a generation or a term but *l'olam va'ed* ("forever"). And God's sovereignty extends *al kol ha'olam kulo* ("over the whole universe in its entirety").

And to what does God's sovereignty refer? When the *machzor* speaks of the "king, king of all the kings," it means the One who "planted the heavens and created the earth" *(shehu noteh shamayim v'yoseid aretz)*[6]—the One, that is, who set into motion immutable laws of nature: the earth revolves around the sun, the moon round the earth, day follows night, winter follows autumn, continental plates shift, volcanoes erupt, glaciers slowly carve the earth, seas cover most of the planet. "The world is charged with the grandeur of God."[7] And the grandeur, the glory, the wonder, the awe, the powerful forces of nature for which we mortals can take no credit, are attributed to *melekh ha'olam,* "ruler of time and space."

God's sovereignty, however, connotes immutable laws not just of nature, but of morality as well. Alas, at present, lamented Rav Joseph Soloveitchik, "the kingdom of God [*malkhut shamayim*] is to be found solely in the natural law. As far as the moral law is concerned ... God's sovereignty is not yet universally accepted."[8]

The problem, Soloveitchik explains, is that "God provided [us] with free will,"[9] and we do not always *choose* to subordinate our will to God's. We follow our *yetzer hara* (our baser inclination), capitulating, perhaps, to the pressure of peers or the unjust will of the state.

The conflicts are legion: advertising makes us want things we do not need, whereas the morality of *malkhut shamayim* forbids coveting what others have; our careers are more easily advanced if we work seven days a week, while *malkhut shamayim* commands a day of rest; even as Washington cuts food stamps, *malkhut shamayim* requires us to feed the hungry; some are tempted into extramarital affairs, even though *malkhut shamayim* prohibits them. Alas, divine sovereignty has yet to be fully established in the moral realm.

Thus, on Rosh Hashanah we pray for what is not yet established: *M'lokh al kol ha'olam kulo* ("Reign, O God, over the whole universe in its entirety").[10] May the norms of goodness one day rule universally, as the laws of nature now do.

Malkhut—the kingship of the divine—is fundamental to both realms. If we could not predict that day would follow night and night follow day, our world would be chaos. So too, without a predictable moral universe, our world becomes "a mess."[11] Perhaps coincidentally—or some prefer, mystically—the root letters of "king" and "sovereignty" *(m.l.kh)* are *at the very center* of the Hebrew alphabet. Quite intentionally, that prayer "Reign, O God, over the whole universe in its entirety" is at the very center of the central blessing of every *Amidah* on Rosh Hashanah, the day on which we pray for the world to be created anew.

Rosh Hashanah is not, however, the only time our liturgy offers us the metaphor of God as king. "God as king" pervades our prayers throughout the entire year: daily, in every morning blessing, every *Kaddish*, every *Mi Khamokhah* (recalling the Song of the Sea), every *K'dushah,* and every *Alenu*. And weekly, every psalm of *Kabbalat Shabbat,* except one, mentions *melekh*. Moreover, God is acknowledged as *melekh ha'olam* in every blessing, day in, day out—a stipulation going back to Rav Yochanan in the Gemara[12] and repeated regularly thereafter.[13]

Now, go ahead, pronounce aloud these formulaic words that introduce our blessings: *Barukh atah Adonai eloheinu melekh ha'olam*. Many of us race through them without noticing the attribute *melekh ha'olam*. Some of us might also race through life without regularly noticing the majesty that pervades our natural world. And we might equally fall prey to behaving in ways that are inconsistent with *ol malkhut shamayim* ("the yoke of the kingdom of heaven").

Perhaps using *and noticing* the name "king of the universe" *(melekh ha'olam)* in our prayers and blessings might increase our awareness of the majesty in nature that does suffuse our world and the moral majesty that ought to suffuse our world.

The central blessing of every *Amidah* on Rosh Hashanah expresses a longing for a time when we, as created beings, will "understand that [no less than] You, [God,] formed us" *(v'yavin kol yatzur ki atah y'tzarto)* and that "God is king and his dominion [is not just *over* everything but also planted] *within* everything" *(V'yomar ... Adonai ... melekh, umalkhuto bakol mashalah),* including our very own human selves.[14] With a whole heart on Rosh Hashanah I do pray, "Rule, O God, over the whole universe in its entirety," longing for the establishment of God's sovereignty in the moral universe, not just the physical one, and hoping for its manifestation in the deeds of all humankind.

From Direct Experience to a World of Words

THE GOD WE STRUGGLE TO KNOW

Rabbi Daniel G. Zemel

Rabbi Daniel G. Zemel is the senior rabbi of Temple Micah in Washington, DC. He contributed to *Who by Fire, Who by Water—Un'taneh Tokef, All These Vows—Kol Nidre, We Have Sinned: Sin and Confession in Judaism—Ashamnu and Al Chet, May God Remember: Memory and Memorializing in Judaism—Yizkor*, and *All the World: Universalism, Particularism and the High Holy Days* (all Jewish Lights).

"The Absolute can be shown but not said," writes philosopher Terry Eagleton.[1] This, as much as anything, captures the Jewish notion of God. Change the word "shown" to "experienced" and we have it. The God of Torah is the absolute who is experienced but never completely captured in the saying. God is the one with the ineffable name.

How ironic, then, to insist that we can pray. How can you call out to someone whose name you never fully get to say? Yet we insist on trying. Time and again, we say *avinu malkeinu!*

What might this mean, or as the Rabbis might have put it, *L'mah hadavar domeh?* "To what can this be compared?"

Possibly, since God has no *name,* we should compare it to a *title.* In the so-called real world, after all, we use titles all the time without a name: "general," "senator," "judge," "sir," "professor," "Dr.," "cabbie," "waiter." It is functional and utilitarian. It uses a title for the roles people play in our dealings with them. The judge is, at best, "Your Honor," never Samuel, Lisa, or Catherine. Yet it is not that these people *have* no names; it is just that the names are irrelevant at the time.

So indeed, *L'mah hadavar domeh?* To what can God be compared? Not to this kind of nameless role-playing, where we call out, "Nurse," or ask for a "rabbi" and get one—any one, nameless even though he/she has a name. This is the I-It realm of Martin Buber. Insofar as they are referred to by their roles, people are "its," in the Buber sense, for we have no particular one of them in mind at the time. Or if we do—if we prefer Smith as our salesperson rather than Jones—it is just because Smith is particularly good at her job, not because we have a genuine relationship with her.

But as Buber saw it, God is (by definition) never an "it." Instead of roles, which any competent person can play, God lives in relationships; there is just one God, moreover, and the purpose of the relationship is the relationship itself. God is the ultimate "Thou" (in Buber's terms) in relationship with whom we come to discover the world and ourselves, so to speak.

So we ask again: *L'mah hadavar domeh?* To what can this be compared?

If we are fortunate, the most important relationship of our lives, the one into which we are born, and the one that provides the ultimate human intimacy of the "I-Thou," evokes the words most similar to what we mean by God: "mom," "mommy," "mother," "dad," "daddy," "father." These too are titles, but titles of a single and singular person whom we know through intimate relationship rather than just an objective description of what that person does. The ones who introduce us to the world, our very first teachers who, we pray, take us lovingly from infancy to independence, from rebellion to responsibility, with them it is always the title of a relationship to which only one single person need apply. Words fail when we struggle to explain what that person means to us. The true depth of the relationship can be shown but not said. *Avinu malkeinu* is such a relationship-title, not a role-title—idealized to the point of being God.

But true relationships are immediately present to us. The very essence of I-Thou relationships is their immediacy, after all. So it is that in the sacred texts we read, God is always known in the immediacy of experience: the pillar of smoke in the wilderness, the bush that burns. No wonder we have trouble with God's "names"—we confuse them with titles for which there are roles, as if God were any king, any parent, just one of many examples that fulfill the dictionary definition. Without the lived experience, we have only the idea of God, a remote thing of theory. We find ourselves limited to reflections on a hypothetical "It," even as our souls hunger for the genuine certainty of "Thou"; we are left with empty titles, Shakespeare's "bare ruined choirs" in place of Elijah's "still small voice."

It wasn't always so. Let us look more carefully at the Bible, where (as I said) God encounters are experiential overflowings of "Thou." Abraham serves food and washes the feet of three visiting strangers who are apparitions of God. God talks to him-/herself in Abraham's presence, wondering how much of his/her plans he/she should share. Abraham feels on good enough terms to tell God that the plan God is undertaking should be reconsidered.

Jacob engages in a nocturnal wrestling match with a muscular God apparition, who wrenches his thigh and sends him off limping. The fierceness of the intimacy has risen in intensity from Abraham's verbal sparring over Sodom to something akin to sibling roughhousing over who must do what first. As dawn breaks and the apparition leaves, Jacob calls the place "God's Face," for as much as it is possible, he has "seen" God there. Still later, when Jacob reconciles with Esau, he says, "Seeing your face is like seeing the face of God" (Genesis 33:10), perhaps recalling the wrestling match of the previous night. Jacob can see the sacred in the merely human.

Moses begins this way too—with direct experience of God. At the burning bush, he takes off his shoes and learns God's name, *ehyeh asher ehyeh*. But what kind of name is that? As past-present-future, it must be the ongoing description of God's immediacy in relationships that will change with time but will always be God as presence, not as theory: the experience itself. Like time, actually—we know time only through experience. Try to define time. Try to explain what time means to a child. Time is the plane on which all experiences happen. This is God's name.

All this changes at Sinai. At Sinai God gives us words. Moses alone now has the direct experience, about which he composes a poetic outburst, such as a lover will sing for his beloved: "Compassionate, gracious, slow to anger, great in kindness and truth, maintaining love, and forgiving!" (Exodus 34:6–7).

From this moment on, our relationship with God moves from intimate to formal. The age of God's miracles is passing. In its place God has given us words. We will ever after struggle to reclaim moments of God's immediacy.

In a way, it is a great loss not to have God in our lives as the patriarchs did, but words are what distinguish humankind. We tell our children, "Use your words!" Sinai, the revelation of words, is the moment of our growing up.

Moses is the transition figure. How ironic that he, of all people, should be trusted to receive Torah, the covenant of words (Jews even call the Ten Commandments *aseret hadibrot,* "the ten words"). He is slow of speech, remember, and he flunks his first test with words when he hits the rock with a staff instead of speaking to it. That very staff had worked before, but now, post-Sinai, God wants words. No more wrestling matches; the age of experience is over.

For Jews, the new world of the words entails commandments. Leviticus follows Exodus, therefore, with ritual after ritual, sacrifice after sacrifice, but not as matters of rote. Rather, like prayer, which the Rabbis will invent in years to come, these are attempts to live through Torah, through word and commandment, but to do so in such a way as to recapture moments of immediacy. Yearning to connect to God, we devise myriad rituals and words to capture relationships: shepherd, rock, savior, warrior, lawgiver, creator, source, peace, master. These are metaphors of *relationship,* however, not of role. They become God's names. And among them, the metaphors of the High Holy Days stand out.

Avinu: We call out to God as we do to our parents—"giver of life, the one we can trust, the one to whom we run when we are frightened, the one who embraces us, takes us in, loves us absolutely." We confront life's ultimate contingency—the miracle that we are alive at all. We yearn for approval and the knowledge that our lives have meaning and purpose.

Malkeinu: We acknowledge that we stand before the sovereign of sovereigns, the creator not just of ourselves but of all the universe, and we know that we come to this place and time to be judged.

Then too, we read on these Days of Awe that we are like clay in the hands of the potter, stone in the hands of the carver. We like to think we shape ourselves, but we do not. We simply cannot control the destiny of our lives. Hence, once again, we think, *malkeinu*—the unpredictable path of life is in God's hands, not our own; and *avinu*—we long, at least, for a divine parent to share our journey with us.

The book from which we pray on these High Holy Days, the same book that belabors the case for God as *avinu* and *malkeinu,* provides, as well, myriad other names that our past has left us. One of these is God as court recorder, the scribe of justice who has another book in hand, the one that records the names and deeds that we will leave behind. Where will our name be written? We pray to the "God who is passionate for life," to write our own names once more in the book of life. When we call *avinu malkeinu*, we beg for our journey to continue.

Appendix A

Avinu Malkeinu through Time

Rabbi Lawrence A. Hoffman, PhD

What follows is a page-by-page listing of the several versions (the *minhagim*, or "rites," as they are called) that are included in the composite liturgy of part 2 (pp.41–64). That composite combines the various rites (Ashkenazi, Sephardi, Yemenite, and so on), so that, at a glance, the great variety of *Avinu Malkeinu* becomes evident. Here, we separate out each rite so that readers can see what they encompass individually. We provide only the English here, but readers can consult the original Hebrew by turning to part 2, where it appears alongside the composite English. The lines here are numbered to coincide with the Hebrew numbering there.

Ashkenazi-Polish Rite (Minhag Polin)

Minhag Polin is the liturgy most likely to be found among Jews worldwide, simply because of the large number of Jews who left Poland (and Eastern Europe generally) to settle in Israel, Europe, and the Americas in the Great Migration that began in 1881. As mentioned in part 1 ("The

History, Meaning, and Varieties of *Avinu Malkeinu*," pp.3–15), it derives from an earlier Ashkenazi Rite, the one developed first in the German Rhineland and known as *Minhag Rinus*. Jews moved from Germany to Poland in the sixteenth and seventeenth centuries, bringing *Minhag Rinus* with them; it eventually evolved to become *Minhag Polin*. With time, however, the influence of Kabbalah saturated much of Eastern Europe, especially those areas where Hasidic Jews predominated. *Minhag Polin*, then, is the Ashkenazi version of prayer that emanated from Germany, evolved further in and around Poland, and was eventually intermixed with influence from kabbalistic lands around the Mediterranean, especially Israel.

To represent *Minhag Polin*, we have selected the classic edition of Philip Birnbaum, published in 1951.[1] Later in these pages, we provide another version of *Minhag Polin*, side by side with *Minhag Rinus* (see section entitled "Ashkenazi-German Rite (Minhag Rinus)").

In general, the texts in this section are translated for the first time from the original Hebrew. For *Minhag Polin*, however, our original translation occurs in part 2 (pp.46–58). Rather

---

[1] Philip Birnbaum, ed., Machzor Hashalem: High Holyday Prayer Book (New York: Hebrew Publishing Co., 1951), 271–75.

than reproduce it here, we provide Birnbaum's English translation, for comparison.

Minhag Polin (Birnbaum, 1951)

¹Our Father, our King, we have sinned before thee.

²Our Father, our King, we have no king except thee.

³Our Father, our King, deal with us kindly for the sake of thy name.

⁴Our Father, our King, renew us for a good year.

⁵Our Father, our King, abolish all evil decrees against us.

⁶Our Father, our King, annul the plans of our enemies.

⁷Our Father, our King, frustrate the counsel of our foes.

⁸Our Father, our King, rid us of every oppressor and adversary.

⁹Our Father, our King, close the mouths of our adversaries and accusers.

¹⁰Our Father, our King, remove pestilence, sword, famine, captivity, destruction, iniquity, and persecution from thy people of the covenant.

¹¹Our Father, our King, keep the plague back from thy heritage.

¹²Our Father, our King, forgive and pardon all sins.

¹³Our Father, our King, blot out and remove our transgressions and sins from thy sight.

¹⁴Our Father, our King, cancel in thy abundant mercy all the records of our sins.

¹⁵Our Father, our King, bring us back in perfect repentance to thee.

¹⁶Our Father, our King, send a perfect healing to the sick among thy people.

¹⁷Our Father, our King, tear up the evil sentence decreed against us.

¹⁸Our Father, our King, remember us favorably.

¹⁹Our Father, our King, inscribe us in the book of a happy life.

²⁰Our Father, our King, inscribe us in the book of redemption and salvation.

²¹Our Father, our King, inscribe us in the book of maintenance and sustenance.

²²Our Father, our King, inscribe us in the book of merit.

²³Our Father, our King, inscribe us in the book of pardon and forgiveness.

²⁴Our Father, our King, cause our salvation soon to flourish.

²⁵Our Father, our King, raise the strength of Israel thy people.

²⁶Our Father, our King, raise the strength of thy anointed one.

²⁷Our Father, our King, fill our hands with thy blessings.

²⁸Our Father, our King, fill our storehouses with plenty.

²⁹Our Father, our King, hear our voice, spare us and have mercy upon us.

³⁰Our Father, our King, receive our prayer with mercy and favor.

³¹Our Father, our King, open the gates of heaven to our prayers.

³²Our Father, our King, dismiss us not empty-handed from thy presence.

³³Our Father, our King, remember that we are but dust.

³⁴Our Father, our King, may this hour be an hour of mercy and a time of grace with thee.

³⁵Our Father, our King, have compassion on us, on our children and our infants.

³⁶Our Father, our King, act for the sake of those who were slain for thy holy name.

³⁷Our Father, our King, act for the sake of those who were slaughtered for proclaiming thy Oneness.

³⁸Our Father, our King, act for the sake of those who went through fire and water for the sanctification of thy name.

³⁹Our Father, our King, avenge the spilt blood of thy servants.

⁴⁰Our Father, our King, do it for thy sake if not ours.

⁴¹Our Father, our King, do it for thy sake and save us.

⁴²Our Father, our King, do it for the sake of thy abundant mercy.

⁴³Our Father, our King, do it for the sake of thy great, mighty, and revered name by which we are called.

⁴⁴Our Father, our King, be gracious to us and answer us, though we have no merit; deal charitably and kindly with us and save us.

Our First Extant Prayer Book, Babylonia, circa 860CE (Seder Rav Amram)

The earliest appearance of *Avinu Malkeinu* as a litany for the High Holy Days is in *Seder Rav Amram*, our first extant comprehensive liturgy, compiled by Rav Amram Gaon (Baghdad, c. 860CE). To the best of our knowledge, Amram's version is the basis for all others, which borrowed from him and then added to, subtracted from, or otherwise emended Amram's lines—not necessarily on purpose, but perhaps as a consequence of the process of oral transmission over time. Our version of Amram's work comes from the scientific edition published by Daniel Goldschmidt, in 1970.[2]

Goldschmidt died just two years later (1972), but to this day he remains unequaled for his work in unearthing and cataloging the manuscript variants of Jewish liturgical texts worldwide. He signed his books "Daniel Goldschmidt" (the practice I follow when citing him here), but he is better known as E.D. Goldschmidt, from "Ernst Daniel," the names given him in Germany, where he was born. Until 1936, he served as librarian in the Prussian State Library of Berlin but then fled the Nazis for Israel, where he began omitting his Germanic name "Ernst." As "Daniel," he devoted the rest of his life to the study of the Jewish People's liturgy, a liturgical extension of Zionism, in a way—as Zionists were intent on gathering in Jews living "in exile," so too, Goldschmidt wished to highlight the ingathering of texts that testified to the many ways that Jews had prayed around the world.

Seder Rav Amram

[1] Our father, our king, we have sinned before You.

[2] Our father, our king, we have no king other than You.

---

[2] Daniel Goldschmidt, Seder Rav Amram Gaon (Jerusalem: Mossad Rav Kook, 1971), 138–39.

³Our father, our king, act with us for the sake of your name.

⁵ᵇOur father, our king, cancel all our burdensome decrees.

⁴ᵃOur father, our king, grant us good new decrees.

⁶ᵇOur father, our king, cancel the plans against us of those who hate us.

⁷Our father, our king, disrupt the schemes of those who are our enemies.

¹⁶Our father, our king, send perfect healing to those among your people who are ill.

¹¹ᵃOur father, our king, stop the plague from your heritage.

¹⁰ᵇOur father, our king, put an end to pestilence, war, famine, and destruction among the people of your covenant.

³³Our father, our king, remember that we are but dust.

⁴⁰ᵃOur father, our king, act for your sake and not for our sake.

¹⁷ᵃOur father, our king, tear up for us the sentence decreed against us.

¹⁴ᵇOur father, our king, erase our notes of debt.

¹²ᵇOur father, our king, forgive and pardon our sins.

¹³ᵃOur father, our king, erase and remove our sins from your sight.

¹⁵Our father, our king, place us again before You in perfect repentance.

¹⁹ᵇOur father, our king, write us in the book of life.

²²ᵃOur father, our king, write us in the book of memory.

²²Our father, our king, write us in the book of merit.

²¹Our father, our king, write us in the book of livelihood and sustenance.

²⁴Our father, our king, cause salvation to flourish for us soon.

²⁹Our father, our king, hear our voice; have compassion and mercy on us.

³⁰Our father, our king, accept our prayer with mercy and favor.

⁴³ᵃOur father, our king, act for the sake of your great name.

⁴²ᵃOur father, our king, act for the sake of your great compassion and have compassion on us.

⁴⁴Our father, our king, be gracious to us and answer us, for we have no merit; act justly and lovingly with us and save us.

France, Eleventh to Twelfth Centuries (Machzor Vitry)

Machzor Vitry is the work, primarily, of Rabbi Simchah of Vitry, a student of the great French commentator Rashi. Rashi had studied in the Ashkenazi academies of the Rhineland, but when they were destroyed in the First Crusade, his own school in France emerged as the predominant representative of Ashkenazi Jewry. As part of its legacy, Simchah collected the liturgical practices of Ashkenaz in this comprehensive work called *Machzor Vitry*.

We rely on the standard edition published first in 1893 and then again in 1923, by a set of German scholars who had hoped to make available a vast number of works from the Jewish past but whose efforts came to an end with the Nazis.[3] That edition, however, had relied on relatively late manuscripts from the thirteenth and fourteenth centuries, the authors of which frequently altered the wording of prayers that they found before them so as to accord with the way liturgical custom had developed by their time. An earlier "Reggio" manuscript (from Reggio Emilia in northern Italy) preserves an earlier and

---

[3] Shimon Halevi Ish Horowitz, ed., Machzor Vitry L'rabbenu Simchah, vol.1 (Nurenberg: M'kitzei Nirdamim, 1923), 384.

more authentic version of the prayers in question, providing us with the Ashkenazi Rite as it was practiced in France during the time of Rashi.

Daniel Goldschmidt (see section entitled "Our First Extant Prayer Book, Babylonia, circa 860CE (Seder Rav Amram)") studied the Reggio manuscript and listed its differences from the printed version. Most of these (in *Avinu Malkeinu*) are minor, just variations in a single word here and there. But Goldschmidt lists also an entirely new line, "Our father, our king, show us a sign of good" *(Avinu malkeinu, aseih imanu ot l'tovah)*.[4]

Machzor Vitry

[1]Our father, our king, we have sinned before You.

[2]Our father, our king, we have no king other than You.

[3a]Our father, our king, act kindly with us for the sake of your name.

[5]Our father, our king, cancel all burdensome decrees against us.

[7b]Our father, our king, disrupt the schemes against us of those who are our enemies.

---

[4] Daniel Goldschmidt, "Nusach Hat'fillot shel Machzor Vitry K'tav Yad Reggio," in Daniel Goldschmidt, *Mechkarei T'fillah Ufiyyut* (Jerusalem: Magnes Press, 1979 [posthumously]), 77.

⁶ᵃOur father, our king, spoil the plans of those who hate us.

⁹ᵃOur father, our king, shut the mouths of our enemies and accusers.

⁹ᵇOur father, our king, side with those who teach our merits.

⁸ᵃOur father, our king, put an end to every one of our adversaries and foes.

¹⁰ᶜOur father, our king, put an end to pestilence, war, famine, captivity, destruction, and plague among the people of your covenant.

¹⁶ᵃOur father, our king, send perfect healing to all those among your people who are ill.

¹¹Our father, our king, prevent the plague among your heritage.

¹²ᵃOur father, our king, pardon and forgive all our sins.

¹⁷Our father, our king, tear up the evil sentence decreed against us.

¹⁴Our father, our king, in your great mercy erase all of our notes of debt.

¹³ᵃOur father, our king, erase and remove our sins from your sight.

¹⁹Our father, our king, write us in the book of good life.

²²ᵇOur father, our king, write us in the book of peace.

²²ᶜOur father, our king, write us in the book of sustaining food.

²¹Our father, our king, write us in the book of livelihood and sustenance.

²⁰ᵇOur father, our king, write us in the book of salvation and redemption.

²⁴Our father, our king, cause salvation to flourish for us soon.

²⁵Our father, our king, give strength to your people Israel.

²⁶Our father, our king, give strength to your messiah.

²⁶ᵇOur father, our king, give strength to your altar.

²⁹Our father, our king, hear our voice; have compassion and mercy on us.

³⁰Our father, our king, accept our prayer with mercy and favor.

⁴²Our father, our king, act for the sake of your great compassion.

⁴³ᵇOur father, our king, act for the sake of your great and revered name by which we are called.

⁴⁰Our father, our king, act for your sake if not for our sake.

⁴¹Our father, our king, act for your sake and save us.

⁴¹ᵃOur father, our king, do not let sin and transgression interrupt our prayer.

³²Our father, our king, do not return us empty-handed from before You.

[34a]"Our father, our king, may this hour and every hour be favorable and an hour of your mercy before You.

[44a]"Our father, our king, be gracious to us and answer us, for we have no justice or love; act with us for the sake of your name and save us.

Italy, Thirteen to Sixteenth Centuries (Machzor Roma)

The dates indicated above (thirteenth to sixteenth centuries) correspond to the period whence manuscripts for this important rite can be dated, but the rite itself is much older than that. *Machzor Roma* (the "Roman *Machzor*," a precursor of what came to be known as the Italian Rite) is the name we give to the order of prayer that emerged in late antiquity throughout many areas of the northern Mediterranean: Italy (first and foremost), but also elsewhere, such as current-day Greece and the Balkan countries, which eventually developed rites of their own (called *Minhag Yavan*, "the Greek Rite," and *Minhag Romaniot*, "the Romanian Rite").

Other than in scholarly works, *Machzor Roma* is rarely cited in surveys of Jewish liturgy, but we have included it here because it is perhaps the earliest instance of independent liturgy outside the two major Jewish communities of late antiquity, the Land of Israel (Palestine) and Babylonia. The version we use comes from

Samuel David Luzzatto (known as ShaDaL = Sh[muel] D[avid] L[uzzatto]), an Italian scholar, philosopher, and commentator, who published an edition of *Machzor Roma* in 1856.⁵

Machzor Roma

¹Our father, our king, we have sinned before You.

²Our father, our king, we have no king other than You.

³Our father, our king, act with us for the sake of your name.

⁵ᵇOur father, our king, cancel all our burdensome decrees.

⁴ᵇOur father, our king, grant us good new tidings.

⁴Our father, our king, grant us a good new year.

⁶Our father, our king, cancel the plans of those who hate us.

⁷Our father, our king, disrupt the schemes of those who are our enemies.

¹⁶Our father, our king, send perfect healing to those among your people who are ill.

---

5   Samuel David Luzzatto, ed., Machzor Kol Hashanah K'fi Minhag K[hillot] K['doshot] Italiani, vol.2 (Livorno, 1856), 39.

[11a] Our father, our king, stop the plague from your heritage.

[10c] Our father, our king, put an end to pestilence, war, famine, captivity, destruction, and plague among the people of your covenant.

[33] Our father, our king, remember that we are but dust.

[17] Our father, our king, tear up the evil sentence decreed against us.

[14a] Our father, our king, erase our note of debt.

[12b] Our father, our king, forgive and pardon our sins.

[13] Our father, our king, erase and remove our sins and our transgressions from your sight.

[15] Our father, our king, place us again before You in perfect repentance.

[32a] Our father, our king, do not return us empty-handed from before You.

[18] Our father, our king, remember us favorably before You.

[19a] Our father, our king, write us in the book of life.

[22] Our father, our king, write us in the book of merit.

[20a] Our father, our king, write us in the book of salvation and comfort.

[21] Our father, our king, write us in the book of livelihood and sustenance.

²³ᵇOur father, our king, write us in in the book of pardon and forgiveness and atonement.

²⁴Our father, our king, cause salvation to flourish for us soon.

²⁹ᵃOur father, our king, hear our voice and have compassion and mercy on us.

³⁰Our father, our king, accept our prayer with mercy and favor.

⁴⁰ᵃOur father, our king, act for your sake and not for our sake.

⁴³ᶜOur father, our king, act for the sake of your great, mighty, and revered name.

⁴²ᵇOur father, our king, act for the sake of your great compassion and your enormous love and have compassion on us.

Ashkenazi-German Rite (Minhag Rinus)

As mentioned (p.264), our baseline Ashkenazi version, the one most commonly found nowadays, hails from Poland and is known as *Minhag Polin* ("the Polish Rite"). It is, however, a later version of an earlier one from Germany proper, known as *Minhag Rinus* ("the Rhineland Rite"), which is still used among communities that hail from modern-day Germany, rather than from Eastern Europe. Daniel Goldschmidt (whose version of *Seder Rav Amram* we use, p.267) left us also with a scientific edition of the Ashkenazi *machzor* for the High Holy Days, in which he compared *Minhag Rinus* with *Minhag Polin*. We provide his comparison of *Avinu Malkeinu* here.

Goldschmidt's version of *Minhag Polin* differs in some tiny respects from the Birnbaum version that we use as our primary text, because he offers a scientific edition based on manuscript comparison. His version is thus more accurate, but not necessarily what Jews today are used to—hence not our selection as "baseline" representative.[6]

Minhag Rinus	Minhag Polin
[1]Our father, our king, we have sinned before You.	[1]Our father, our king, we have sinned before You.
[2]Our father, our king, we have no king other than You.	[2]Our father, our king, we have no king other than You.
[3]Our father, our king, act with us for the sake of your name.	[3]Our father, our king, act with us for the sake of your name.
[4]Our father, our king, grant us a good new year.	[4]Our father, our king, grant us a good new year.
[5]Our father, our king, cancel all burdensome decrees against us.	[5]Our father, our king, cancel all burdensome decrees against us.
[6]Our father, our king, cancel the plans of those who hate us.	[6]Our father, our king, cancel the plans of those who hate us.

---

[6] Daniel Goldschmidt, Machzor Layamin Hanora'im, vol.1 [Rosh Hashanah] (New York: Leo Baeck Institute, 1970), 131–32.

⁷Our father, our king, disrupt the schemes of those who are our enemies.

⁸Our father, our king, put an end to every one of our adversaries and foes.

⁹Our father, our king, shut the mouths of our adversaries and accusers.

¹⁰Our father, our king, put an end to pestilence, war, famine, captivity, destruction, sin, and extermination among the people of your covenant.

¹¹Our father, our king, prevent the plague among your heritage.

¹⁶Our father, our king, send perfect healing to those among your people who are ill.

¹⁵Our father, our king, place us again before You in perfect repentance.

¹²Our father, our king, forgive and pardon all our sins.

¹³ᵃOur father, our king, erase and remove our sins from your sight.

¹⁷Our father, our king, tear up the evil sentence decreed against us.

---

⁷Our father, our king, disrupt the schemes of those who are our enemies.

⁸Our father, our king, put an end to every one of our adversaries and foes.

⁹Our father, our king, shut the mouths of our adversaries and accusers.

¹⁰Our father, our king, put an end to pestilence, war, famine, captivity, destruction, sin, and extermination among the people of your covenant.

¹¹Our father, our king, prevent the plague among your heritage.

¹²Our father, our king, forgive and pardon all our sins.

¹³ᵃOur father, our king, erase and remove our sins from your sight.

¹⁴Our father, our king, in your great mercy erase all of our notes of debt.

¹⁵Our father, our king, place us again before You in perfect repentance.

¹⁶Our father, our king, send perfect healing to those among your people who are ill.

¹⁴Our father, our king, in your great mercy erase all of our notes of debt.

³³Our father, our king, remember that we are but dust.

¹⁸Our father, our king, remember us favorably before You.

¹⁹Our father, our king, write us in the book of good life.

²²Our father, our king, write us in the book of merit.

²¹Our father, our king, write us in the book of livelihood and sustenance.

²⁰Our father, our king, write us in the book of redemption and salvation.

²³Our father, our king, write us in in the book of forgiveness and pardon.

²⁴Our father, our king, cause salvation to flourish for us soon.

²⁵Our father, our king, give strength to your people Israel.

²⁶Our father, our king, give strength to your messiah.

²⁹Our father, our king, hear our voice; have compassion and mercy on us.

¹⁷Our father, our king, tear up the evil sentence decreed against us.

¹⁸Our father, our king, remember us favorably before You.

¹⁹Our father, our king, write us in the book of good life.

²⁰Our father, our king, write us in the book of redemption and salvation.

²¹Our father, our king, write us in the book of livelihood and sustenance.

²²Our father, our king, write us in the book of merit.

²³Our father, our king, write us in in the book of forgiveness and pardon.

²⁴Our father, our king, cause salvation to flourish for us soon.

²⁵Our father, our king, give strength to your people Israel.

²⁶Our father, our king, give strength to your messiah.

²⁷Our father, our king, fill our hands from among your blessings.

²⁸Our father, our king, fill our storehouses with plenty.

²⁹Our father, our king, hear our voice; have compassion and mercy on us.

³⁰Our father, our king, accept our prayer with mercy and favor.

³¹Our father, our king, open the gates of heaven to our prayer.

³³Our father, our king, remember that we are but dust.

³²Our father, our king, do not return us empty-handed from before You.

³⁴Our father, our king, may this hour be an hour of mercy and a time of favor before You.

³⁶Our father, our king, act for the sake of those killed for your holy name.

³⁷Our father, our king, act for the sake of those slaughtered for your oneness.

³⁸Our father, our king, act for the sake of those who go through fire and water for your holy name.

³⁹Our father, our king, avenge the spilled blood of your servants.

³⁰Our father, our king, accept our prayer with mercy and favor.

³²Our father, our king, do not return us empty-handed from before You.

³⁶Our father, our king, act for the sake of those killed for your holy name.

³⁷Our father, our king, act for the sake of those slaughtered for your oneness.

³⁸Our father, our king, act for the sake of those who go through fire and water for your holy name.

³⁹Our father, our king, avenge the spilled blood of your servants.

⁴⁰Our father, our king, act for your sake if not for our sake.

⁴¹Our father, our king, act for your sake and save us.

⁴²Our father, our king, act for the sake of your great compassion.

⁴³Our father, our king, act for the sake of your great, mighty, and revered name by which we are called.

⁴⁴Our father, our king, be gracious to us and answer us, for we have no merit; act justly and lovingly with us and save us.

⁴⁰Our father, our king, act for your sake if not for our sake.

⁴¹Our father, our king, act for your sake and save us.

⁴²Our father, our king, act for the sake of your great compassion.

⁴³Our father, our king, act for the sake of your great, mighty, and revered name by which we are called.

⁴⁴Our father, our king, be gracious to us and answer us, for we have no merit; act justly and lovingly with us and save us.

England, Turn of the Twentieth Century (Minhag Sepharad)

The Sephardi Rite, the tradition, originally, of Jews in pre-expulsion Spain and Portugal, exists in two main versions: (1) the liturgy of the exiles who sailed across the Mediterranean to countries ruled by the Ottoman Turks, including the Land of Israel; and (2) those who moved north to Holland (and from there to the New World and to England). Jews in the first group who reached the Land of Israel were influenced by Kabbalah and, eventually, developed a version of the

Sephardi Rite known as *Minhag Ari*, named after the most famous spiritual guide there, "the Ari," an acronym for "the Divine Rabbi Isaac" (Ha'elohi Rabbi Isaac)—Isaac Luria. The Sephardi Rite proper, however, the version that emerged among Jews in Holland, England, and the Americas, was issued by Rabbi David Aaron de Sola (1796–1860) of the Bevis Marks Synagogue in London, in 1836–1837, and republished by the great British scholar and rabbi Moses Gaster at the turn of the twentieth century. His version is the one we use here.[7]

Minhag Sepharad

[2] Our father, our king, we have no king other than You.

[3] Our father, our king, act with us for the sake of your name.

[4] Our father, our king, grant us a good new year.

[5a] Our father, our king, cancel all burdensome and evil decrees against us.

---

[7] Moses Gaster, ed., Book of Prayer and Order of Service according to the Custom of the Spanish and Portuguese Jews with an English Translation Based Principally on the Work of the Late Rev. D.B. De Sola, Minister of the Congregation Bevis Marks, London, vol.2 [Rosh Hashanah] (London: Oxford University Press Warehouse, 1903), 92.

⁶Our father, our king, cancel the plans of those who hate us.

⁷Our father, our king, disrupt the schemes of those who are our enemies.

⁸Our father, our king, put an end to every one of our adversaries and foes.

¹⁰ᶜOur father, our king, put an end to pestilence, war, famine, captivity, destruction, and plague among the people of your covenant.

¹⁶Our father, our king, send perfect healing to those among your people who are ill.

¹¹Our father, our king, prevent the plague among your heritage.

³³Our father, our king, remember that we are but dust.

¹⁹Our father, our king, write us in the book of good life.

²¹Our father, our king, write us in the book of livelihood and sustenance.

²⁰Our father, our king, write us in the book of redemption and salvation.

¹⁸ᵃOur father, our king, remember us favorably before You.

²⁴Our father, our king, cause salvation to flourish for us soon.

²⁵Our father, our king, give strength to your people Israel.

²⁶ᵇOur father, our king, give strength to your altar.

¹⁵Our father, our king, place us again before You in perfect repentance.

²⁹Our father, our king, hear our voice; have compassion and mercy on us.

⁴⁰Our father, our king, act for your sake if not for our sake.

³⁰Our father, our king, accept our prayer with mercy and favor.

³²ᵃOur father, our king, do not return us empty-handed from before You.

Yemenite Tikhlal (the Baladi Rite)

Jews settled in Yemen early on, prior to the birth of Islam, but quickly fell under Islamic rule with Islam's rise and spread in the seventh century.

The region has enjoyed a wide variety of liturgical customs, preserved orally for many centuries. These local practices existed alongside—and intermixed with—traditions from the Land of Israel.

Toward the end of the nineteenth century, modernity (in general) and the advent of widespread printing (in particular) fostered a comparison of the various local Yemenite practices. Those that were deemed to have been influenced by the Land of Israel were called "Al-Shami," meaning "of the Sham," *Sham* being the Arabic term for the general geographic area of Israel.

The practices deemed local in nature were dubbed "Baladi" ("local") and collected in a printed book called in Yemini Arabic the *Tikhlal* ("comprehensive").

For our versions of *Avinu Malkeinu*, we have drawn from a contemporary reprinting of the *Tikhlal* with a commentary by Yachya Tsalich (the MaHaRITZ), an esteemed halakhic authority for Yemenite Jews from the eighteenth century. His many works, composed in manuscript form only, were later published in printed format and included *Etz Chayim* ("Tree of Life"), a commentary on the *Tikhlal*, published first in 1894.[8]

Minhag Yemen

[2]Our father, our king, we have no king other than You.

[3]Our father, our king, act with us for the sake of your name.

[4]Our father, our king, grant us a good new year.

[5a]Our father, our king, cancel all burdensome and evil decrees against us.

[6]Our father, our king, cancel the plans of those who hate us.

---

[8] Hatikhlal Ham'foar Or MaHaRITZ: Nusach Baladi, Rosh Hashanah (Bnei Brak, 2004), 150–51.

⁷ᵃOur father, our king, disrupt the schemes of all those who are our enemies.

⁸Our father, our king, put an end to every one of our adversaries and foes.

¹⁰ᵃOur father, our king, put an end to pestilence, war, famine, captivity, pillage, destruction, plague, Satan, evil inclination, and bad diseases from among the people of your covenant.

¹⁶Our father, our king, send perfect healing to those among your people who are ill.

¹¹Our father, our king, prevent the plague among your heritage.

³³Our father, our king, remember that we are but dust.

¹⁹Our father, our king, write us in the book of good life.

²¹Our father, our king, write us in the book of livelihood and sustenance.

²³ᵃOur father, our king, write us in the book of forgiveness and pardon and atonement.

²⁰Our father, our king, write us in the book of redemption and salvation.

¹⁸ᵃOur father, our king, remember us favorably before You.

²⁴Our father, our king, cause salvation to flourish for us soon.

²⁵Our father, our king, give strength to your people Israel.

²⁶ᵃOur father, our king, give strength to your messiah.

¹⁵Our father, our king, place us again before You in perfect repentance.

²⁹Our father, our king, hear our voice; have compassion and mercy on us.

⁴⁰Our father, our king, act for your sake if not for our sake.

³⁰Our father, our king, accept our prayer with mercy and favor.

³²ᵃOur father, our king, do not return us empty-handed from before You.

Chabad (Minhag Lubavitch, Minhag Ari as adapted by Rabbi Schneur Zalman of Liadi, the founder of Chabad)

As previously mentioned, Sephardi liturgy traveled with Spanish exiles across the Mediterranean to the Ottoman Empire, where (especially in the Land of Israel) they encountered kabbalistic teachings by a number of authorities, chief among them Isaac Luria, known as the Ari (see section entitled "England, Turn of the Twentieth Century (Minhag Sepharad)"). Traditions of prayer that combined Sephardi liturgy with the practices of the Ari are known as *Minhag Ari*. But we do not know for sure when *Minhag Ari* actually took shape—or even if the Ari himself actually used it.

The Ari (1534–1572) grew up in Egypt and probably used the Sephardi Rite as it had come from Spain. His most influential disciple, Chaim Vital (1543–1620), altered that rite by (among other things) adding kabbalistic meditations to it. These were later associated with the Ari himself, even though they may go back only to Vital. In any case, this altered Sephardi tradition made its way to Hasidic circles in modern-day Ukraine, where Ashkenazi customs were added. To this day,*Minhag Ari* exists in various forms, among them, the version established by Rabbi Schneur Zalman of Liadi (1745–1812), the founder of Lubavitch Hasidism, known broadly today as Chabad. It corresponds quite thoroughly to Ashkenazi tradition in Poland, with intermixtures of whatever Schneur Zalman had received as the authentic tradition of Isaac Luria.[9]

Minhag Lubavitch

[2]Our father, our king, we have no king other than You.

---

[9] For our version, we rely on Rabbi Nissen Mangel, ed., Machzor for Rosh Hashanah, Annotated Version, according to the Custom of Those Who Pray Nusach Ha-Ari Zal as Arranged by Rabbi Schneur Zalman of Liadi (New York: Merkoz L'inyanei Chinuch, 2014), 152–54.

³Our father, our king, act with us for the sake of your name.

⁴Our father, our king, grant us a good new year.

⁵Our father, our king, cancel all burdensome decrees against us.

⁶Our father, our king, cancel the plans of those who hate us.

⁷Our father, our king, disrupt the schemes of those who are our enemies.

⁸ᵃOur father, our king, put an end to every one of our adversaries and foes.

⁹ᶜOur father, our king, shut the mouths of our adversaries and accusers.

¹⁰ᵈOur father, our king, put an end to pestilence, war, famine, captivity, and destruction among the people of your covenant.

¹¹Our father, our king, prevent the plague among your heritage.

¹⁵Our father, our king, place us again before You in perfect repentance.

¹⁶Our father, our king, send perfect healing to those among your people who are ill.

¹⁷Our father, our king, tear up the evil sentence decreed against us.

¹⁸Our father, our king, remember us favorably before You.

¹⁹Our father, our king, write us in the book of good life.

²⁰Our father, our king, write us in the book of redemption and salvation.

²¹Our father, our king, write us in the book of livelihood and sustenance.

²²Our father, our king, write us in the book of merit.

²⁴Our father, our king, cause salvation to flourish for us soon.

²⁵Our father, our king, give strength to your people Israel.

²⁶Our father, our king, give strength to your messiah.

²⁷Our father, our king, fill our hands from among your blessings.

²⁸Our father, our king, fill our storehouses with plenty.

²⁹Our father, our king, hear our voice; have compassion and mercy on us.

³⁰Our father, our king, accept our prayer with mercy and favor.

³¹Our father, our king, open the gates of heaven to our prayer.

³³Our father, our king, remember that we are but dust.

³²Our father, our king, do not return us empty-handed from before You.

³⁴Our father, our king, may this hour be an hour of mercy and a time of favor before You.

³⁵Our father, our king, have compassion on us and on our children.

³⁶Our father, our king, act for the sake of those killed for your holy name.

³⁷Our father, our king, act for the sake of those slaughtered for your oneness.

³⁸Our father, our king, act for the sake of those who go through fire and water for your holy name.

³⁹Our father, our king, avenge the spilled blood of your servants.

⁴⁰Our father, our king, act for your sake if not for our sake.

⁴¹Our father, our king, act for your sake and save us.

⁴²Our father, our king, act for the sake of your great compassion.

⁴³Our father, our king, act for the sake of your great, mighty, and revered name by which we are called.

⁴⁴Our father, our king, be gracious to us and answer us, for we have no merit; act justly and lovingly with us and save us.

Appendix B

Alternatives to Avinu Malkeinu*

[* We cited the following works as they appear in their original sources. This concerns text, spelling, and punctuation.]
Rabbi Dalia Marx, PhD

From Israel: Kavanat Halev, Reform, 1989

After the traditional *Avinu Malkeinu*, the following two poems appear.[10]

Eloheinu Shebashamayim:
Our God in Heaven (Selections from a Sephardic Piyyut)

Our God in heaven, hear our voice and willingly accept our prayer.
Our God in heaven, remember your covenant and do not forget us.
Our God in heaven, we seek You, reveal Yourself to us.

אלהינו שבשמים

אֱלֹהֵינוּ שֶׁבַּשָּׁמַיִם שְׁמַע קוֹלֵנוּ
וְקַבֵּל תְּפִלָּתֵנוּ בְּרָצוֹן.
אֱלֹהֵינוּ שֶׁבַּשָּׁמַיִם בְּרִיתְךָ זְכוֹר
וְאַל תִּשְׁכָּחֵנוּ.
אֱלֹהֵינוּ שֶׁבַּשָּׁמַיִם דְּרַשְׁנוּךָ
הִמָּצֵא לָנוּ.

---

[10] Kavanat Halev contains another poetic alternative version for Avinu Malkeinu by Rabbi Motti Rotem.

Our God in heaven, have mercy upon us and our infants and children.	אֱלֹהֵינוּ שֶׁבַּשָּׁמַיִם חֲמַל עָלֵינוּ וְעַל עוֹלָלֵנוּ וְטַפֵּנוּ.
Our God in heaven, purify us from our sins.	אֱלֹהֵינוּ שֶׁבַּשָּׁמַיִם טַהֲרֵנוּ מֵעֲוֹנֵינוּ.
Our God in heaven, inscribe us in a book of sustenance and good providence.	אֱלֹהֵינוּ שֶׁבַּשָּׁמַיִם כָּתְבֵנוּ בְּסֵפֶר מְזוֹנוֹת וּפַרְנָסָה טוֹבָה.
Our God in heaven, fulfill the desires of our heart for good.	אֱלֹהֵינוּ שֶׁבַּשָּׁמַיִם מַלֵּא מִשְׁאֲלוֹת לִבֵּנוּ לְטוֹבָה.
Our God in heaven, redeem us from our foes.	אֱלֹהֵינוּ שֶׁבַּשָּׁמַיִם פְּדֵנוּ מִידֵי אוֹיְבֵינוּ.
Our God in heaven, justify us in your judgments.	אֱלֹהֵינוּ שֶׁבַּשָּׁמַיִם צַדְּקֵנוּ בְּמִשְׁפָּטֶיךָ.
Our God in heaven, bring the day of redemption near to us.	אֱלֹהֵינוּ שֶׁבַּשָּׁמַיִם קָרֵב לָנוּ יוֹם הַיְשׁוּעָה.
Our God in heaven, bring us near to your service.	אֱלֹהֵינוּ שֶׁבַּשָּׁמַיִם קָרְבֵנוּ לַעֲבוֹדָתֶךָ.
Our God in heaven, see the affliction of your people Israel.	אֱלֹהֵינוּ שֶׁבַּשָּׁמַיִם רְאֵה בָּעֳנִי עַמְּךָ יִשְׂרָאֵל.
Our God in heaven, heal the sick among your people Israel.	אֱלֹהֵינוּ שֶׁבַּשָּׁמַיִם רְפָא חוֹלֵי עַמְּךָ יִשְׂרָאֵל.
Our God in heaven, grant peace on earth.	אֱלֹהֵינוּ שֶׁבַּשָּׁמַיִם תֵּן שָׁלוֹם בָּאָרֶץ.
Our God in heaven, we call and You shall answer.	אֱלֹהֵינוּ שֶׁבַּשָּׁמַיִם נִקְרָא וְאַתָּה תַעֲנֶה.

Shekhinah M'kor Chayeinu: Shekhinah, Source of Our Lives (Rabbi Yehoram Mazor)

Shekhinah, source of our lives—
hear our voice, have mercy and compassion upon us.
Shekhinah, source of our lives—
remember that we are your sons and daughters.
Shekhinah, source of our lives—
help us to acknowledge our limitations.
Shekhinah, source of our lives—
guide us on pleasant paths.
Shekhinah, source of our lives—
teach us compassion and righteousness.
Shekhinah, source of our lives—
act for those who struggle for peace and justice.
Shekhinah, source of our lives—
turn our sorrow to joy and our grief to gladness.
Shekhinah, source of our lives—
bless our soil and all the works of our hands.
Shekhinah, source of our lives—
gather your children from the four corners of the land to their borders.
Shekhinah, source of our lives—
complete the restoration of Jerusalem, our Holy City.

שכינה מקור חיינו
(הרב יהורם מזור)

שְׁכִינָה מְקוֹר חַיֵּינוּ —
שִׁמְעִי קוֹלֵנוּ חוּסִי וְרַחֲמִי עָלֵינוּ.
שְׁכִינָה מְקוֹר חַיֵּינוּ —
זִכְרִי כִּי בָּנֶיךָ וּבְנוֹתַיִךְ אֲנַחְנוּ.
שְׁכִינָה מְקוֹר חַיֵּינוּ —
חַנְּכִי אוֹתָנוּ לְהַכִּיר בְּמִגְבְּלוֹתֵינוּ.
שְׁכִינָה מְקוֹר חַיֵּינוּ —
הַדְרִיכִי אוֹתָנוּ בְּדַרְכֵי נֹעַם.
שְׁכִינָה מְקוֹר חַיֵּינוּ —
לַמְּדִי אוֹתָנוּ רַחֲמִים וּצְדָקָה.
שְׁכִינָה מְקוֹר חַיֵּינוּ —
עֲשִׂי לְמַעַן הַנֶּאֱבָקִים לְשָׁלוֹם וּלְצֶדֶק.
שְׁכִינָה מְקוֹר חַיֵּינוּ —
הִפְכִי אֶבְלֵנוּ לְשָׂשׂוֹן וִיגוֹנֵנוּ לְשִׂמְחָה.
שְׁכִינָה מְקוֹר חַיֵּינוּ —
בָּרְכִי אַדְמָתֵנוּ וְכָל מַעֲשֵׂה יָדֵינוּ.
שְׁכִינָה מְקוֹר חַיֵּינוּ —
קַבְּצִי בָּנַיִךְ וּבְנוֹתַיִךְ מֵאַרְבַּע כַּנְפוֹת הָאָרֶץ לִגְבוּלָם.
שְׁכִינָה מְקוֹר חַיֵּינוּ —
הַשְׁלִימִי בִּנְיַן יְרוּשָׁלַיִם עִיר קָדְשֵׁנוּ.

From the UK: Forms of Prayer (Draft Edition), Reform, 2014

Avinu Malkeinu

Rabbi Paul Freedman, *Forms of Prayer: Erev Rosh Hashanah Machzor*, Draft Edition (London: 2014), 81–82.

אָבִינוּ מַלְכֵּנוּ חָטָאנוּ לְפָנֶיךָ.
גּוֹאֲלֵנוּ סוֹמְכֵנוּ, הַחֲזִירֵנוּ בִּתְשׁוּבָה שְׁלֵמָה לְפָנֶיךָ.
הוֹדֵנוּ פָּאֲרֵנוּ, הָרֵם קֶרֶן יִשְׂרָאֵל עַמֶּךָ.
זוֹכְרֵנוּ קוֹנְנֵנוּ, מְחוֹק בְּרַחֲמֶיךָ כָּל־שִׁטְרֵי חוֹבוֹתֵינוּ.
טְהוֹרֵנוּ שׁוֹמְרֵנוּ, סְלַח וּמְחַל לְכָל־עֲוֹנוֹתֵינוּ.
שְׁכִינָתֵנוּ תִּקְוָתֵנוּ, חַדְּשִׁי עָלֵינוּ שָׁנָה טוֹבָה.
יוֹצְרֵנוּ רוֹפְאֵנוּ, שְׁלַח רְפוּאָה שְׁלֵמָה לְחוֹלֵי עַמֶּךָ.
חוֹסְנֵנוּ צוּרֵנוּ, זְכוֹר כִּי עָפָר אֲנָחְנוּ.
וַתִּיקֵנוּ עָזְרֵנוּ, אַל תְּשִׁיבֵנוּ רֵיקָם מִלְּפָנֶיךָ.
דּוֹרְשֵׁנוּ נוֹטְרֵנוּ, כַּלֵּה כָּל־צַר וּמַשְׂטִין מֵעָלֵינוּ.
בּוֹרְאֵנוּ לְבוּבֵנוּ, עֲשֵׂה לְמַעַנְךָ אִם לֹא לְמַעֲנֵנוּ.
אָבִינוּ מַלְכֵּנוּ חָנֵּנוּ וַעֲנֵנוּ, כִּי אֵין בָּנוּ מַעֲשִׂים, עֲשֵׂה עִמָּנוּ צְדָקָה וָחֶסֶד וְהוֹשִׁיעֵנוּ.

א״מ Our Father, our King, we have sinned before You.

ג״ס Our Redeemer who supports us, help us to return to You in complete repentance.

ה״פ Our Crown and Glory, raise the honour of Your people Israel.

ז"ק You who remember us, having created us, in Your abundant mercy, wipe out all records of our sins.

ט"ש Perfect One who watches over us, pardon us and forgive all our iniquities.

כ"ת God who dwells among us, our Everpresent Hope, renew this year for us as a good year.

י"ר You who formed and heal us, bring true healing to our sick.

ה"צ Our Strength, our Rock, remember that we are but dust.

ו"ע Ancient One who continues to be our Help, do not send us away empty from Your presence.

ד"נ You who seek us out and protect us, keep us safe from all trouble and persecution.

ב"ל Our Creator, our Beloved, act for Your sake if not for ours.

Avinu Malkeinu, answer us with Your grace, for we lack good deeds; deal with us in charity and love, and save us.

From North America: Mahzor Lev Shalem, Conservative, 2010

Avinu Malkeinu: Alternate Version

Rabbi Edward Feld, reprinted with the permission of The Rabbinical Assembly from

Mahzor Lev Shalem (New York: Rabbinical Assembly, 2010), 93–94.

Avinu Malkeinu, we have sinned in Your presence.	אָבִינוּ מַלְכֵּנוּ! חָטָאנוּ לְפָנֶיךָ.
Our creator, who blesses us, we have no sovereign but You.	בּוֹרְאֵנוּ מְבָרְכֵנוּ, אֵין לָנוּ מֶלֶךְ אֶלָּא אָתָּה.
Our redeemer, who guards us, act kindly toward us in accord with Your name.	גּוֹאֲלֵנוּ מְשַׁמְּרֵנוּ, עֲשֵׂה עִמָּנוּ לְמַעַן שְׁמֶךָ.
You who seek us out and sustain us, make this new year a good one for us.	דּוֹרְשֵׁנוּ מְפַרְנְסֵנוּ, חַדֵּשׁ עָלֵינוּ שָׁנָה טוֹבָה.
You who are our glory, our savior, annul every harsh decree against us.	הוֹדֵינוּ מוֹשִׁיעֵנוּ, בַּטֵּל מֵעָלֵינוּ כָּל־גְּזֵרוֹת קָשׁוֹת.
Ancient One, our rescuer, nullify the designs of our foes.	וָתִיקֵנוּ מְפַלְּטֵנוּ, בַּטֵּל מַחְשְׁבוֹת שׂוֹנְאֵינוּ.
Provider, our refuge, rid Your covenanted people of disease, war, hunger, captivity, and destruction.	זָנֵנוּ מְנוּסֵנוּ, כַּלֵּה דֶבֶר וְחֶרֶב וְרָעָב וּשְׁבִי וּמַשְׁחִית עָוֹן וּשְׁמַד מִבְּנֵי בְרִיתֶךָ.
You who are our strength, who gives us life, rid us of every oppressor and adversary.	חוֹסֵנוּ מְחַיֵּינוּ, הָפֵר עֲצַת אוֹיְבֵינוּ.
You who purify us and have mercy on us, forgive and pardon all our sins.	טַהֲרֵנוּ מְרַחֲמֵנוּ, סְלַח וּמְחַל לְכָל־עֲוֹנוֹתֵינוּ.

יוֹצְרֵנוּ מְלַמְּדֵנוּ,	*You who form us and instruct us,*
הַחֲזִירֵנוּ בִּתְשׁוּבָה שְׁלֵמָה לְפָנֶיךָ.	*return us to Your presence, fully penitent.*
כּוֹנְנֵנוּ מְכַלְכְּלֵנוּ,	You who establish us and provide
שְׁלַח רְפוּאָה שְׁלֵמָה לְחוֹלֵי עַמֶּךָ.	for us, send complete healing to the sick among Your people.
לְבוּבֵנוּ מְגַדְּלֵנוּ,	*You, our beloved, who raised us,*
זָכְרֵנוּ בְּזִכָּרוֹן טוֹב לְפָנֶיךָ.	*remember us favorably.*
אָבִינוּ מַלְכֵּנוּ,	Avinu Malkeinu, inscribe us for
כָּתְבֵנוּ בְּסֵפֶר חַיִּים טוֹבִים.	good in the Book of Life.
אָבִינוּ מַלְכֵּנוּ,	*Avinu Malkeinu, inscribe us in the*
כָּתְבֵנוּ בְּסֵפֶר גְּאֻלָּה וִישׁוּעָה.	*Book of Redemption.*
אָבִינוּ מַלְכֵּנוּ,	Avinu Malkeinu, inscribe us in
כָּתְבֵנוּ בְּסֵפֶר פַּרְנָסָה וְכַלְכָּלָה.	the Book of Sustenance.
אָבִינוּ מַלְכֵּנוּ,	*Avinu Malkeinu, inscribe us in the*
כָּתְבֵנוּ בְּסֵפֶר זְכִיּוֹת.	*Book of Merit.*
אָבִינוּ מַלְכֵּנוּ,	Avinu Malkeinu, inscribe us in
כָּתְבֵנוּ בְּסֵפֶר סְלִיחָה וּמְחִילָה.	the Book of Forgiveness.
נוֹטְרֵנוּ מְפַלְטֵנוּ,	Our protector and savior, cause
הַצְמַח לָנוּ יְשׁוּעָה בְּקָרוֹב.	our salvation to flourish soon.
סוֹמְכֵנוּ מַצִּילֵנוּ,	*Our support and rescuer, cause*
הָרֵם קֶרֶן יִשְׂרָאֵל עַמֶּךָ.	*Your people Israel to be exalted.*
עוֹזְרֵנוּ מַקְשִׁיבֵנוּ שְׁמַע קוֹלֵנוּ,	Our helper, who listens to us, hear
חוּס וְרַחֵם עָלֵינוּ.	our voice, be kind, sympathize with us.
פּוֹדֵנוּ מְשַׁמְּרֵנוּ,	*Our redeemer, who watches over*
קַבֵּל בְּרַחֲמִים וּבְרָצוֹן אֶת־תְּפִלָּתֵנוּ.	*us, accept our prayer, willingly and lovingly.*
צוּרֵנוּ מְנוּסֵנוּ,	Our fortress, who is our refuge, do
נָא אַל תְּשִׁיבֵנוּ רֵיקָם מִלְּפָנֶיךָ.	not send us away empty-handed.
	Holy One, who justifies us,
	remember that we are but dust.
	Merciful One, who gives us life, have compassion for us, our infants, and our children.

קָדוֹשֵׁנוּ מַצְדִיקֵנוּ,
זְכוֹר כִּי עָפָר אֲנָחְנוּ.
רַחֲמֵנוּ מְחַיֵּינוּ,
חֲמוֹל עָלֵינוּ וְעַל עוֹלָלֵינוּ וְטַפֵּינוּ.
שׁוֹמְרֵנוּ מוֹשִׁיעֵנוּ,
עֲשֵׂה לְמַעַן הֲרוּגִים עַל שֵׁם קָדְשֶׁךָ.
תּוֹמְכֵנוּ מְסַעֲדֵנוּ,
עֲשֵׂה לְמַעַנְךָ אִם לֹא לְמַעֲנֵנוּ.
אָבִינוּ מַלְכֵּנוּ, חָנֵּנוּ וַעֲנֵנוּ,
כִּי אֵין בָּנוּ מַעֲשִׂים,
עֲשֵׂה עִמָּנוּ צְדָקָה וָחֶסֶד
וְהוֹשִׁיעֵנוּ.

Guardian, who grants us victory, do this for the sake of those who were martyred for Your holy name.

Benefactor, who provides for our welfare, do this for Your sake if not for ours.

Avinu Malkeinu, have mercy on us, answer us, for our deeds are insufficient; deal with us charitably and lovingly, and redeem us.

From North America: Mishkan HaNefesh, Reform, 2015

Avinu Malkeinu—Almighty and Merciful

Rabbi Janet Marder and Rabbi Shelly Marder, *Mishkan HaNefesh: Machzor for the Days of Awe* (New York: CCAR Press, forthcoming), 220, introduction to *Avinu Malkeinu* (can serve also as an alternative version).

Loving father
Infinite Power
Gentle, forgiving
Lofty, inscrutable
Avinu

Malkeinu
Compassionate Mother
Omnipotent Lord
Comforting presence
Fathomless mystery
Avinu
Malkeinu
Our Rock and Redeemer
Life of the Universe
Close to us always
Impossibly far
Avinu
Malkeinu
Embracing
Confounding
Accepting our frailty
Decreeing our end
Avinu
Malkeinu
None of these are true
None of these are You
Yet we stand as those before us have stood
Summoned to judgment, longing for love
Avinu, Malkeinu
May these words be a bridge
They come from our hearts
May they lead us to You

From North America: Kehilla Community Machzor, Renewal, 2014

Avinu Malkeinu

Rabbi Burt Jacobson, *Kehilla Community Machzor* (2014; originally published in the High Holy Day supplement of Congregation Mishkan Shalom, Philadelphia).

Our Father, our King, teach us how to make this year a new beginning.

Our Mother, our Queen, teach us how to grow from the harshness of life.

Our Source and our Destiny, teach us how to accept what we must accept.

Our Guide and our Truth, teach us to change what must be changed.

Our Father, our King, teach us how to face disease and death.

Our Mother, our Queen, teach us how to enjoy the gifts of life.

Our Source and our Destiny, teach us how to make peace with our enemies.

Our Guide and our Truth, teach us how we can best help our people Israel.

Our Father, our King, teach us how we can best help all humanity.

Our Mother, our Queen, let us find pardon for our wrongdoings.

Our Source and our Destiny, let us return to You, wholly and completely.

Our Guide and our Truth, teach us how to help those who are ill.

Our Father, our King, let us write our names in the Book of Life.

Our Mother, our Queen, help us to find meaningful work.

Our Source and our Destiny, help us to find inner freedom.

Our Guide and our Truth, help us to learn how to love.

Our Father, our King, receive our prayers.

Our Mother, our Queen, teach us how to be good lovers.

Our Source and our Destiny, teach us how to be good parents.

Our Guide and our Truth, teach us how to be good children.

Our Father, our King, teach us how to be good friends.

Our Mother, our Queen, teach us how to be good Jews.

Our Source and our Destiny, teach us how to be good people.

Our Guide and our Truth, teach us how to be one with Your universe.

Avinu malkeinu, chaneinu va'aneinu ki ein banu ma'asim

Asai imanu tzedakah va'chesed, Ve'hoshi'einu

Avinu malkeinu, grant us justice and bring us salvation,
Grant us justice and loving kindness and bring us salvation.

אָבִינוּ מַלְכֵּנוּ, חָנֵּנוּ וַעֲנֵנוּ,
כִּי אֵין בָּנוּ מַעֲשִׂים,
עֲשֵׂה עִמָּנוּ צְדָקָה וָחֶסֶד
וְהוֹשִׁיעֵנוּ.

Notes

The History, Meaning, and Varieties of Avinu Malkeinu, by Rabbi Lawrence A. Hoffman, PhD

[1] *Seder Rav Amram*, ed. E.D. Goldschmidt, part 2, section 108, p.138.

[2] The full tale is discussed elsewhere in this volume. See, e.g., Boeckler, "Why 'Our Father'?", pp.92–98; Gelfand, "Would You Still Love Me If...?" pp.226–230; Goldberg, "*Avinu Malkeinu* and the New Reform Machzor (Mishkan HaNefesh)," pp.154–163; Kaunfer, "Prayer and Character: The Story Behind *Avinu Malkeinu*," pp.99–106; Marx, "Empowerment, Not Police: What Are We to Do with Problematic Liturgical Passages?," pp.119–137.

[3] Literally, "went down before the ark," a term in the Babylonian Talmud to describe the act of leading the congregation in the *Amidah*.

[4] The usual eighteen blessings of the daily *Amidah* plus eight others, discussed in Mishnah Ta'anit 2:2–5.

[5] *Seder Rav Amram*, part 1, section 98, p.46.

[6]   "Our father, our king, our God, be gracious to us and answer us. We have no merit. For your sake, deal righteously with us [Avinu malkeinu eloheinu, choneinu va'aneinu. Ein banu ma'asim. Aseih imanu l'ma'an sh'mekha tz'dakah]." *Siddur Rav Saadiah Gaon,* ed. Israel Davidson, Simchah Assaf, Issachar Joel, p.24.

[7]   *Abudarham Hashalem,* Wertheimer ed., p.119.

"Our Father and King": The Many Ways That Liturgy Means, by Rabbi Lawrence A. Hoffman, PhD

[1]   For the first, see illustrations in Thomas R. Cole, *The Journey of Life* (Cambridge: Cambridge University Press, 1992), 11; or his rhyme from fifteenth- to seventeenth-century Germany: "10 Years—a child; 20 years—youth; 30 years—a man; 40 years—standing still; 50 years—settled and prosperous; 60 years—departing; 70 years—protect your soul; 80 years—the world's fool; 90 years—scorn of children; 100 years—God have mercy." For the second, see *Pirkei Avot* 5:21: "5 years—Bible; 10

years—Mishnah; 13 years—the *mitzvot*; 15 years—Talmud; 18 years—marriage; 20 years—to pursue [a living]; 30 years—strength; 40 years—understanding; 50 years—counsel; 60 years—old age; 70 years—ripe old age; 80 years—special strength; 90 years—bowed over; 100 years—as if dead and passed from the world."

[2] Philosopher Ludwig Wittgenstein imagines himself talking to someone who affirms a theological postulate like the last judgment—something Wittgenstein denies. What this amounts to is not so much a difference of opinion as, "I think differently ... I have different pictures" (Ludwig Wittgenstein, *Lectures and Conversations on Aesthetics, Psychology and Religious Belief*, ed. Cyril Barrett [Berkeley: University of California Press, nd], 55).

[3] Victor Erlich, cited by Terence Hawkes, *Structuralism and Semiotics* (Berkeley: University of California Press, 1977), 71.

[4] Ibid., 81.

[5] Terry Eagleton, *How to Read Literature* (New Haven, CT: Yale University Press, 2013), 192.

[6] Archibald Macleish, *Ars Poetica*.

[7] 2 Maccabees 3:14–20, 10:16.

[8] Talmud, Ta'anit, 25b. For textual variants, cf. Lawrence A. Hoffman "The History, Meaning, and Varieties of *Avinu Malkeinu*," pp.3–15, and Elie Kaunfer, "Prayer and Character: The Story behind *Avinu Malkeinu*," pp.99–106.

[9] Stefanos Alexopoulos, "Litany," in *The New Westminster Dictionary of Liturgy and Worship*, ed. Paul Bradshaw (Louisville, KY: Westminster John Knox Press, 2002), 281–83.

[10] Sir Philip Sidney, *Defense of Poetry* (1595), cited in Marjorie Garber, *The Use and Abuse of Literature* (New York: Anchor Books, 2012), 188.

[11] See Lawrence A. Hoffman, ed., *My People's Prayer Book*, vol.2, The Amidah, p.73, and vol.4, Seder K'riat Hatorah *(The Torah Service)*, p.125 (Woodstock, VT: Jewish Lights, 1998 and 2000, respectively).

Who's Your Daddy?, by Chazzan Danny Maseng

[1] Abraham Isaac Kook, *Abraham Isaac Kook: The Lights of Penitence, Lights of Holiness: The Moral Principles, Essays, Letters, and*

Poems, trans. Ben Zion Bokser (Mahwah, NJ: Paulist Press, 1978), 203.
[2] Ibid., 262–263.
[3] To hear Chazzan Danny Maseng's *Avinu Malkeinu,* visit www.dannymaseng.com.

Biblical Precursors: Father, King, Potter, by Dr. Marc Zvi Brettler

[1] On the kingship of God in Rabbinic literature, see Reuven Kimelman, "Rabbinic Prayer in Late Antiquity," in *The Cambridge History of Judaism,* vol.4, *The Late Roman-Rabbinic Period,* ed. Steven T. Katz (Cambridge, UK: Cambridge University Press, 2006), 600–609.
[2] These examples are taken from relations hiprx.utk.edu.

Father or King: A View from the Psalms, by Rabbi Jonathan Magonet, PhD

[1] Each of these sections (Psalm 145:4–10, 14–20) is itself constructed around the central theme of God's attributes. In the first section, verses 8 and 9 present our Exodus quotation itself (described above);

in the second, verse 17 provides a parallel description of God as righteous and loving: *tzaddik adonai b'khol d'rakhav v'chasid b'khol ma'asav,* "Righteous is Adonai in all His ways, and loving in all His deeds." The two sets of attributes stand out because they objectively describe the qualities of God, whereas the verses before and after denote the relationship between God and people. In the first section (vv. 4–7, 10), people address God directly, offering praise to God; the second section (vv. 14–16, 18–20), inverts the relationship, describing what God does for people. If the model is that of a royal court, one approaches the king with words of praise (what we give to God, part one) and departs with gifts (what God gives to us, part two).

[2] For a more detailed study of Psalm 145, see Jonathan Magonet, *A Rabbi Reads the Psalms,* 2nd rev. ed. (London: SCM Press, 2004), 32–40.

[3] The three terms for "sin" are difficult to translate but reflect quite different concepts. The weakest, *chata'ah,* usually translated as "sin," means to miss the mark, to fail to reach a goal, and thus to go astray. The stronger term, *avon,*

sometimes translated as "iniquity," comes from the root "to be crooked," hence the sense of habitual wrong behavior. The third (and strongest) term, *paesha,* means "rebellion" and is used for the rebellion of a vassal state against its imperial master.

Why "Our Father"?, by Dr. Annette M. Boeckler

[1] A research overview and a detailed bibliography can be found in Annette Boeckler, *Gott als Vater im Alten Testament. Traditionsgeschichtliche Untersuchungen zur Entstehung und Entwicklung eines Gottesbildes,* 2nd ed. (Gütersloh: Gütersloher Verlagshaus, 2002); see also Annette Boeckler, "Keine väterliche Züchtigung! Zur Exegese von Prov. 3,12b," *Biblische Notizen* 96 (1999): 12–18; Annette Boeckler, "Mal barmherzig, mal autoritär. Die Entwicklungsgeschichte einer Gottesvorstellung," *Zeitzeichen* 2 (2001): 22–24; Annette Boeckler, "Unser Vater," in *Metaphor in the Hebrew Bible,* ed. Pierre van Hecke (Leuven: Uitgeverij Peeters, 2005), 249–61.

[2] For references to Akkadian sources, see Boeckler, *Gott als Vater* 49–52; sources are given in the footnotes.

[3] Similar but without using the sonship image is Psalm 110. See Boeckler, *Gott als Vater*, 197–211. On the sonship ideology in Israel, see Werner Schlisske, *Gottessohne und Gottessohn im alten Testament. Phasen der Entmythisierung im Alten Testament* (Stuttgart: W. Kohlhammer, 1973); Manfred Görg, *Mythos und Mythologie: Studien zur Religionsgeschichte und Theologie* (Wiesbaden: Harrassowitz, 2010), 317ff; Geoffrey P. Miller, *The Ways of a King: Legal and Political Ideas in the Bible* (Göttingen: Vandenhoeck & Ruprecht, 2011); Shawn W. Flynn, *YHWH Is King: The Development of Divine Kingship in Ancient Israel* (Leiden: Brill, 2014).

[4] An analysis of the relationship between adult religion and traumatic child experiences revealed that maltreatment by fathers has negative effects on the religiosity of the victims, a consequence of the religious image of God as "father." See Alex Bierman, "The Effects of Childhood Maltreatment on Adult Religiosity and Spirituality: Rejecting God

the Father Because of Abusive Fathers?" *Journal for the Scientific Study of Religion* 44, no.3 (Sept. 2005): 349–59.

Prayer and Character: The Story behind Avinu Malheinu, by Rabbi Elie Kaunfer, DHL

[1]   Many manuscripts are missing this.
[2]   Most manuscripts do not include this.
[3]   Devora Steinmetz offers a similar analysis in "Perception, Compassion, and Surprise: Literary Coherence in the Third Chapter of *Bavli Ta'anit*" (*Hebrew Union College Annual*, forthcoming). My gratitude to Dr. Steinmetz for sharing this article with me and discussing this theme.

Divine Epithets and Human Ambivalence, by Rabbi Reuven Kimelman, PhD

[1]   See Deuteronomy 26:17–18 for the reworking of the language of marriage into a metaphor of the covenant.
[2]   It is advisable to use "father" rather than "parent," since metaphorical language for God should be rooted in human

experience. In human experience, parents are engendered as fathers and mothers. Accordingly, God should be called, when appropriate, father or mother (e.g., Isaiah 42:14, 45:10, 46:3–4, and 49:15, where the appropriate mother images for God are used). The images of God are constantly in flux in the liturgy, but they are always concrete, as in the end of the penitential prayer *Aneinu*, where God is called *misgav imahot* ("the fortress of the matriarchs"), *avie yetomim* ("father of orphans"), and *dayyan almanot* ("judge of widows").

[3] *Olam* in the liturgy frequently refers to the human world, not the physical world.

[4] *The Special Laws* 2.165.

[5] *Against Apion* 2.168.

[6] *The Twelfth, or Olympic, Discourse*, 55, 74–75.

[7] Plato, *The Second Epistle* 312E.

[8] By Clement of Alexandria *(The Exhortation to the Greeks* 6[60], *Stromateis* 5.103.1), by Celsus (Origen, *Contra Celsum* 6.18), and by Numenius (Eusebius, *Preparation for the Gospel* 11.18.3).

[9] Fragment 12 (Numenius, *Fragments*, p.54).

[10] Ed. H. Hobein, 17:5. He also refers to "the God who is the father and creator

of all" (39:5), as does his contemporary Celsus, as cited by Origen, *Contra Celsum* 8.68.

[11] Tertullian, *Apology* 24.3.

[12] Justin, *Dialogue with Trypho* 1.

[13] *Octavius of Marcus Minucius Felix* 18, 11, p.82.

[14] For the whole issue of divine kingship in Late Antiquity, see Reuven Kimelman, "Blessing Formulae and Divine Sovereignty in Rabbinic Liturgy," in *Liturgy in the Life of the Synagogue: Studies in the History of Jewish Prayer*, ed. Ruth Langer and Steven Fine (Winona Lake, IN: Eisenbrauns, 2005), 1–39.

[15] See Reuven Kimelman, "Testing Abraham: Justice in Sodom before Loyalty in the Akedah," TheTorah.com, http://thetorah.com/justice-in-sodom-before-loyalty-in-the-akedah.

[16] See Uri Ehrlich, *The Weekday Amidah in Cairo Genizah Prayerbooks: Roots and Transmission* (Jerusalem: Yad Ben-Zvi Press, 2013), 99 [in Hebrew].

[17] A similar distinction is found in the Sabbath prayer: "Grant us rest, Adonai our God, for You are our father, and reign over us quickly, for You are our king" *(Seder Rav Amram Gaon,* ed. E.D.

Goldschmidt [Jerusalem: Mosad Harav Kook, 1971], 2:34, p.79, line 5 [in Hebrew]).

[18] The peroration of the fourth (middle) blessing of the Yom Kippur *Amidah* uses both terms together to cover all eventualities: "For You are the pardoner of Israel and the forgiver of the tribes of Yeshurun in every generation. And besides You we have no king who forgives and pardons. Blessed are You, Adonai, who forgives and pardons our offenses" (E.D. Goldschmidt, *Mahzor La-Yamim Ha-Nora 'im* [Jerusalem: Koren, 1970], 2:5–6 [in Hebrew]).

[19] For extensive commentary on these two blessings, see Reuven Kimelman, "The Penitential Part of the *Amidah* and Personal Redemption," in *Seeking the Favor of God*, vol.3, *The Impact of Penitential Prayer beyond Second Temple Judaism*, eds. Mark J. Boda, Daniel K. Falk, and Rodney A. Werline (Atlanta, GA: Society of Biblical Literature, 2008), 71–84.

Our Father, Our King: Old and New Parables, by Dr. Wendy Zierler

[1] For a discussion of the king metaphor in biblical literature, see Marc Brettler, *God Is King: Understanding an Israelite Metaphor* (Sheffield, UK: Sheffield Academic Press, 1989).

[2] On the use of such tales, see Daniel Boyarin, *Intertextuality and the Reading of Midrash* (Bloomington: Indiana University Press, 1990), 89.

[3] See Lamentations 1:1, 1:3. Translation adapted from *The Midrash Rabbah: Lamentations*, trans. H. Freedman and Maurice Simon (London: Soncino, 1977), 72.

[4] David Stern, *Parables in Midrash: Narrative and Exegesis in Rabbinic Literature* (Cambridge, MA: Harvard University Press, 1991), 100.

[5] S.Y. Agnon, "The Kerchief," in *Twenty-One Stories*, ed. Nahum Glatzer (New York: Schocken Books, 1970), 47.

[6] Yehuda Amichai, *Patuach, Sagur, Patuach* (Jerusalem: Schocken Books, 1998), 8; my translation.

Empowerment, Not Police: What Are We to Do with Problematic Liturgical Passages?, by Rabbi Dalia Marx, PhD

[1] *Kol Haneshamah: Prayerbook for the Days of Awe*, ed. David A. Teutsch (Wyncote, PA: Reconstructionist Press, 1999), 453.

[2] See "The History, Meaning, and Varieties of *Avinu Malkeinu*," by Rabbi Lawrence A. Phoffman, PhD, in this volume.

[3] *Kol Haneshamah*, 453.

[4] An exception to this rule is Marcia Falk's new *machzor: The Days Between: Blessings, Poems, and Directions of the Heart for the Jewish High Holiday Season* (Waltham, MA: Brandeis University Press, 2014).

[5] The generative phase of the Hebrew Bible—its creation and redaction—for the most part is hidden from our eyes. It has undergone a long editing process, and we know little about its canonization. For example, the numerous stories about King David reveal indirect criticism of our most important king. Rabbinic literature preserves controversies regarding the inclusion of some biblical books—e.g.,

Ecclesiastes and Esther (see Mishnan Yadayim 3:5–6; Talmud, Shabbat 30a; Megillah 7a)—and the exclusion of others—e.g., Ben Sirach (Ecclesiasticus), a Jewish wisdom book, similar in style to Job and Proverbs (c. second or third century BCE). The Rabbis occasionally refer to Ben Sirach (they even cite it) but maintain that it is not canonical (Tosefta, Yadahim 2:5). It is part of the "external" books, known also as the Apocrypha. See Joel M. Hoffman, *The Bible's Cutting Room Floor* (New York: St. Martin's Press, 2014).

[6] This is only one use of *k'rei* and *k'tiv*; in most cases the changes deal with spelling of words.

[7] According to the Babylonian custom, the entire Torah was read every year; in the old *Eretz Yisrael* Rite, it was read in the course of about three and a half years.

[8] Many Reform *machzorim* replaced this reading with the more edifying text of Deuteronomy 29:9–30. But then the thought-provoking tension between the ritual-oriented Torah reading and the moral invocation of the prophet is lost.

[9] For more on some of these methods, see Moshe Zipor, "The Blessing of the Priests

Is Not Read and Not Translated?," *Textus* 24 (2009): 221–38.

[10] Jakob J. Petuchowski, *Guide to the Prayerbook* (Cincinnati, OH: HUC Press, 1967), 54–55.

[11] P. Hyman, "Changing from the Inside," in *Jewish Women in America: An Historical Encyclopedia,* ed. P. Hyman and D. Dash Moore (New York: Routledge, 1997), vol.2, xxxi.

[12] See, e.g., *Mishkan T'filah* (New York: CCAR Press, 2007), 24.

[13] *Poked sarah* ("the One who remembers Sarah") was chosen over the wording from the North American Reform *ezrat sarah* ("the help of Sarah") because it echoed Genesis 21:1, "And God remembered *[pakad et]* Sarah."

[14] In this case the liturgy just follows the biblical text, where both Moses and Miriam led the people in the "Song of the Sea."

[15] Vanessa Ochs, *Inventing Jewish Ritual* (Philadelphia: Jewish Publication Society, 2007), 47–56.

[16] For the term "innovative" as applied to such rituals, see Elyse Goldstein, "My Pink Tallit," in *New Jewish Feminism,* ed.

Elyse Goldstein (Woodstock, VT: Jewish Lights, 2009), 81–89.

[17] See, e.g., Debra Orenstein, ed., *Lifecycles: Jewish Women on Life Passages & Personal Milestones* (Woodstock, VT: Jewish Lights, 1994).

[18] Chava Weissler, "Meanings of Shekhinah in the 'Jewish Renewal' Movement," *Nashim*, 10 (2005): 53–83.

[19] Judith Plaskow, "The Right Question Is Theological," in *On Being a Jewish Feminist*, ed. S. Heschel (New York: Schocken Books, 1983), 228.

[20] For detailed discussion of these four levels of engendered liturgical language, see Dalia Marx, "Gender Language in Liberal Israeli Liturgy," in *New Jewish Feminism: Probing the Past, Forging the Future*, ed. Elyse Goldstein (Woodstock, VT: Jewish Lights, 2008), 206–17.

[21] *Gates of Forgiveness: The Union Selichot Service; A Service of Preparation for the Days of Awe*, ed. Chaim Stern (New York: Central Conference of American Rabbis, 1980), 45.

[22] Ibid., 39. I highlighted the changed words.

[23] Matthew Berke, "God and Gender in Judaism," *First Things*, June 1996, www.fi

rstthings.com/article/1996/06/003-god-and-gender-in-Judaism.

[24] *Gates of Repentance,* ed. Chaim Stern (New York: Central Conference of American Rabbis, 1978), 189–90, 121–22.

[25] On *Avinu Malkeinu* on Shabbat, see Asher Lopatin, pp.231–234.

[26] *Machzor Ruach Chadashah,* ed. Andrew Goldstein and Charles H. Middleburgh (London: Liberal Judaism, 2003), xi, 73, 137.

[27] *Avinu Malkeinu,* Paul Freedman, ed., in *Forms of Prayer: Erev Rosh Hashanah Machzor,* draft ed. (London: 2014), 82.

[28] *Kol Haneshamah,* 453.

[29] Ibid.

[30] Ibid., 456.

[31] Ibid.

[32] Ibid.

[33] Ibid.

[34] *Mahzor Lev Shalem,* ed. Edward Feld (New York: Rabbinical Assembly, 2010), 94.

[35] *Mishkan HaNefesh: Machzor for the Days of Awe,* ed. Edwin Goldberg, Janet Marder, Sheldon Marder, and Leon Morris (New York: CCAR Press, forthcoming).

[36] Additional sheets for High Holy Day prayers, Navah Tehila (2014).

[37] Jakob J. Petuchowski, *Prayerbook Reform in Europe* (New York: UAHC Press, 1968), 128–213.

[38] Interestingly, some Israelis are experimenting lately with a combined-gender speech. For example, instead of saying *chaverim v'chaverot* ("friends," in both genders), they would say *chaverotim*. Time will tell whether these tentative initiatives will find wider resonance in the Israeli realm.

[39] I thank Rabbi Lawrence A. Hoffman, the editor of this book, and Rabbi Shelton Donnell for their many helpful comments while I was writing this essay. I also thank the following rabbis for allowing me to cite their work and for making it accessible: Edward Feld, Paul Freedman, Burt Jacobson, Ruth Gan-Kagan, Carol Levithan, Yehoram Mazor, and Hara Person. Every effort has been made to trace and acknowledge the copyright holders for the material included in this chapter and Appendix B. I apologize for any errors or omissions that may remain and ask that any omissions be brought to my

attention so that they may be corrected in future editions.

Why We Say Things We Don't Believe, by Rabbi Karyn D. Kedar

[1] This article is a revision of "The Metaphor of God," in *New Jewish Feminism: Probing the Past, Forging the Future,* ed. Rabbi Elyse Goldstein (Woodstock, VT: Jewish Lights, 2009).

A British Father and a British King?, by Rabbi Paul Freedman

[1] Neil Gillman, *Sacred Fragments: Recovering Theology for the Modern Jew* (Philadelphia: Jewish Publication Society, 1990), 80.
[2] *Siddur Lev Chadash* (London: Union of Liberal and Progressive Synagogues, 1995), xx.
[3] See Lawrence A. Hoffman, ed., *My People's Prayer Book,* vol.10, *Shabbat Morning* (Woodstock, VT: Jewish Lights, 2007), 177–93.
[4] Israel Abrahams, *A Companion to the Authorised Daily Prayerbook: Historical and Explanatory Notes* (New York: Hermon Press, 1966), 171.

[5] *Forms of Prayer*, vol.1, *Daily and Sabbath Prayers* (London: J. Wertheimer & Co., 1841), introduction, ix.

Avinu Malkeinu and the New Reform Machzor (Mishkan HaNefesh), by Rabbi Edwin Goldberg, DHL

[1] The members of the core editorial team of the *machzor* are Rabbi Edwin Goldberg, Rabbi Janet Marder, Rabbi Sheldon Marder, and Rabbi Leon Morris. Rabbi Hara Person is the managing editor.

[2] The editors are also aware that when it comes to petitionary prayer, repetition can be a valuable rhetorical device. Petition does more than merely ask God to act; it also encourages self-reflection on even our hidden hopes.

[3] The version in the current Reconstructionist *machzor* has nineteen lines, for instance, compared with the traditional forty-four-line version found in many traditional *machzorim*. At one point we thought about creating a set of approximately twelve verses for each service—some consistent in each and

every service, and others specific to the service in question and drawn from the "treasury" of the classic *machzor*. We eventually abandoned that plan, seeing that it would not actually work.

[4] Actually, we did think of possible alternatives to *avinu malkeinu*—for example, *sh'khinah imeinu,* "nurturing presence" (more literally, "mothering presence"); *m'kor binateinu,* "source of insight and understanding"; *tzur chayeinu,* which we thought of as "unweathered stone, steadying strength beneath us"; and *Y'did Nafshoteinu,* "intimate soul companion."

[5] In the words of fellow editor Rabbi Sheldon Marder, "We're not looking for literal word-for-word equivalents. We are looking for clear, elegant, poetic language that captures the sense and spirit of the Hebrew and sounds good when read aloud."

[6] On the Jewish view of sin, see Lawrence A. Hoffman, ed., *Prayers of Awe, We Have Sinned: Sin and Confession in Judaism—Ashamnu and Al Chet* (Woodstock, VT: Jewish Lights, 2012).

[7] Jay Michaelson explains in *Everything Is God: The Radical Path of Nondual Judaism*

(Boston: Trumpeter, 2009) that non-dualism is where the atheist and the mystic shake hands.

What Is God's Name?, by Rabbi David A. Teutsch, PhD

[1] Lawrence A. Hoffman, ed., *Prayers of Awe, We Have Sinned: Sin and Confession in Judaism—Ashamnu and Al Chet* (Woodstock, VT: Jewish Lights, 2012), 94–95.

[2] On which, see Lawrence A. Hoffman, ed., *My People's Prayer Book,* vol.10, *Shabbat Morning:* Shacharit *and* Musaf (Woodstock, VT: Jewish Lights, 2007), 177–93.

[3] Joel Rosenberg, trans., in *Kol Haneshamah: Shabbat Vechagim* (Wyncote, PA: Reconstructionist Press, 1994), 452. Cf. technical translation and commentary in Hoffman, *My People's Prayer Book,* vol.10, *Shabbat Morning,* 177–93.

Changing God's Names: The Liturgy of Liberal Judaism in Great Britain, by Rabbi Andrew

Goldstein, PhD, and Rabbi Charles H. Middleburgh, PhD

[1] Israel Movement for Progressive Judaism, *Machzor,* 1989, 71f.
[2] Ruth F. Brin, *Harvest: Collected Poems and Prayers* (New York: Reconstructionist Press, 1959), 4.
[3] *Mahzor Lev Shalem,* ed. Edward Feld (New York: Rabbinical Assembly, 2010), 93–94.

So Near and Oh So Far, by Rabbi Laura Geller

[1] The revised edition of *Gates of Repentance,* which came out in 1996 (New York: Central Conference of American Rabbis, 1978), had already made the same change.
[2] Talmud, Yoma 69b; see Rachel Adler, *Engendering Judaism* (Philadelphia: Jewish Publication Society, 1998), 61.

Rescuing the Father-God from Delray Beach, by Rabbi Jeffrey K. Salkin, DMin

[1] Richard Levy, ed., *On Wings of Awe: A Machzor for Rosh Hashanah and Yom Kippur*

(Washington, DC: B'nai B'rith Hillel Foundations, 1985), 275–76.
[2] *Exodus Rabbah* 23:8.
[3] I am grateful to Harold Bloom for prodding my expanded thinking in this area. See Harold Bloom, *Jesus and Yahweh: The Names Divine* (New York: Riverhead, 2005).
[4] *Lamentations Rabbah*, proem 24.
[5] Talmud, Bava Metzia 59b.

I Do Not Know Your Name, by Rabbi Sandy Eisenberg Sasso, DMin

[1] *Exodus Rabbah* 29:1.
[2] *Pesikta D'rav Kahana* 12:25.
[3] *Exodus Rabbah* 29:1.

Abracadabra: The Magic of Naming, by Rabbi Bradley Shavit Artson, DHL

[1] Elijah Judah Schochet, *Animal Life in Jewish Traditions: Attitudes and Relationships* (New York: Ktav, 1984), 11.
[2] Midrash *Genesis Rabbah* 17:4
[3] Midrash *Genesis Rabbah* 17:4
[4] *Tikkunei HaZohar* 17a

My Name Is Vulnerability, by Rabbi Tony Bayfield, CBE, DD

[1] Abraham Joshua Heschel, *Heavenly Torah: As Refracted through the Generations*, ed. Gordon Tucker (New York: Continuum, 2005).

[2] See Arthur A. Cohen, *The Natural and the Supernatural Jew* (London: Vallentine, Mitchell, 1967), 234–59.

[3] Maybaum emphasizes the connection between the destruction of the First Temple (the first *churban*), the destruction of the Second Temple (the second *churban*), and the Shoah (which he calls the third *churban*).

[4] Talmud, Gittin 58a.

[5] Heschel, *Heavenly Torah*, 118. The citation from the school of Rabbi Ishmael is *Mekhilta D'rabbi Yishmael, Shirata* 8.

[6] *Mekhilta D'rabbi Yishmael, Pischa* 14.

[7] *Exodus Rabbah* 2:5.

[8] Heschel, *Heavenly Torah*, 120.

[9] *Lamentations Zuta* 1:18.

[10] A phrase used by, among others, Richard Rubenstein. See Richard Rubenstein, *Morality and Eros* (New York: McGraw-Hill, 1970), 185–6.

[11]   This biblical phrase is central to Eliezer Berkovits, *Faith after the Holocaust* (New York: Ktav, 1973).

Two Pockets, by Rabbi Joshua M. Davidson

[1]   Mishnah Sanhedrin 4:5.
[2]   Rabbi Milton Steinberg in "Rosh Hashanah 5765—First Day," Rabbi Dr. Analia Bortz.
[3]   *Un'taneh Tokef*, trans. Rabbi Chaim Stern, in *Gates of Repentance: The New Union Prayerbook for the Days of Awe* (New York: Central Conference of American Rabbis, 1978, rev. 1996), 315.
[4]   Ibid., 313.
[5]   *Deuteronomy Rabbah* 11:10.
[6]   Mishnah Sanhedrin 4:5.
[7]   Rabbi Jerome Malino in "To Look at the Sky," Rabbi Jerome K. Davidson, Rosh Hashanah Eve 1987, unpublished manuscript.
[8]   *Gates of Repentance*, 410.
[9]   Ibid., 521.
[10] Rabbi Dr. Norman J. Cohen, *Moses and the Journey to Leadership: Timeless Lessons of Effective Management from the Bible and Today's Leaders* (Woodstock, VT: Jewish Lights, 2007), 171.

[11] Bachya ibn Paquda, *Chovot Ha-l'vavot*.
[12] Rabbi Allen S. Maller, "Hassidic Wisdom: Sayings and Stories."

Re-imaging God, by Rabbi Lawrence A. Englander, CM, DHL, DD

[1] See, e.g., Lawrence A. Hoffman, ed., *Who by Fire, Who By Water—Un'taneh Tokef* (Woodstock, VT: Jewish Lights, 2010), esp. 29ff.
[2] Marcia Falk, "Notes on Composing New Blessings," *Journal of Feminist Studies in Religion* (Spring 1987): 44. For one of the groundbreaking works in this field, see Sallie McFague, *Metaphorical Theology: Models of God in Religious Language* (Philadelphia: Fortress Press, 1982).
[3] See Lawrence A. Hoffman, ed., *My People's Prayer Book*, vol.2, *The Amidah* (Woodstock, VT: Jewish Lights, 1998), 164ff.
[4] See Lawrence A. Hoffman, *The Journey Home* (Boston: Beacon Press, 2002), 135–44.
[5] See Lawrence A. Hoffman, ed., *We Have Sinned: Sin and Confession in*

Judaism—Ashamnu and Al Chet (Woodstock, VT: Jewish Lights, 2012), 94–95.

"Would You Still Love Me If...?," by Rabbi Shoshana Boyd Gelfand

[1] See Barry Johnson, *Polarity Management: Identifying and Managing Unsolvable Problems* (Amherst, MA: HRD Press, 2014).

Celebrating a Conflicted Relationship with God, by Rabbi Asher Lopatin

[1] See Michael Chernick, "*S'udah Sh'lishit:* A Rite of Modest Majesty," in Lawrence A. Hoffman, ed., *My People's Prayer Book,* vol.7, *Shabbat at Home* (Woodstock, VT: Jewish Lights, 2004), 30–37.

God the Cashier: A Parable of the Dubner Maggid's, by Rabbi Jack Riemer

[1] From *Yigdal,* a popular morning hymn that encapsulates the thirteen principles of faith composed by prominent medieval

philosopher Moses Maimonides (1135–1204). See Lawrence A. Hoffman, ed., *My People's Prayer Book,* vol.5, Birkhot Hashachar *(Morning Blessings)* (Woodstock, VT: Jewish Lights, 2001), 99–105.

Piety and Protest, by Rabbi Dennis C. Sasso, DMin

[1] Dedicated to the memory of my beloved father, Colman Abraham Sasso *(z"l),* who died during the week that I completed this essay. His life reflects the ideals of this prayer.

The Most Difficult Name for God, "You"—Or, How Is Prayer Possible?, by Rabbi Jonathan P. Slater, DMin

[1] On which, see, e.g., Samuel J. Levine, "An Introduction to Self-Incrimination in Jewish Law, with Application to the American Legal System: A Psychological and Philosophical Analysis," *Loyola of Los Angeles International & Comparative Law Review* 257 (2006): 257–77, http://digitalcommons.lmu.edu/ilr/vol28/iss2/2.

[2] *The Zohar*, Pritzker ed., trans. and ed. Daniel C. Matt (Stanford, CA: Stanford University Press, 2012), 7:465–66.

[3] Ibid., 466 n339.

[4] Norman Fischer, *Opening to You: Zen-Inspired Translations of the Psalms* (New York: Viking Compass, 2002), xviii.

Machzor and Malkhut: The Challenge of Naming a King, by Rabbi David Stern

[1] Marianne Moore, "Poetry," in *The Norton Anthology of Modern Poetry*, eds. Richard Ellman and Robert O'Clair (New York: W.W. Norton, 1973), 421.

[2] David Hartman, *A Heart of Many Rooms* (Woodstock, VT: Jewish Lights, 1999), xxii – xxiii.

[3] Elyse Frishman and Peter Knobel, *Mishkan T'filah* (New York: Central Conference of American Rabbis, 2007), ix.

[4] Translation from Daniel C. Matt, *The Essential Kabbalah* (Edison, NJ: Castle Books, 1997), 22.

"We Guess; We Clothe Thee, Unseen King," by Rabbi Margaret Moers Wenig, DD

[1] Gerard Manley Hopkins, from his poem "Nondum."

[2] From *Un'taneh Tokef*, a *piyyut* added to the Rosh Hashanah and Yom Kippur *Musaf Amidah* in Ashkenazi *machzorim*. See Lawrence A. Hoffman, ed., *Prayers of Awe, Who by Fire, Who by Water—Un'taneh Tokef* (Woodstock, VT: Jewish Lights, 2010), 47.

[3] I am coauthor, with Naomi Janowitz, of the privately published 1975 *Siddur Nashim*, the first to use female images and feminine pronouns for God, and the author of the 1990 sermon "God Is a Woman and She Is Growing Older."

[4] From the *Alenu*. See Lawrence A. Hoffman, ed., *My People's Prayer Book*, vol.6, *Tachanun and Concluding Prayers* (Woodstock, VT: Jewish Lights, 2000), 133.

[5] From the liturgy surrounding the reading of Torah. See Lawrence A. Hoffman, ed., *My People's Prayer Book*, vol.4, Seder K'riat

Hatorah: *The Torah Service* (Woodstock, VT: Jewish Lights, 2000), 49.

[6] From the *Alenu.* See Hoffman, *My People's Prayer Book*, vol.6, *Tachanun and Concluding Prayers*, 133.

[7] Gerard Manley Hopkins.

[8] Dr. Arnold Lustiger, *Machzor Mesoras HaRAv, Rosh Hashanah Machzor, with Commentary Adapted from the Teachings of Rabbi Joseph B. Soloveitchik* (Khal Publishing and the Orthodox Union, 2007), 535.

[9] Ibid.

[10] From the middle blessing of the Rosh Hashanah *Amidah*. See note 12, below.

[11] In the words of former U.S. secretary of state Madeline Albright.

[12] Talmud, Berakhot 60a.

[13] "Any blessing *[b'rakhah]* in which there is no mention of the name [of God] and the sovereignty [of God] is not a [proper] blessing, unless it is adjacent to a neighboring [blessing that does meet these requirements]" *(Mishneh Torah,* Blessings 1:5).

[14] From *Eloheinu velohei avoteinu m'lokh al kol ha'olam kulo,* the central prayer of every Rosh Hashanah *Amidah.*

From Direct Experience to a World of Words: The God We Struggle to Know, by Rabbi Daniel G. Zemel

[1] Terry Eagleton, *Culture and the Death of God* (New Haven, CT: Yale University Press, 2014), 98.

Glossary

The glossary presents names and Hebrew words used regularly throughout this volume and provides the way they are pronounced. Sometimes two pronunciations are common, in which case the first is the way the word is sounded in Hebrew, and the second is the way it is sometimes heard in common speech, under the influence of English or, sometimes, of Yiddish, the folk language of Jews in northern and eastern Europe (a combination, mostly, of Hebrew and German). Our goal is to provide the way that many Jews actually use these words, not just the technically correct version.

The pronunciations are divided into syllables by dashes.

The accented syllable is written in capital letters.

"Kh" represents a guttural sound, similar to the German (as in "sprach").

The most common vowel is "a" as in "father," which appears here as "ah."

The short "e" (as in "get") is written as either "e" (when it is in the middle of a syllable) or "eh" (when it ends a syllable). Similarly, the short "i" (as in "tin") is written as either "i" (when it is in the middle of a syllable) or "ih" (when it ends a syllable).

A long "o" (as in "Moses") is written as "oe" (as in the word "toe") or "oh" (as in the word "Oh!")

Ahavah Rabbah (pronounced ah-hah-VAH rah-BAH or, commonly, ah-HAH-vah RAH-bah): Literally, "Great Love"; the first two Hebrew words and, thus, the title of a prayer introducing the morning and evening synagogue recitation of the *Sh'ma*, and proclaiming God's love for Israel. Here, however, it is used to describe a mode of Jewish music (see **mode**).

Al Chet (pronounced ahl-KHET): Literally, "For the sin"; the larger of the two confessions that mark the Yom Kippur liturgy. Known also as "the long [or great] confession" *(vidu'i rabbah*, pronounced vee-DOO-i rah-BAH or, commonly, VEE-doo-i RAH-bah). (See Lawrence A. Hoffman, ed., *We Have Sinned: Sin and Confession in Judaism—Ashamnu and Al Chet, Prayers of Awe* series [Woodstock, VT: Jewish Lights, 2012].)

Amidah (pronounced ah-mee-DAH or, commonly, ah-MEE-dah): Literally, "standing," that is, "the prayer that is said standing"; the second of two central units in the worship service, the first being the *Sh'ma* and Its Blessings. (See Lawrence A. Hoffman, ed., *My People's Prayer Book*, vol.1, *The* Sh'ma *and Its Blessings*, and vol.2, *The Amidah* [Woodstock, VT: Jewish Lights, 1997 and 1998].)

Ashkenaz: See **Ashkenazi.**

Ashkenazi (pronounced ahsh-k'-nah-ZEE or, commonly, ahsh-k'-NAH-zee): From the Hebrew word *Ashkenaz*, meaning the geographic area of northern (and, by extension, eastern) Europe. Ashkenazi is the adjective, describing the liturgical rituals and customs practiced there, as opposed to *Sephardi*, meaning the liturgical rituals and customs that are derived from Sepharad, Spain (see **Sephardi**).

Bimah (pronounced bee-MAH or, commonly, BEE-mah): Literally, "stage," "platform," or "pulpit"; in context here, the area in a worship space from which the worship service is conducted and the Torah publicly read.

Chiasm (pronounced KYE-asm): A literary term for poetry or prose arranged in mirror-like form, so that the last half mirrors the first in reverse: a five-line poem, for example, such that the topical arrangement of the last two lines inverts that of the first two, that is, a poem arranged as A1, B1, C, B2, A2.

Gaon (pronounced gah-OHN; pl. *Geonim*, pronounced g'-oh-NEEM): Title for the leading rabbis in Baghdad and vicinity (present-day Iraq) from about 750 to 1038. From a biblical word meaning "glory," and equivalent in title to "your Excellency."

Geonim (pronounced g'-oh-NEEM): plural of *gaon*. See **Gaon**.

Kavyokhl: See **Kiv'yakhol**.

Ketubah (pronounced k'-too-BAH or, commonly, k'-TOO-bah): The rabbinically ordained marriage certificate, a legal document drawn up by the groom and given to the bride; originally, and still today in traditional quarters, a statement of his obligations to her and the conditions in default of which she may later sue for divorce; among liberal Jews, however, often rewritten to reflect the spiritual bases by which both members of the couple enter their marriage.

Kiddush (pronounced kee-DOOSH or, commonly, KIH-dihsh): Literally, "sanctification"; the prayer for the eve of Shabbat and holidays intended to announce the arrival of sacred time, and accompanied by wine. Hence, *Kiddush* cup: the cup, generally artistic in design, from which the wine is drunk.

Kiv'yakhol (pronounced kih-v'-yah-KHOHL or, in Yiddish, *kavyokhl*, pronounced kah-v'-YUH-khl). Literally, "so to speak" or "if it could be said"; a rabbinic caveat frequently modifying an anthropomorphic reference to God, as if to indicate that such a thing really cannot be posited of God, even though, for conversation sake, we imagine that it can. In Yiddish the expression evolved into *kavyokhl*, an actual noun referring to God: e.g., *hot kavyokhl gezogt*, "God said."

Kol Nidre (pronounced kohl need-RAY or, commonly, kohl NIHD-ray): Literally, "All vows"; the opening words and, thus, the name for the prayer that dominates the opening evening service for Yom Kippur. (See Lawrence A. Hoffman, ed., *All These Vows:* Kol Nidre,*Prayers of Awe* series [Woodstock, VT: Jewish Lights, 2011].)

Litany: A literary pattern for many prayers, composed of a series of lines or verses, each one consisting of a repetitive word or words to which variant endings are added.

L'mah Hadavar Domeh (pronounced l'MAH hah-dah-VAHR doh-MEH): Literally, "To what can the matter be compared?" A rhetorical question in classical rabbinic literature calling for elaboration on a point being made, often a parable or an analogy that further explains it.

Machzor (pronoundced makh-ZOHR or, commonly, MAKH-zohr): The collection of prayers for holy days, as opposed to the *siddur* (pronounced see-DOOR or, commonly, SIH-d'r), the "order" of prayer for daily and Shabbat worship (see **Siddur**). Originally, however, a collection of liturgy for prayers of the entire year, including daily and Shabbat liturgy—from the Hebrew root *ch.z.r*, "to return," that is, the prayers that return according to an annual cycle.

Machzor Vitry (pronounced makh-ZOHR veet-REE or, commonly, MAKH-zohr VEET-ree): Literally, the collection of prayers for the annual cycle (the *machzor*) composed by [Simchah of the French community named] Vitry. An eleventh- to twelfth-century compendium that provides our earliest comprehensive picture of Jewish liturgy in Ashkenaz (see **Ashkenazi**).

Malkhut (pronounced mahl-KHOOT): Literally, "kingdom, realm" and used prominently in *Malkhut Shamayim* (pronounced mahl-KHOOT shah-MAH-yeem), "The kingdom or realm of heaven [that is, God]" in opposition to kingdoms or realms ruled by human beings.

Melekh (pronounced MEH-lehkh): Literally, "king, ruler."

Minhag (pronounced mihn-HAHG or, commonly, MIHN-hahg): Literally, "custom"; the way that a given set of Jews pray, a "rite," as in *Minhag Ashkenaz* or *Minhag Sepharad* (the prayer customs or rite of Jews in Ashkenaz or Sepharad (see **Ashkenazi, Sephardi**).

Mode: The basic building block of synagogue chants. Unlike the Western musical tradition, which is based on an octave of whole and half notes, liturgical chant within Judaism is built on various combinations of melodic patterns, one of which is called *Ahavah Rabbah*, taking its name from the *Ahavah Rabbah* prayer, with which the cantor introduces the mode into the *shacharit* (morning) service of Shabbat (see **Ahavah Rabbah**).

Piyyut (pronounced pee-YOOT): See ***piyyutim***.

Piyyutim (pronounced pee-yoo-TEEM; sing. *piyyut*, pronounced pee-YOOT): Literally, "poems, poetry"; used here for poetic insertions into the standardized prayers, common especially for liturgy on holy days.

Rashi (pronounced RAH-shee): An acronym for R[abbi] SHlomo I[tzchaki], hence RaSHI (France, 1040–1105). A giant of rabbinic literature, the best-known commentator on the meaning of the Hebrew Bible and Talmud.

Rite: See **Minhag.**

Seder (pronounced *SAY-dehr)*: Literally, "order," hence the name given to the order of prayer and foods that constitute the Passover-eve meal; and also an early name for the order of Jewish prayer, as in *Seder Rav Amram* (pronounced SAY-dehr rahv ahm-RAHM or, commonly, SAY-dehr rahv AHM-rahm), "the order of prayer compiled by Rav Amram," our earliest extant comprehensive order of Jewish prayer, compiled around 860 by Rav Amram of Babylonia (present-day Iraq).

Seder Rav Amram: See **Seder.**

Sepharad: See **Sephardi.**

Sephardi (pronounced s'-fahr-DEE or, commonly, s'-FAHR-dee): From the Hebrew word *Sepharad* (pronounced s'-fah-RAHD), denoting the geographic area of modern-day Spain and Portugal. *Sephardi* is the adjective, describing not just the inhabitants but also the liturgical rituals and customs practiced there, as opposed to *Ashkenazi,* meaning those derived from *Ashkenaz,* northern and eastern Europe (see **Ashkenazi**).

Sh'ma (pronounced sh'-MAH): The central prayer in the first of the two main units in the worship service, the second being the *Amidah* (see **Amidah**).*Sh'ma,* meaning "hear," is the first word of the first line, "Hear O Israel: Adonai is our God; Adonai is One," the paradigmatic statement of Jewish faith, the Jew's absolute commitment to the presence of a single and unique God in time and space.

Siddur (pronounced see-DOOR or, commonly, SIH-d'r): From the Hebrew word *seder* (see **Seder**) meaning "order" and, therefore, by extension, the name given to the "order of prayers" or prayer book, usually just for the daily and Sabbath service. The equivalent collection for holy-day liturgy is called *machzor* (see **Machzor**).

Siddur Saadiah: The *siddur* (order of prayer) by Saadiah Gaon, our second extant comprehensive prayer book, c. 920, composed roughly sixty years after the first one, by Amram Gaon, c. 860 (see **Gaon** and **Seder Rav Amram**).

Un'taneh Tokef (pronounced oo-n'-TAH-neh TOH-kehf): Literally, "Let us acknowledge the power," the first two Hebrew words and, thus, the title of a central liturgical poem (a *piyyut*) exploring the fragility of human life; associated with a legend about a Jewish martyr in the Crusades, but actually authored by a poet named Yannai, from late antiquity. (See Lawrence A. Hoffman, ed., *Who By Water, Who By Fire*—Un'taneh Tokef, *Prayers of Awe* series [Woodstock, VT: Jewish Lights, 2010].)

Yizkor (pronounced yihz-KOHR, or, commonly, YIHZ-k'r): Literally, "May He [God] Remember," the first Hebrew word, and hence, the title, of the main prayer in the Memorial Service; and, by extension, the title of that service as a whole. (See Lawrence A. Hoffman, ed., *May God Remember: Memory and Memorializing in Judaism—Yizkor, Prayers of Awe* series [Woodstock, VT: Jewish Lights, 2013].)

Front Cover Flap

PRAYERS OF AWE

"The High Holy Days confirm in us the conviction that we are mortal beings capable of great goodness, but of the evil we call "sin" as well; that there is a divine presence before whom we stand and give account; and that, with proper repentance and resolve, we can wipe the slate clean and begin anew to realize all the promise of a world re-created, a child reborn, a mind re-formed, and a conscience reawakened. This series aims at such a liturgical reawakening."

—Rabbi Lawrence A. Hoffman, PhD

***

Few prayers demonstrate so clearly the process by which Jewish liturgy grew through the ages as does *Avinu Malkeinu*. While it is not until the Middle Ages that it makes its way into Jewish liturgy worldwide, the images of God as father and king go back to the Bible; the beginning of a prayer addressed to *Avinu Malkeinu* is presented in the Talmud as going back to the second century.

This fascinating sixth volume in the *Prayers of Awe* series examines how this prayer developed through time to become what it is today and how that history—of both words and melody—illustrates Jewish liturgical creativity. It mines the disciplines of philosophy, literature and linguistics for the liturgical theory behind the prayer and the matter of naming, answering how and why we began to refer to God as father and king in the first place. And it wrestles with the modern and feminist challenges of translating and owning its masculine imagery.

Featuring traditional Hebrew text and modern translation—as well as several contemporary versions from the Ashkenazi, Sephardi, Hasidic and even Yemenite communities—this book lets you know exactly what the prayers say. Commentaries from people across the gamut of Jewish tradition and in every walk of life examine this prayer from the viewpoints of the ancient Rabbis and modern theologians, as well as biblical, mystical, Talmudic, halakhic, linguistic, feminist, community and personal perspectives.

***

Prayers of Awe Series

To see all volumes in the series, see section entitled "Also in the Prayers of Awe Series"

Back Cover Flap

RABBI LAWRENCE A. HOFFMAN, PhD, has served for more than three decades as professor of liturgy at Hebrew Union College – Jewish Institute of Religion. He is a world-renowned liturgist and holder of the Stephen and Barbara Friedman Chair in Liturgy, Worship and Ritual. His work combines research in Jewish ritual, worship and spirituality with a passion for the spiritual renewal of contemporary Judaism.

His many books, written and edited, include the previous five volumes in the *Prayers of Awe* series: *Who by Fire, Who by Water—Un'taneh Tokef*; *All These Vows—Kol Nidre*; *We Have Sinned: Sin and Confession in Judaism—Ashamnu and Al Chet*; *May God Remember: Memory and Memorializing in Judaism—Yizkor*; and *All the World: Universalism, Particularism and the High Holy Days*.

Hoffman also edited the ten-volume series *My People's Prayer Book: Traditional Prayers, Modern Commentaries*, winner of the National Jewish Book Award; and coedited *My People's Passover Haggadah: Traditional Texts, Modern Commentaries*, a finalist for the National Jewish Book Award (all Jewish Lights).

Rabbi Hoffman cofounded and developed Synagogue 2/3000, a transdenominational project to envision and implement the ideal synagogue of the spirit for the twenty-first century. In that

capacity, he wrote *Rethinking Synagogues: A New Vocabulary for Congregational Life* (Jewish Lights).
Also Available

Rosh Hashanah Readings Yom Kippur Readings
Inspiration, Information, Contemplation
Edited by Rabbi Dov Peretz Elkins Section introductions from Arthur Green's *These Are the Words*

From a variety of inspiring sources—ancient, medieval, modern, Jewish and non-Jewish—a selection of readings, prayers and insights.

Back Cover Material

An illuminating in-depth exploration of the complexities—and perhaps audacity—of naming the unnameable.

One of the oldest and most beloved prayers—known even to Jews who rarely attend synagogue—is *Avinu Malkeinu* ("Our Father, Our King"), a liturgical staple for the entire High Holy Day period. "Our Father, Our King" has resonance also for Christians, whose Lord's Prayer begins "Our Father."

Despite its popularity, *Avinu Malkeinu* causes great debate because of the difficulties in thinking of God as father and king. Americans no longer relate positively to images of royalty; victims of parental abuse note the problem of assuming a benevolent father; and feminists have long objected to masculine language for God.

Through a series of lively introductions and commentaries, almost forty contributors—men and women, scholars and rabbis, artists and thinkers from all Jewish denominations and from around the world—wrestle with this linguistic and spiritual conundrum, asking, "How do we name God altogether, without recourse to imagery that defies belief?"

***

PRAYERS OF AWE

A multi-volume series designed to explore the High Holy Day liturgy and enrich the praying experience for everyone—whether experienced worshipers or guests who encounter Jewish prayer for the very first time.

***

Contributors

Rabbi Bradley Shavit Artson, DHL
Rabbi Tony Bayfield, CBE, DD
Dr. Annette M. Boeckler
Dr. Marc Zvi Brettler
Dr. Erica Brown
Gordon Dale, MA
Rabbi Joshua M. Davidson
Rabbi Lawrence A. Englander, CM, DHL, DD
Rabbi Paul Freedman
Rabbi Shoshana Boyd Gelfand
Rabbi Laura Geller
Rabbi Edwin Goldberg, DHL
Rabbi Andrew Goldstein, PhD
Dr. Joel M. Hoffman
Rabbi Lawrence A. Hoffman, PhD
Rabbi Elie Kaunfer, DHL
Rabbi Karyn D. Kedar

Rabbi Reuven Kimelman, PhD
Rabbi Asher Lopatin Catherine Madsen
Rabbi Jonathan Magonet, PhD
Rabbi Dalia Marx, PhD
Chazzan Danny Maseng
Ruth Messinger
Rabbi Charles H. Middleburgh, PhD
Rabbi April Peters
Rabbi Jack Riemer
Rabbi Jeffrey K. Salkin, DMin
Rabbi Dennis C. Sasso, DMin
Rabbi Sandy Eisenberg Sasso, DMin
Rabbi Jonathan P, Slater, DMin
Rabbi David Stern
Rabbi David A. Teutsch, PhD
Rabbi Margaret Moers Wenig, DD
Rabbi Daniel G. Zemel
Dr. Wendy Zierler

www.ingramcontent.com/pod-product-compliance
Lightning Source LLC
Chambersburg PA
CBHW010717300426
44114CB00022B/2882